SECOND LANGUAGE ACQUISITION BY ADULT IMMIGRANTS: A FIELD MANUAL

Clive Perdue, Editor

THE EUROPEAN SCIENCE FOUNDATION PROJECT

NEWBURY HOUSE PUBLISHERS, INC.
ROWLEY, MASSACHUSETTS 01969
ROWLEY • LONDON • TOKYO
1 9 8 4

Library of Congress Cataloging in Publication Data
Main entry under title:

Second language acquisition by adult immigrants.

   (Cross-linguistic series on second language research)
   Bibliography: p.
   Includes indexes.
   1. Language acquisition--Handbooks, manuals, etc.
I. Perdue, Clive.   II. Series.
P118.S35   1984   401'.9   84-1158
ISBN 0-88377-281-7

NEWBURY HOUSE PUBLISHERS, INC.

Language Science
Language Teaching
Language Learning

ROWLEY, MASSACHUSETTS 01969
ROWLEY • LONDON • TOKYO

Originally published by the European Science Foundation.

                                   First printing: October 1984
Printed in the U.S.A.   5   4   3   2   1

CROSS-LINGUISTIC SERIES
ON SECOND LANGUAGE RESEARCH

Roger W. Andersen, Editor

Second language research within the United States has tended historically to focus on the acquisition of English as a second language. The purpose of this series is to expand the focus of second language research to include a wider variety of languages, and to approach such research from a more inter-disciplinary perspective. In addition to language acquisition, the series will deal with second language use and its related psychological, social and anthropological concerns. Other volumes in the series include *Pidginization and Creolization as Language Acquisition*, Roger W. Andersen, Editor and *Second Languages*, Roger W. Andersen, Editor.

CONTENTS

Preface

1 Aims of the Field Manual

This field manual has been prepared by researchers engaged in a Research Activity of the European Science Foundation[1] entitled "The Ecology of Adult Language Acquisition" and constitutes a detailed description of this project at the end of its pilot year. The field manual has a major and a minor purpose. Its major purpose is to provide a theoretical and practical framework for the whole project; its minor purpose is to serve as a source of information about this activity for other researchers and organizat~~ions~~ ~~will briefly comment on both~~ aims.

(a) A framework for the projec~~t~~ ~~The project is a~~ co-ordinated, comparative ~~study of the untutored acquisition of~~ a second language by adult ~~immigrant workers. It will be~~ carried out by teams working in five European countries and will involve five different target languages - <u>Dutch</u>, <u>English</u>, <u>French</u>, <u>German</u>, Swedish - and six different source languages - Arabic, Finnish, Italian, Punjabi, Spanish and Turkish. In all countries, the social and linguistic situation is similar enough to justify a parallel and co-ordinated investigation; but there are nevertheless differences. For example, in Sweden, but not in other countries, <u>there is a certain amount of teaching for virtually all immigrant workers,</u> and the social status of the Finnish minority, which constitutes the largest foreign population, is generally higher than that of immigrant workers elsewhere. In Great Britain, very many "foreign" workers have some form of British citizen-

---

[1] The European Science Foundation is based in Strasbourg, France. It provides a forum for the exchange of ideas and information for its 48 member research organizations from 18 European countries, and supports a limited number of European research projects, such as this.

Foundation in 1980. Much of chapter 1 of the field manual is based on ideas discussed by these researchers in elaborating the proposal.

Everybody engaged in the pilot year has contributed to the field manual. That is to say that contributions have come from five different teams, or about twenty different individuals. Their specific research interests are not always identical, and some differences in what each team sees as the project's priorities have given rise to long discussions. This edition of the field manual is essentially the outcome of piloting work undertaken by the Swedish and German teams - and to a lesser extent the other teams - and of these discussions. In other words, it represents a compromise which satisfies everybody partially, and nobody fully.

The intense, and invaluable, overall participation in the writing of this document makes it difficult always to give credit where it is due for the many comments all contributors have made on each other's work. In what follows, main authors are mentioned, together with those who have made written contributions to the content of each chapter:

Chapter 1. Wolfgang Klein, with contributions from Jens Allwood, Rainer Dietrich, Guus Extra and Clive Perdue.

Chapter 2. Wolfgang Klein and Clive Perdue.

Chapter 3. Angelika Becker and Rainer Dietrich; Guus Extra; Christine de Hérédia and Michèle Mittner; Sven Strömqvist.

Chapter 4. Margaret Simonot and Jens Allwood; Sian Dodderidge, Colin Hindmarch, Tom Jupp, Clive Perdue, Hugh Pigeon, Celia Roberts, Peter Sayers, Sven Strömqvist.

Chapter 5. Clive Perdue, with contributions from Wolfgang Klein.

Chapter 6. Rainer Dietrich and Clive Perdue, with contributions from Jens Allwood (6.2.2 & 6.2.4) and Guus Extra (6.2.5).

Chapter 7. Wolfgang Klein, with contributions from Angelika Becker.

Chapter 8. Clive Perdue, with contributions from everybody, and in particular the German, Swedish and French teams: Angelika Becker, Rainer Dietrich, Ani Garmirian, Wolfgang Klein;

ship; this is generally not the case for immigrants to the other
target countries. In Germany, one often finds relatively self-con-
tained ghettos of Turkish workers who have very little contact with
the surrounding German community: this phenomenon has some parallels
in the other countries, but is not the majority case.

It would be unwise for the success of the project simply to
ignore such differences, thus a certain flexibility is needed. On the
other hand, a comparative project such as this cannot be run unless
the central parts of the study are done in parallel. This field manual
sets out to define what has to be done in parallel. It specifies the
type and number of informants to be studied in each country as well
as the areas of linguistic investigation; it also describes in detail
the common core of methods of data collection to be used. However, it
is not fully specified, leaving some freedom as to the weight which
is attribut_____esting
supplement_____owance is
made for t_____ns and
to the spe_____rs taking
part in the_____rch teams
will stick _____ed here.

(b) A source of information. As far as second language studies are
concerned, there are at least five aspects of this project which,
to our knowledge, go beyond previous related research.[2] Firstly, the
number of languages - both source and target - which are simultaneously studied; secondly, the attempt to carry out a co-ordinated longitudinal study of 2 1/2 years in these different linguistic environments; thirdly, the range and type of linguistic phenomena (from
prosody to discourse skills) whose acquisition is investigated;
fourthly, the attempt to relate these multiple skills to each other
and to various non-linguistic factors which may determine their acquisition; and finally, the range and variety of data collection
techniques used.

---

[2] See chapters 2 and 3. The expression 'our' in this sentence, and many
first person plurals in the text, refers to the contributors of the field
manual. However, the editor must take responsibility for any misuse of these
expressions.

Having a detailed account of the overall organization of the project,
the topics which have been selected for investigation, the methods which
will be used for data collection and for analysis, and finally the
heuristic considerations that caused the project to be organized in the
way it is, might be helpful for other researchers in the field. If researchers do find in this manual some ideas on what may be worthwhile
to investigate in similar projects, we hope they will contact the Max-Planck-
Institut für Psycholinguistik, Nijmegen, or the co-ordinators of the national teams[3] so that mutual findings may be discussed.

More generally, the phenomenon of immigration and of relationships
between the host and immigrant communities is one which has become
important for the countries in which this project will be carried out.
In the majority of these countries, it is being studied intensively from
different perspectives (in France, for example, there is an interdisciplinary laboratory within the Conseil National de la Recherche Scientifique whose research is directed specifically towards international
migration). We hope that this manual will also give some indication
to researchers in other fields and organizations who are concerned with
this problem, of the contribution that researchers in the field of
linguistics can make to a better understanding of the communication and
relationships between majority and minority communities.

2 Organization of the Field Manual

Chapters 1 and 2 contain an overall description of the project.
Chapter 1 discusses from a more theoretical point of view the objectives
of the project, the questions to be investigated and the linguistic
topics and type of informant relevant for this investigation. In chapter
2, the overall organization will be outlined from a more practical point
of view: the researchers and informants involved, time-schedule, combination of target and source languages, etc.

---

[3] All affiliations and addresses are given in chapter 2. Comments on
the field manual are most welcome, and can be sent to any of the central
or local co-ordinators.

Chapter 3 contains a brief account of previous research on the spontaneous acquisition in the chosen target countries by adult learners. Other research results of immediate concern to some aspect of the project are mentioned at the appropriate places in the following chapters.

In chapters 4-7, the central chapters, the topics of research will be discussed in detail: why we think these topics are important for our investigation, what the specific hypotheses are, how they arise out of previous work, and how we will try to approach them.

To answer the questions raised there, we will need data of very different kinds - data, for example, which will be suitable for the experimental analysis of prosody as well as data about attitudes or differing background knowledge. Thus we require both a broad range of data collection techniques, and precise indications on how to use these techniques in a co-ordinated and comparable way. In chapter 8, these techniques and ways of combining them are discussed, together with a sample plan of the actual work each team will have to accomplish during the data collecting phase of the project.

Despite the presence of about 11 million foreign workers in the countries concerned, the number of informants suitable for the planned longitudinal study is small at present. Furthermore, these informants' co-operation for a period of about three years has to be assured, and we neither wish nor would be able to treat them as pure research sub-jects. All these problems and the ethics of our research will be discussed in chapter 9.

3 Contributors and acknowledgements

This is an update of the ESF edition of the manual. A revised and much extended version will appear towards the end of the project. It will then be possible to incorporate, in particular, findings from preliminary anal-ysis of data, and accounts of the linguistic and cultural backgrounds from which our informants come.

The aims and overall structure of the project - including the data collection techniques described in chapter 8 - were defined by Jens Allwood and Wolfgang Klein in a proposal accepted by the European Science

Jens Allwood, Sven Strömqvist, Kaarlo Voionmaa; Daniel Faïta, Christine de Hérédia, Michèle Mittner, Colette Noyau, Daniel Véronique, Jens Allwood and the Swedish team contributed particularly in the elaboration of the techniques of action interview, video-recorded self-confrontation, film-watching and self-recording.

Chapter 9.   Clive Perdue, with contributions from the Swedish and German teams.

The whole manuscript was extensively edited by Clive Perdue. Other people have taken the trouble to read draft versions of this manual, and we have greatly benefitted from their comments. Our thanks must go to the project's steering committee[4] (particularly to Dan Slobin and Ayhan Aksu for the time they have devoted and for their valuable advice), and also to Aladin Akyürek, Anne Dunlea, John Hawkins, Eric Kellerman, K.J. Mattheier, Susan Ervin-Tripp and Lily Wong-Fillmore.

Sylvia Aal, Marlene Arns, Marion Klaver, Rolf Koenig, Uschi de Pagter, Edith Sjoerdsma and Peter Wittenburg of the Max-Planck-Institut in Nijmegen have provided greatly appreciated help and support throughout this first period of the project: we express our gratitude to all of them.

Finally, we are especially grateful to Willem Levelt of the Max-Planck-Institut and Monique Flasaquier of the European Science Foundation for all their help in bringing this project into being, and to Roger Andersen for his help and advice with this version of the Field Manual.

---

[4] John Lyons, Ayhan Aksu, Norbert Dittmar, Willem Levelt, Bengt Nordberg, Dan Slobin, and, more recently, Tom Jupp.

1. Objectives of the Project

1.1 Objectives of the project

This project deals with the spontaneous second language acquisition (henceforth "SSLA") of foreign workers and their communication with speakers of the language of the country where they work. The term "foreign worker" includes, for our purposes, workers and the adult members of their family, and "foreign" refers to language rather than to citizenship. Taken in this sense, there are at present about 11 million foreign workers living in the industrialized western European countries. Various political measures have reduced, and, in some countries, almost halted their arrival during the past few years; but it is to be expected that their number will increase again after Spain and Portugal are fully integrated into the European Economic Community.

The social, political, and linguistic situation of foreign workers differs to some extent in the various host countries, and the following remarks on the general background of the project give a simplified, but typical picture.

As a rule, foreign workers do not speak or understand the language of their new social environment when they arrive; there are some exceptions, particularly in Great Britain, but this is untypical. Regular adult language tuition is rare, except in Sweden; in Germany, for example, less than 5 % of all adult foreign workers ever go to a language course. In their daily lives, foreign workers acquire what is most urgently needed, and some even attain a certain fluency. But normally, their acquisition slows down and even stops at a level that is far removed from the language of the world they have to live in.

This is a problem from a social, an educational, and a scientific point of view.

From a social point of view

It is obvious that foreign workers are strongly disadvantaged by their

language problems. This concerns almost every aspect of their social
life: from everyday contacts at work or in leisure time to all in-
stitutional situations (authorities, courts, education). Moreover,
their lack of knowledge of the language often makes it extremely
difficult for them to get to know their social, economic and political rights.

There is indeed a general and reciprocal lack of understanding between the host and immigrant communities of the way in which language affects their interaction (cf. 1.3.3). This can lead to language problems being evoked by the former as an excuse for direct
or indirect discriminatory action, and to strong resentment against
the host community on the part of the latter. An important aim of
this project will be to lessen this lack of understanding, by making
its results known to relevant organizations, and by contributing,
albeit indirectly, to appropriate language pedagogy (cf. 1.2).

From an educational point of view

Changing this situation would require, amongst other things, systematic and intensive language teaching programmes. The chances of establishing programmes of this kind are presently very poor. There are
economic problems: these programmes are expensive. There are attitudinal difficulties: there are elements in some countries which are
not interested in measures that could lead to full integration and
perhaps permanent residence of foreign workers; some of the foreign
workers feel that stronger integration into the host society would
have to be paid for by a loss of their own cultural identity, indeed
language. However, there are also more specifically educational ob-
stacles. Second language teaching in general is a well-established
field with a rich variety of programmes and methods; but most of
them are designed for different types of learner and different learning situations, and it is difficult, if not impossible, to adapt them
to the specific situation and to the specific needs of foreign workers. Over the past years, some experience has been gained in this
field, but as compared to second language teaching for other populations, it is still relatively limited. This project will attempt to
contribute further information on these issues (cf. 1.4.1).

From a scientific point of view

Most foreign workers acquire some, often very restricted, knowledge of the language of their social environment. We have called this process "spontaneous second language acquisition". A careful and systematic analysis of this process under various conditions could give us insight into:

I.   the factors on which acquisition depends;

II. the general structure of second language acquisition with respect to

    a. the order in which elements of the language are acquired and

    b. the speed and success of the acquisition process;

III. the characteristics of communication between native and non-native speakers of a language.

These insights would not only advance our understanding of how languages are processed, they could also function as a basis for systematic and more efficient teaching. It is not too far-fetched to assume that until we really know the ecological principles of un-tutored language learning, language teaching is an art based on practical experience and more or less mastered according to individual pedagogical gifts; but it lacks any significant and reliable scientific foundation. Indeed, much work has been undertaken in recent years to explain the discrepancy between what teachers think they teach in the classroom and the learner's resultant knowledge of the language.

A systematic investigation into the process and determining factors of the ecology of second language acquisition seems therefore important on social, educational, and scientific grounds. Such an investigation is the aim of this project.

During the course of the project, a major and a minor question will be asked. The major question concerns the investigation of the acquisition process as regards both its determining factors and the linguistic structure of the developing system from the very early stages of acquisition. The minor question is closely linked to the major question, while placing it in a larger context: it concerns the investigation of communication between native target language speakers and foreign workers who have been resident in the host country for some time, and whose situation is such that further acquisition from a relatively stabilized 'plateau' may occur. We return to the minor question in 1.4.

1.2 Related topics which are not objectives of the project

Before commenting in more detail on the objectives of the main study, it might be helpful to explain why we are restricting the scope of the project in certain ways:

(a) The study will be restricted to the process of second language acquisition of individuals who are 18 years or older as the process
starts. It is felt that this is a strong restriction, but to include
other types of acquisition would clearly be beyond our means.
Work has been, and is being, undertaken where the acquisition of
one language by different learner-types (child L1, child L2, adult
L2, and some more specific cases) is studied to see what aspects
of the learning process are comparable across learner-types, and
what aspects are due to the linguistic, or cultural-cognitive
development of the learner. This approach, and the cross-linguistic
approach adopted here, can be seen as complementary, rather than
contradictory.
A further and, we think, important reason for concentrating on
adults is that more work has been accomplished overall on child
language acquisition than on adult acquisition. For wide-reaching
comparisons to be made, the empirical gap on the side of adult
language acquisition must be filled, and we hope to be able to
contribute to doing so.

(b) The study will, in principle, be restricted to spontaneous language
acquisition; that is, it is not interested in the effects of systematic teaching, or in the results of specific teaching methods.
This does not mean that learners who have been exposed to some
teaching should necessarily be excluded from the population to be
studied; but this explicit intervention into their acquisition
process should be viewed simply as only one of the variables which
must be taken into account.

(c) The project does not intend to develop teaching material. It is
     expected, and as we have said, it is an important motivation for
     this project that its results contribute to establishing a scien-
     tific basis for language teaching, thus going some way towards
     remedying social and educational disadvantage.
     As well as information on the communicative needs of foreign workers,
     we can provide here at least partial indications as to the extent
     that variations in cultural-cognitive and motivational factors
     influence acquisition, and specifically, the type of awareness of
     the TL object that occurs in SSLA (norms, difficulties, etc.). It
     seems to be generally agreed that language teaching to adults as
     it exists today, is essentially a metalinguistic activity and it
     would seem important therefore to take into account the represen-
     tations of the TL that hitherto untutored learners would bring to
     the classroom.
     It would be a wrong ambition, however, and clearly beyond our com-
     petence, to aim at the concrete design of language courses and
     teaching material.

1.3 The main study: spontaneous second language acquisition in the early stages

1.3.1 Objectives. In investigating SSLA from the early stages of acquisition, we will set ourselves three closely related objectives, aiming
to find at least partial answers to the following questions:

I.   Determining factors:
     What are the psychological and social factors that determine the
     structure and tempo of language acquisition in adult language
     learners? How do these factors interact?
II. The acquisition process:
     a. What is the structure of the acquisition process itself?
     Given the cultural-cognitive development of adults (as opposed to
     children, cf. 1.2), what communication devices are available to
     them at the onset of learning? What devices specific to the lan-
     guage are acquired? in what order? and at what rate relative to
     each other?

b. What regulates the overall acquisition tempo? That is, what accelerates it, what slows it down, and what causes, possibly, its virtual halt (fossilization) at a level which is sometimes still very far from the language of the social environment?

Answers to these questions can contribute to a better understanding of the social interaction of (representatives of) the host and immigrant communities, as in order to study them we will have to consider the structure of the learner's language at a specific time (his "intermediate system") and the way that this intermediate system is put to use in daily interaction (this problem is placed in a wider perspective in 1.4). This provokes our next question:

III. Language use:

What does a learner's language look like at a given time in the acquisition process? That is, what are its grammatical properties? How is it used in daily interaction? This includes a study of particular phenomena such as avoidance strategies, paraphrase techniques, or nonverbal communication used as a suppletive device, and, on a more general level, how successful or unsuccessful this interaction is, or is felt to be by the learner and the target language speaker (cf. 1.3.3).

All of these problems are closely linked, and require a detailed analysis of the actual structure and tempo of the acquisition process, and an investigation of the various factors that influence or determine it, including the specific language needs and communicative problems of foreign workers. They will be approached by (a) a cross-linguistic and (b) a longitudinal investigation:

(a) It will be important to identify those phenomena in the acquisition process which are language- or culture-specific, and those which are recurrent, i.e. generalizable, if we are to propose a more universal account of language acquisition by adults. An investigation which compares the acquisition of many target languages (TLs) by speakers of many source languages (SLs), although it is not the only way of approaching this problem, nevertheless seems to us the best way. We will be studying the acquisition of the following TLs: Dutch, English, French, German, Swedish, by speakers of the follow-

ing SLs: Arabic, Finnish, Italian, Punjabi, Spanish, Turkish. See
the discussion in 2.2.

(b) There is little detailed longitudinal information (cf. chapter 3)
about the process of adult language acquisition. Most work has concentrated on cross-sectional studies of adult learners at different
levels of proficiency, from which hypotheses can be formulated as
regards the acquisition process: but these hypotheses have to be
tested. The best way of doing this at present seems to be a mixed
procedure with longitudinal case studies controlled by supplementary, cross sectional data, in which it will be possible to follow
this process in some detail.

This "qualitative" (i.e. non-statistical) approach seems, moreover,
to be necessary as a first step towards explaining the general existence
of non-native, fossilized varieties of the TLs. In other words, some of
the linguistic aspects of the present interaction between adult workers
and members of the target society have to be explained diachronically.
Clearly this is only a first step, but the hypotheses we should be able
to offer at the end of the investigation are essential for a firmer
foundation to any future co-variational study requiring representative
samples of non-native TL speakers.

1.3.2 Motivations. The selection and combination of the three objectives
is motivated by various considerations. The starting point is the obvious fact that almost everything that a foreign worker learns is learned
in communication, basically in everyday contacts. This leads the foreign
worker into a seemingly paradoxical situation: in order to communicate,
he has to learn the language, and in order to learn the language, he
has to communicate. This is no real paradox, of course, since first,
communication may run on different levels of language fluency, and
second, it is not entirely based on language in the sense of a purely
verbal system. Since the learner already masters a first language,
he may draw on a rich repertoire of communicative skills which are not
(or only partially) bound to a specific language; they include nonverbal
means, such as iconic gestures, pointing, etc., as well as various
discourse skills, such as recounting events with many sub-events in an

"unmarked" sequence which does not require explicit tense marking, etc.
As a consequence, any deeper understanding of SSLA seems impossible
unless we also study how the learner's "intermediate system" at a given
point is put to use - that is, how he applies his restricted repertoire
of lexical items and grammatical rules in order to communicate, and how
these repertoires interact with more general communicative skills,
such as particular nonverbal means and specific discourse techniques.
This immediately motivates the third objective of the project, but it
also bears on the other two.

A second and no less salient feature of SSLA is the fact that it
results in quite different stages of language mastery. Some learners
reach a variety which is almost indistinguishable from that of a native
speaker; others will never go beyond a vocabulary of fifty words, a few
elementary syntactic constructions and a couple of idiomatic expressions.
This is in clear contrast to first language acquisition, and in partial
contrast to second language acquisition by teaching where both extremes
occur more rarely. This elementary fact immediately raises the following questions:

(a) What are the general factors that determine the exact course of
the acquisition process (if we assume there is one process),
that lead possibly to different acquisition processes (if we
assume that there are real structural differences) and that, in
any event, are responsible for its temporal characteristics,
such as acceleration, slowing down, halt?

(b) Looked at from a different point of view: are the different
"stable varieties" (fossilization) the outcome of different
acquisition processes, or do they represent different stages in
one acquisition process which, due to unknown factors which we
wish to understand, comes to an early halt in one case, whereas
it goes on and thus reaches a higher level in the other case?

These two main questions motivated the first and second objectives of
the project, and make clear the necessity of undertaking longitudinal
studies from (near) the beginning of the acquisitional process.

Mastering a language requires skills of various sorts - including,
for example, the ability to produce and to recognize certain sounds and

prosodic patterns, the ability to recall lexical items, and to put them into well-organized sequences, the ability to associate certain words, like deictic expressions, with features of the speech situation, the ability to monitor not only one's own production, but also to obtain indications of the listener's understanding, the ability to discover why something was said, and finally to take into account possible differences between one's own and the listener's knowledge and assumptions. Learning a language means acquiring all these abilities to a greater or lesser extent. Hence, if we are taking our own objectives seriously, namely to investigate the whole process of language acquisition and its determinants, all of these abilities should ideally be taken into account. Obviously, this is impossible, first because it would clearly be beyond the scope of any reasonable research project, and second, because the present state of language sciences is far from permitting such an enterprise. But it is intended to select and to approach a broad variety of topics (cf. 1.5 and chapters 4 - 7) which, in our opinion, are representative for a large part of the abilities involved. Thus, it will not be possible to trace the process of language acquisition in its totality, but at least to grasp many of its important aspects.

In what follows, we will first outline some of the factors that can influence or determine the acquisition process, and then justify in some detail the areas of investigation chosen.

1.3.3 <u>Determining factors in acquisition</u>. There are many determining factors. For heuristic purposes, we may divide them into three major groups:

(a) Cognitive, perceptual and motor factors, that is, the totality of the learner's acquisition potentiality, for example:
    - the ability to break up sequences of sounds into smaller units,
    - the ability to discriminate between sounds,
    - the ability to identify recurring elements and to associate them with particular functions or meanings,
    - the ability to produce combinations of both segmental and supra-segmental sound features,
      etc.

Clearly, everyone who is able to learn a second language to some
extent must have a set of such cognitive/perceptual prerequisites.
Although they are partly biologically given, they will be subsequently influenced by learning experience, in particular in first
language acquisition. As regards learning experience we are not
entitled to assume that these prerequisites are identical for all
learners, and hence, the project has to take into account this
group of factors.

(b) Propensity factors dependent on the learner's needs, attitudes and
motivations - first of all, the learner's communicative needs and
wishes and the resulting interest in learning the language of his
social environment. Learning a second language is a considerable
cognitive effort, and it may be said that the process starts off
and goes on until a certain balance is reached between cognitive
effort and communicative needs. "Needs" has to be understood here
in a broad sense, ranging from the wish to buy a loaf of bread to
the wish to act as a normal and non-conspicuous member of society,
or, on the contrary, to achieve communicative efficiency without
sacrificing one's own SL identity. There is a second component
in learning propensity which in fact is often difficult to separate from "needs", namely the attitude towards the target language
and the society which uses this language and one's awareness of
different aspects of the language. Both needs and attitude (besides
what has been discussed in (a) of this paragraph) constitute the
learner's propensity. We may assume that this learning propensity
is the most important though not the only factor for the temporal
characteristics of the acquisition process. Hence, it has to be
taken into account.

(c) Exposure to the language. There are two interrelated factors here
which, at the expense of simplifying the problem, we will discuss
separately: the first is the type and quantity of the TL that a
learner hears (this we will call "input"); the second concerns his
interaction, as a social being speaking a foreign language, with
social beings for whom this language is a first language (this we
will call the "right to speak").

Input

Ascertaining the type and quantity of the TL to which adult workers
are exposed is more difficult than in the case of the classroom
learner of a foreign language. For the latter case, "input" would
approximately correspond to the syllabus, and the teacher's own
use of the TL. For SSLA, however, we need to know what varieties
of the TL are spoken in the learner's environment, whether TL
native speakers address the learner in the same way as they address
other TL native speakers of this environment (the clearest case
where this is not true is the use of "foreigner talk" to foreign
workers), what discourse domains and communicative situations are
recurrent, and what the frequency is of these recurrent situations.
Moreover, these situations will reflect, at least to a certain
extent, the communicative rules obtaining in the different cultures of the participants. From the learner's point of view, un-
familiarity with these differences - e.g., the relative verbosity
of the target culture, the appropriate way of expressing different
communicative functions - may be supposed to affect his acquisition,
and will have to be taken into account.

The right to speak

In the previous paragraph, the "input" (as the metaphor from information science suggests) is objectivized: we need to know what
sounds, words, sentence types, etc. the learner hears, and how
often.
In any situation, however, some participants have more the right to
speak than others, and people speak differently to different people,
in different situations. One of the reasons for this is, obviously,
the respective social positions of the participants. (Labov, 1972a
and b, Bourdieu, 1977, Bourdieu & Passeron, 1970, have given detailed
accounts, from different perspectives, of how one's social position
determines one's right to speak and also one's way of speaking, and
conversely, how one's way of speaking determines one's right to
speak and the hearer's perception of one's social position, personality, culture, etc.) In other words, the variety of language
a speaker uses will influence a hearer's perception of the

speaker's personality, social desirability, etc. Certain prosodic
and morphosyntactic phenomena, and factors of conversation management, which are attended to usually on a sub-conscious level, can
allow a listener to project a stereotype - e.g., "he speaks pidgin",
and all the negative implications of this - onto the speaker and
hence find these phenomena confirmed in reality.

Keeping to linguistic phenomena, we may say that a speaker of a
foreign language is typically at a disadvantage from this point of
view. (This approximation is true for this project. We will not be
confronted with situations where, for example, the economic weight
of a particular language allows its speakers to hold the floor
whatever the language being used.) This disadvantage can, and does,
result in the learner having little confidence in his use of the
TL (which is reflected in the deprecating comments he can make on
his own use of it), and therefore low expectations of any interaction involving native speakers.

Furthermore, the potential for misunderstanding, and for verbal
aggression, which exists between native speakers of different
varieties of a language is heightened in the case of a foreign
speaker of a language, whose speech is often judged negatively by
members of the majority community. Language is not a trivial factor
in the breakdown of communications and relationships between members of different socio-linguistic communities - indeed it can
often be the overt trigger. Language is, of course, not the only
factor in causing breakdown.

If we are to take the social problem mentioned in 1.1 seriously,
we will have to examine in some detail the "right to speak" of our
informants in linguistic interactions, and its effect on acquisition.

1.4 Long resident foreign workers

1.4.1 The inclusion of "long residence groups" (LRGs) in the project. As
we said in 1.3.1, a longitudinal investigation from the very early
stages of acquisition is necessary to understand how fossilization comes
about, i.e. to contribute some explanation for the general existence of

relatively stable, non-native varieties of the TLs in the target countries. It would not be too presumptuous to suppose that some understanding of this phenomenon can contribute to the efficacy of any future
measures to help newly-arrived immigrant workers with their language
problems.

It should be pointed out that, independently of possible political
decisions taken in the future - such as Spain's or Portugal's joining the
Common Market - the arrival on the job market of newly arrived foreign
workers will be a <u>structural</u> aspect of the economies of host countries
such as those in which this project will be carried out, for at least
the next decade. Prospective figures published in France, where immigration is now officially at a halt, show that family reunions will
continue (as will, in any case, immigration which is initially clandes-
tine), and that as a result, large numbers of women will be looking for
employment: a frequent plan for them will be (a) to join their families,
(b) to work unofficially, (c) to work officially (Silberman et al.,
1980:35).

However, the majority of immigrant workers at present active in the
target countries are those who have been established for some years,
and whose socio-linguistic problems remain acute. We propose to study
- in three countries: England, Germany and Sweden - groups of such
informants. In doing so, we hope to address more fully the project's
third objective (cf. 1.3.1) - the investigation of the use of non-native
varieties of the TL in everyday interaction - and thus to obtain more insights into what the communicative needs and motivations for language learning of foreign workers are.

1.4.2 <u>Questions to be investigated</u>. In studying the LRGs, we will be interested in two main questions:

(a) What factors govern the general situation whereby foreign workers,
    who have been settled in a country for several years and who have
    acquired certain linguistic skills, nevertheless have great diffi-
    culty in making themselves clearly and successfully understood
    for many important aspects of their daily lives? On a wider level,
    what are the links between language and social disadvantage for
    this type of population?

In attempting to answer these questions, we will be looking
essentially at everyday linguistic interaction between native TL-
speakers and members of the LRGs either directly (to the extent
that this is possible, cf. 8.1) or indirectly, using the formal
data collection techniques at our disposal (cf. 8.3 & 4). All the
topics of investigation are relevant in this respect, but more
particularly chapter 4: Understanding, Misunderstanding, Breakdown.

(b)   After some years' residence, these informants' command of the TL
will in all likelihood - as we have said - have become fossilized:
we do not know however, whether this process of fossilization will
apply to all aspects of informants' TL capacities and in all circumstances.

We hypothesize that external circumstances acting independently,
and also acting on motivation - rather than the informants' cognitive
prerequisites (cf. 1.3.3) - will have determined fossilization (with
the possible exception of pronunciation: cf. Neufeld, 1979). If
this is indeed the case, it should also be the case that a change
in the informants' external circumstances - family situation, change
or loss of job - will provoke further acquisition (or, possibly,
regression). We therefore propose to choose, for the LRGs, informants whose life is undergoing or has just undergone an important
change of circumstances, in order to ascertain whether there is
indeed a perceptible link between use and knowledge of the TL at
this non-initial level.

To our knowledge, this type of potential acquisition/loss has
hitherto received relatively little attention, cf. chapter 3:
Previous Work.

1.5   Areas of investigation

All descriptions of SSLA, and all previous investigations into
SSLA (cf. chapter 3), have concentrated on selected linguistic phenomena,
be they phonological, syntactic, lexical, discourse or whatever. This is
inevitable since, although acquisition takes place simultaneously in all
these domains, it is beyond the scope of any research project to explore

them all. As was stated in 1.3.2, a choice must be made. For our part, we have selected four areas of investigation which do not correspond to the traditional linguistic domains mentioned above, but rather bring together selected questions from each domain - and from others (in particular, cultural background knowledge, emotional attitude and linguistic awareness) - which bear interdependently on more general hypotheses about the process of SSLA, and about the factors which may explain it. These four broad areas of investigation are described in detail in chapters 4 - 7; here, we will attempt to justify the approach adopted.

1.5.1 <u>The learner's analytic problem</u>. As has been pointed out in 1.3.2, SSLA is language acquisition in everyday communication. The learner is faced at the outset with a basic communication problem - understanding messages and having his/her own messages understood - in a difficult, sometimes hostile, environment (cf. 4.2.1; we return to the question of environment below), and must display and simultaneously develop a wide range of verbal and nonverbal skills.

As far as <u>comprehension</u> is concerned, the learner is faced in the early stages of acquisition with the basic problem of decomposing stretches of TL speech into smaller units, which may or may not coincide with the units into which a native speaker decomposes his language. (This latter problem may result in the learner taking in, and subsequently using, unanalyzed or "formulaic" expressions, cf. 6.2.5.) We may call this task the learner's <u>analytic problem</u>, and it partially motivated the choice of the first area of investigation: Understanding, Misunderstanding, Breakdown, cf. chapter 4.

In choosing this theme, we are seeking to trace how the learner goes about solving this task with the cognitive/perceptual disposition (including background knowledge) he has. In situation, the learner can make use of many clues to meaning (nonverbal as well as verbal). We may therefore imagine that a particular message be understood on a particular occasion without the acquisition process being affected. Thus, we are faced with the problem of identifying, from our inferences as to the perceptual strategies at work in individual situations, those which can plausibly be taken to be recurrent, and of mapping their use onto

the acquisition process. (The investigation of the structural properties of the acquisition process and of informants' language use, cf.
1.3.1, is indissociable here.) Obviously, this is a difficult task,
and one which requires control over at least some aspects of the actual
input to the learner, as well as his own spontaneous output and introspection. Furthermore, the study of comprehension in SSLA is difficult
(and this perhaps explains its relative neglect in previous work),
the more so as the very nature of our informants precludes the type of
test developed for formally educated adult L1 speakers (cf. Gleitman &
Gleitman, 1970).

We therefore propose to concentrate on a limited number of questions, and attempt to answer them by inference from spontaneous production, completed by self-confrontation, film-watching and informal experiments as well as ad hoc translation tasks (cf. 2.5.2 for a description of these techniques). In brief, we are inferring how the different
cognitive/perceptual disposition, and general background knowledge, of
each learner intervenes in his acquisition of the TL by examining (some
aspects of) how he analyses the TL in situation, and subsequently
checking these inferences with the learner.

In order to solve the analytic problem, the learner cannot rely
on the structure of the TL since this is exactly what he has to analyse.
His decomposition may be guided by various phonological clues, such as
pauses, intonation breaks, etc., which, he thinks, mark boundaries in
the speech stream. He may also apply to the task of understanding the
speech stream the principles underlying the SL: these principles may be
grammatical "look for the verb at the end", functional "look for new/
important information at the end", "contiguous elements are likely to
be semantically related", or abstract "x and y cannot be related since
they are separated by two cyclic nodes". (For many of the principles
plausibly at work here, cf. Slobin, 1973.) If the principles applied
are shared by the SL and the TL, the task may be facilitated.

In addition, the learner may be guided by his interpretation in
context of the utterance and some of its parts. When faced with an
utterance like "Peter was here", he may know that the sequence /pi:tə/
refers to an acquaintance, thus allowing an interpretation of /pi:tə/
and /wəzhiə/ as distinct units.

Similarly, if for example successful communication with native speakers
involves correct and recurrent manipulation of specific objects in
some environment, the recurrent association (e.g., by gesture) of a
sequence of sounds and an object by native speakers will help the learner
in decomposing the speech stream, and in acquiring the lexical items in
question (cf. 4.3.2 and 6.2.1). What remains for the learner is then to
infer the semantic relationships between the items he recognizes. We
will return to this problem in 1.5.3 below.

More generally, the learner's "stored knowledge" (knowledge of the
world as shaped by his own culture, cf. 4.2.2) may allow him to interpret
- or misinterpret - some aspects of messages in situation: an Italian
in England on even his first visit to a supermarket can infer that the
first (and probably only) tone unit uttered by the cashier after ringing
up the total will refer to the figures on the till; this inference may
on the other hand not be at all obvious for a newly-arrived Punjabi.
In other words, the greater the assumptions shared by source and target
cultures, the more successful the learner's inferences will be.

Lastly, the learner may try to give himself the wherewithal to
verify that he has indeed understood the message, by repetition or
other meta-linguistic means (cf. 4.4).

1.5.2 <u>Areas of investigation</u>. The areas we will be concerned with in
relation to what may broadly be called "processing the input" are therefore the role of cultural background knowledge in (mis)understanding
(cf. 4.3), feedback processes (cf. 4.4), the integration of contextual and
uttered information (cf. 4.3.2, and chapter 7), and two broad perceptual
strategies: "segmenting frames" (cf. 6.2.5) and "looking for important
words" (cf. 4.3.2). For this latter strategy, on the assumption that
important words will be taken in and subsequently re-used, the exhaustive lexicon for each SL-TL-pair that we will be establishing for the
early stages of acquisition will serve as a check (cf. 1.5.4 and 6.3).

The use of the term "important" in the last paragraph implies that
propensity factors will also play a role in the analytic task of the
learner. Formulaic expressions, for example, may be acquired precisely
because they are perceived to fulfill important communicative functions
in everyday interaction. This should be placed in a wider perspective,

however, as it will be important to examine the role of both success
and failure - i.e., understanding vs misunderstanding and breakdown -
in the acquisition process.

The learner's "right to speak" (cf. 1.3.3) is partially governed
by native speakers' reactions in linguistic communication. As we said
above, this communication can be difficult, and native speakers' reactions sometimes hostile, leading them to consider the learner as in-
competent or inferior - linguistically, but perhaps also intellectually
and socially -; this being one basis for negative stereotypes (cf. 4.2.1).
Misunderstandings may have a positive or negative effect on the learner's
propensity, either making him linguistically more aware and prepared
consciously to learn the TL (cf. von Stutterheim, 1982), or leading him
to avoid all but inevitable linguistic contact with TL native speakers,
thus provoking early fossilization. We propose to examine the role of
misunderstandings, and communicative breakdown, which inevitably heighten
the social/psychological distance (Schumann, 1978) between the learner
and the TL community, on the attitudes and emotions of our informants,
and to attempt to determine to what extent this leads to avoidance and
early fossilization (cf. 4.5).

These selected aspects of the learner's analytic task therefore
seem a propitious area for all three objectives of the project, as well
as providing partial answers to the relative role of language specific
vs generalisable phenomena in the acquisition process.

1.5.3 <u>The learner's synthetic problem</u>. However the learner accomplishes
this analytic task, he will eventually (after, perhaps an initial
"passive" phase, cf. 4.6) come up with a certain number of items which
are important for his own communication in the TL. He is then faced
with a <u>synthetic problem</u>, that is, the task of arranging these items
so that they form meaningful utterances. Which principles will he
follow in this respect? He has by now, we suppose, some hunches about
the TL based on the initial analysis of the input. As comprehension and
production are interactive and henceforth simultaneous activities for
the learner, we may expect the arrangement of items which he has, to
follow grammatical, functional and more abstract principles similar to
those mentioned in 1.5.1, whose efficiency for TL communication will be

measured by the degree of comprehension of his interlocutors, as evidenced e.g., by the type of feedback they give (cf. 4.4). This arrangement of items in utterances will be completed by his own use of contextual features, etc., as he attempts to have his message understood.

In other words, we expect, broadly speaking, similar phenomena to be at work in comprehension and production, and will select some aspects of production which can be compared with the areas of investigation of 1.5.1.

First, however, we would like to mention two crucial aspects of the learner's synthetic problem which have received relatively little attention in previous studies: ranking of functions (1.5.3.1) and alternatives in expression (1.5.3.2).

1.5.3.1 Ranking of functions. The question here is how the necessity of expressing certain functions, such as quantification, attribution, modality, temporal, causal and other relations between items, intervenes in the learner's synthetic problem. (Note that this problem parallels the task the learner has in inferring relationships between items he recognizes in the interlocutor's utterances, cf. 1.5.1.)

There is a rich variety of such functions, and there is no reason to assume that all of them are equally important for the learner when communicating; the functions he learns to express will therefore presumably reflect his communicative needs. More generally, there is no reason to suppose that all of them are equally basic to communication tout court: the fact that some languages have developed devices to express some of these functions to a high degree of differentiation while leaving others at a more rudimentary level seems to suggest that there are clear communicative priorities among them. Both of these facts should influence the order in which the corresponding means are developed in second language acquisition.

An example of what is meant by this is the following:
Previous research (Heidelberger Forschungsprojekt "Pidgin-Deutsch", 1978; hereafter "HPD") into the spontaneous acquisition of German by Spanish and Italian adults has shown that noun phrases are developed by and large in the following order (for illustrative purposes, this description is somewhat simplified here. It will be taken up again in 7.2.2.3):

(a) proper names and common nouns (plus forms for "I" and "you")
(b) nouns with a quantifier (both uninflected)
(c) nouns with an article
(d) nouns with an adjective
(e) combinations of (b) to (d)
(f) more complex attributes.

Obviously, this development goes from simple to more complex in terms of the number of elements, but this does not explain, for example, why numerals (b) are learned before determiners (c), and determiners before adjectives (d). A possible, although at present speculative assumption might be that among all the functions of the noun phrase and its parts, "pure" reference (that is, evoking an object, person, idea, etc. and leaving implicit such distinctions as generic vs specific) is fundamental, quantification is more "important" for communication than determination (there are languages without definite and indefinite articles, but no languages without numerals), which in turn is more "important" than attribution. Alternatively (or perhaps interdependently) the order of acquisition reflects the order of urgency that learners feel in expressing these functions.

We may also speculate (cf. 1.5.1 and 4.3.2), that in <u>analysing</u> the speech stream, the learner will first identify nouns, then an association of a noun with a numeral, and so on.

1.5.3.2 <u>Alternatives in expression</u>. This question is in a way the counterpart to 1.5.3.1. As a rule, basic functions like reference, predication, setting in time and space, modality are not uniquely linked to just one expressive device, say a particular type of syntactic construction, or to a particular set of suffixes; there is rather a repertoire of different possibilities which may be used simultaneously or alternatively. Different languages may give different priorities to these possibilities while the functions as such are more or less shared by all languages. Hence, the learner by virtue of his first language competence knows how to apply these functions, but he has to learn how to express them in the target language. Which of the various possibilities he is faced with does he choose first, and how is the balance shifted from certain elementary devices to more complex ones until he (possibly)

disposes of the full repertoire offered by the target language? Again,
we will illustrate the problem by an example taken from the acquisition
of German by Spanish and Italian workers (HPD, 1978). In German (just
as in all other target languages) <u>temporality</u> is expressed essentially
by four devices: (a) tense marking of the verb (or auxiliary), (b)
simple deictic or non-deictic temporal adverbs, (c) complex adverbial
constructions formed with prepositions and conjunctions (for acquisition studies, (b) and (c), though functionally similar, should be kept
apart), and (d) some discourse principles such as "first event first"
or "jumps in temporal sequence must be explicitly marked". In the early
stages of acquisition, (a) and (c) are never used, and (b) is extremely
restricted, that is, the morphological and syntactic devices are never,
or almost never used; temporality is exclusively expressed on the one
hand, by a limited number of simple adverbs and by pure nouns in temporal
function (<u>vacation</u> in the sense of "when I was on vacation"), and on the
other hand, by discourse principles. As the acquisition process goes on,
simple adverbials consisting of preposition and noun are learned, and
morphological tense marking of analytic forms (modal or auxiliary
plus infinitive or participle) are developed, and the balance is slowly
shifted to these expressive means.

In relation to this, we wish to see (cf. 7.4) whether this linguistic progression noted here ~~~~~~~~~~~~~~~~~~~~~~~~~~~~~~~ - for
all cases of acqu ~~~~~~~~~~~~~~~~~~~~~~~~~~~~~~~~~~~ether
it is specific to ~~~~~~~~~~~~~~~~~~~~~~~~~~~~~~~~~ or
more generalizable,, and, for each learner, why the progression - if
there is progression - happens.

To summarize, the following questions seem to us to be important
in investigating the learner's synthetic problem:
- the relationship between the analytic and the synthetic problem;
- the relative communicative importance the learner assigns to different
  functions such as reference, quantification, attribution, etc., and
  why this should be;
- the shift from one set of devices for expressing these functions to
  another set, and why this shift occurs.

These questions bear necessarily on all three objectives of the
project, and on the role of phenomena specific to a language vs that of

more generalizable phenomena in second language acquisition.

1.5.4 <u>Areas of investigation</u>. The areas of investigation we have chosen
in relation to 1.5.3 include problems of <u>linearization</u> and <u>reference to
people, space and time</u>.

Levelt (1982b) points out that many of the principles governing the
way a speaker arranges an amount of complex information in temporal
order (the linearization problem) are independent of specific languages
and cultures, and exist both to facilitate retrieval of pieces of information on the part of the speaker and to facilitate the listener's
comprehension.

We are asking three questions here: what principles govern the
temporal order of learners' utterances with respect to each other? What
principles govern learners' arrangement of items within an utterance?
How does a learner's use of these principles develop, or change, over
time? For the first question, previous work with L1 speakers (cf. 5.1)
has shown that different principles operate in different discourse
domains: we will limit ourselves to the study of learners' organization
of states, events and processes in time (cf. 7.4.2.3). It is hypothesized
that learners will initially use TL-independent principles in expressing these relationships, and that TL-specific devices will progressively be introduced, as in the example of 1.5.3.2.

Within the utterance, we will examine how the learner makes use
both of the principles governing the order of utterances in discourse,
and of pragmatic constraints such as what information is given at a
particular point, or what an utterance is about, as well as local
principles such as "semantically related items are placed together",
in order to structure information. Three devices for signalling <u>the
thematic structure of utterances</u> (cf. chapter 5) will be particularly
studied: stress/intonation, word order and anaphora. It is hypothesized
that in the early stages learners will structure their utterances essentially along pragmatic - i.e., largely TL-independent - principles, and
that TL-specific (or TL-variety-specific, cf. 5.1.4) syntactic devices
will progressively play a greater role. This hypothesis is obviously
very broad: the typological distance between SL and TL in a given pair,
and the fact that our informants are adults are likely to affect the

extent to which it is true (cf. 5.2.1).

Referring to persons, space and time has already been mentioned several times in this section. Any utterance uttered by a speaker necessarily contains at least some aspects of such reference (cf. the moi-ici-maintenant of Benveniste, 1966, or the origo of Bühler, 1934). It is therefore independent of any specific discourse domain; and the acquisition of TL devices for expressing such reference is a central problem for any learner. This immediately justifies its inclusion as a major research topic.

Furthermore, the formal and semantic properties of this area have been well described for the TLs as systems, and the acquisition of these systems by L1 and L2 learners has received much previous attention: we may therefore see how the results of previous work apply across our ten linguistically distinct cases of SSLA. Two further characteristics of this area make its investigation particularly interesting for a project such as this:

Firstly, all languages seem to have developed two different means of expressing such reference: deictically (the problem addressed by Benveniste and Bühler), and non-deictically. Deictic means crucially hinge on the ability to associate certain situational features to certain expressions. There is no reason to assume that the way in which this is done is very different from one language to another; hence, a large part of deictic reference need not be learned; what has to be learned are some language specific words and some language specific semantic oppositions (cf. here-there in English as opposed to aqui-alli-alla in Spanish). Non-deictic reference, on the other hand, is less context-dependent and hinges much more on verbal means; therefore, we may assume that it requires much more learning than deictic reference, and its full use should develop later.

Secondly, spatial, temporal and personal reference differ in the degree to which they are obligatory - both between each other and between the various languages under study. Thus, temporal reference is, except for elliptical sentences, obligatory in all languages involved; it automatically goes with verb inflection; personal deictic reference is obligatorily marked by pronouns in all target languages, but only in some source languages. Spatial reference is always optional. It may be assumed that optional or obligatory marking also influences the learner's approach to these categories in the target languages.

Both of these areas therefore allow us fully to address the questions summarized in 1.5.3.2.

The final major area of investigation is termed <u>processes in the developing vocabulary</u>. Here, we are seeking to identify in selected lexical fields (see below), the semantic processes at work as the learner builds up his vocabulary. An attempt will be made to relate them to some of the factors determining the acquisition processes which were discussed in 1.3 of this chapter. If, for example, successful communication with native speakers of the TL involves recurrent use of specific items in some environment, then it can be hypothesized that the corresponding lexical field will exhibit a high degree of precise differentiation. Or, if an environment is perceived to correspond closely to some environment of the SL culture, the corresponding lexical field may be structured according to SL principles. These considerations motivate the choice of the areas "home", "work", "social relations" for investigation.

An attempt will also be made to identify what have come to be known as lexical gap fillers: strategies used to compensate for the lack of a specific word, such as gestures, paraphrasing and code-switching. As the relative communicative success of the use of these strategies presumably influences further acquisition, this topic is directly relevant for the second and third objectives of the project (cf. 1.3.1).

However, this area of investigation is extremely difficult on various grounds. Although lexical semantics is a classical and well-established field of linguistics, a full and systematic description of more than small subdomains of the lexicon is still an almost impossible enterprise, even for well-explored languages like English, German or French. Furthermore, the methods developed in lexical semantics are designed to describe more or less stable systems, and although in historical linguistics, there are numerous studies dealing with semantic change, they are restricted to a few items and a few aspects of semantic development. To our knowledge, there is no elaborated descriptive technique which would allow a systematic description of full semantic systems in evolution. A final problem has to do with the specific kind of data we have access to in this project. Usually, the semantics of some lexical item or some lexical field is described on the basis of the linguist's knowledge of the language in question. He knows what the various words mean in various contexts, and he has to integrate this knowledge into some coherent description. In the case of learner varieties, however, he has no immediate access to the "language" he wants to describe. He may be able to understand at least a part of the learner's utterance. He is able to do so on the basis of his competence in the target language (and, to a lesser extent, his competence in the source language). But this presupposes that the learner uses the lexical items with the same internal set of semantic features as the TL native speaker does. We may also wonder whether, in all cases, the learner <u>perceives</u> a lexical item in this way. Two examples of what is meant here are the following:

(a) HPD (1978) found that the verb <u>kommen</u> was strongly overgeneralized by initial learners to denote all kinds of movements, including abstract changes of state.

This fact is interesting for two reasons: - it may indicate the functional importance of the origo (Bühler, 1934) in the early stages of acquisition (cf. 7.3.2.4, and, for pronouns, 7.2.2.1); - it may be that the learner perceives native speakers' use of <u>kommen</u> as meaning, generically, "move".

(b) It was also found by HPD that a word such as <u>Kuh</u> was correctly used (and, presumably, perceived) as denoting "cow", but also incorrectly used, by extension, to denote all farm animals.

Our main preoccupation in this area will therefore be to identify, for each lexical field (cf. 6.2), processes such as extension and overgeneralization, taking as the principal data base the learner's utterances, completed, however, by self-confrontation (cf. 8.4.4), where learners will be asked to make explicit their use and understanding of relevant lexical items.

Other areas of investigation chosen here are metalinguistic vocabulary, expressions of emotional attitude, modality and formulaic expressions. We have already discussed the communicative importance of the latter, and the opportunity they give us to investigate the strategy of segmenting frames. Modality was chosen since, like reference to people,

space and time, it is a fundamental characteristic of any utterance
(and indeed interdependent with reference to time in the TLs). The first
two were chosen as we consider linguistic awareness and emotional attitude to be important propensity factors in acquisition (cf. 1.3.3) and
wish to study to what extent learners can verbalize them. And on a
very practical level, some time will inevitably be spent during the
investigation in talking to informants about these subjects. Thus for
metalinguistic vocabulary, we will be looking for expressions such as
"French is difficult", "What does this mean?" as well as for the (much
less likely) occurrence of terms such as "adjective", "predicate", etc.

Finally, as we mentioned in 1.5.1, this area will serve as a check
on the perceptual strategies of the learner. The strategies used for
identifying important words will presumably result in the acquisition
of these words and their subsequent production. The exhaustive lexicon
(cf. 6.3) for each SL-TL-pair which we are establishing - at least for
the early stages of acquisition - will allow us to determine, for each
informant, the order of appearance and frequency of use of lexical items
and formulaic expressions.

2. Lay-out of the Whole Project

2.1 Personnel and organizations involved in the project

The project will run over five years with a staff of about 20 full-time researchers. It is planned as a longitudinal comparative study in five European countries: France, (Federal Republic of) Germany, Great Britain, The Netherlands, and Sweden. In each of these countries, a local research group has been set up, which, in principle, consists of three researchers; the co-ordinator of each group may, but need not belong to these three. Depending on the local situation, changes in the composition of these work groups may be necessary. The local centres and their co-ordinators are:

1. Université de Paris VIII - Vincennes à St. Denis,
   Groupe de Recherches sur l'Acquisition des Langues,
   2, Rue de la Liberté, 93526 Saint-Denis, Cedex 02, France.
   Co-ordinators: Colette Noyau & Daniel Véronique.

2. Universität Heidelberg, Seminar für Deutsch als
   Fremdsprachenphilologie, Plöck 55, 6900 Heidelberg, FRG.
   Co-ordinator: Rainer Dietrich.

3. National Centre of Industrial Language Training,
   Havelock Road, Southall, Middlesex UB2 4NZ, Great Britain.
   Co-ordinators: Margaret Simonot & Celia Roberts.

4. Katholieke Hogeschool Tilburg, Subfaculteit Letteren,
   Hogeschoollaan 225, 5000 LE Tilburg, Netherlands.
   Co-ordinator: Guus Extra.

5. Göteborgs Universitet, Institutionen för Lingvistik,
   Erik Dahlbergsgatan 11B VI, Göteborg, Sweden.
   Co-ordinator: Jens Allwood.

Local arrangements are also being made for co-operation with interested researchers and other relevant projects: for example, a university consultative group exists in Britain to maintain links with relevant university departments and more especially to stimulate interest in this area of research in British universities; the French team is a member of the CNRS interdisciplinary laboratory (GRECO 13) on international migration and is in regular contact with some of the other member teams on matters relating to this project; in Germany co-operation has been arranged with the Berlin project on communication strategies used by Turkish learners of German (Freie Universität: co-ordinator N. Dittmar). In Sweden, co-operative arrangements have been established with the EIFO project on second generation immigrants. Finally, regular meetings are planned with researchers working on the Neuchâtel project on bilingualism (Université de Neuchâtel: co-ordinators B. Py and G. Lüdi), and with researchers at the University of California, Los Angeles.

The project has been approved by the ESF's Social Sciences and Humanities committees, and by its General Assembly. It is supported by the following ESF member organizations: Max-Planck-Gesellschaft (FRG); the Social Science Research Council (Britain); the Nederlandse Organizatie voor Zuiver Wetenschappelijk Onderzoek (Netherlands); the Humanistik Samhällsvetenskapliga Forsknigsrådet (Sweden); the Academy of Finland; the Fonds National Suisse de la Recherche Scientifique (Switzerland); the Conseil National de la Recherche Scientifique (France); the Fonds National Belge (Belgium) and the CNR (Italy).

The project's central co-ordination is at the Max-Planck-Institut für Psycholinguistik, Berg en Dalseweg 79, NL 6522 BC Nijmegen, Netherlands. The project directors are Wolfgang Klein (Max-Planck-Institut) and Jens Allwood; the central co-ordinator is Clive Perdue (Max-Planck-Institut). For matters concerning the European Science Foundation, the project is organized by Jostein Mykletun, ESF, 1, Quai Lezay Marnésia, F-6700 Strasbourg.

In addition, a "Steering Committee" has been set up which meets regularly, advises the project members in their work and reports to the ESF on the project's progress. It is composed as follows:

John Lyons, University of Sussex (Chairman)
Ayhan Aksu, Boğaziçi Üniversitesi, Istanbul

Norbert Dittmar, Freie Universität, Berlin
Willem Levelt, Max-Planck-Institut, Nijmegen
Bengt Nordberg, Uppsala Universitet
Dan Slobin, University of California

In the following sections, we shall outline in turn the languages to be studied, the type of informants required, the time schedule of the project and the data collection techniques to be used.

2.2   Source and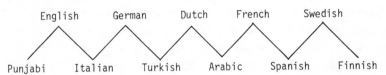

The target languages were English, German, Dutch, French and Swedish. For each target language two source languages were selected. The selection was essentially based on two criteria. First, those languages with the greatest number of native speakers (in a given target country) were given priority. Second, it should be possible to make linguistically interesting comparisons; this means that paired comparisons should be made of the acquisition of one target language (TL) by speakers of source languages (SL) with very different structures, and of the acquisition of two TLs by speakers of the same SL. Only such an arrangement allows a systematic analysis of the impact which a particular SL has on the second language acquisition of a learner and allows us therefore to identify generalizable phenomena in the acquisition process. The two criteria lead to the following combination of target and source languages:

English   German   Dutch   French   Swedish

Punjabi   Italian   Turkish   Arabic   Spanish   Finnish

Hence, Arabic, Spanish, Turkish and Italian are represented in two host countries, each. Punjabi and Finnish remain singles; they are the most important source languages in Great Britain and Sweden, respectively, but they play no significant role elsewhere. Three out of the six source languages are non-Indo-European.

Although this combination is in the circumstances an almost optimal solution, some drawbacks and problems remain, which should be mentioned:

30—Lay-out of the whole project

(a)   Four of the five TLs are Germanic. Although it would have been
      linguistically more interesting to have a typologically broader
      range of TLs, it was felt that these five should be chosen as they
      are the most important European languages for foreign workers
      (ranging from German with about 6 million potential learners to
      Dutch with about half a million).
(b)   Arabic and Spanish show some syntactic similarities. They were
      nevertheless chosen for TL French as they are important SLs in
      France and allow the paired comparisons with TLs Dutch and Swedish
      mentioned above.
(c)   Most languages show some internal variation. This is most apparent
      in the case of Arabic, but holds for the other SLs as well, though
      to a lesser extent. It also plays a role for the TLs. Excluding
      the media, foreign workers in Germany for example are usually ex-
      posed not to standard German but to a local vernacular, which in
      many cases, if spoken by one of its native speakers, is incompre-
      hensible for other speakers of German. The variety of Swedish spo-
      ken in the Göteborg area has certain word order possibilities and
      intonational phenomena not found in other dialects of Swedish.
      Regional variation between the French spoken in the Paris and
      Marseilles areas will have to be taken into account as the French
      study will be undertaken in both these places.
(d)   The grammatical descriptions which are available for some of these
      languages may prove to be unsatisfactory for our purposes. Given
      the continuing debate about even the most salient features of the
      best-explored language of the world - standard English - such as
      the progressive form or pronominalization, we should not expect
      the available descriptions of Punjabi or Turkish, despite all
      their merits, to be sufficient for our purposes. In addition, the
      available descriptions are - with some exceptions - restricted to
      structural properties; they do not deal so much with language in
      use, that is, with phenomena such as ellipsis, consonant cluster
      simplification, quantitative features, etc.; but it is language in
      use which supplies the input for the learner. And above all, for
      most of the dialects and vernaculars, we have no systematic de-
      scriptions at all.

Hence, there are three inevitable consequences for our investigation:

(1) We cannot rely for informant selection on simple categorizations such as "speaker of Turkish" (the more so as many "Turks" among the foreign workers are actually Kurdish); it will be necessary to control as much as possible for their actual native language variety.

(2) As was stated in 1.3.3, we will have to collect data about the language which is actually spoken in the social environment of our informants (including possible variety switches). This will involve some observation and interviewing of native TL speakers (see the following section).

(3) We have to ensure that descriptions of the varieties in question are reliable. In particular, it may become necessary to work out such descriptions for at least some aspects of the "target varieties" on the basis of our own data.

2.3 Time schedule and informants

The whole project will run over five years. It has two phases:

1. Phase A (3 years). This phase is planned for field work, preparation of data (selection for analysis and transcription) and first analysis.

2. Phase B (2 years). This phase will involve the detailed data analysis and the completion of the project report.

The field work and analysis phases are not completely separated; it seems sensible to start with some exemplary analysis in phase A, and it might be necessary to collect some additional data in Phase B.

Essentially, the project is planned as a longitudinal study on small samples of learners, completed by smaller cross-sectional studies (see below). In each of the five target countries, two groups of four informants (one group per source language) will be studied. Their language acquisition will be observed over 30 months (phase A). All of them should be adults between 18 and 30 years at the start of the project, and at the beginning of observation, they should have preferably none, or at least extremely restricted knowledge of the target language.

All learners should be working class people, and in each of the ten
groups, both men and women should be represented. It seems pointless to
subdivide the groups according to further variables; but for each learner, a careful and detailed record of possibly relevant factors (education, job, intensity of contacts with TL) has to be worked out and - if
these factors change - regularly updated.

This summary description of the main sample of informants does not
mention the practical problems inherent in this longitudinal study.
These will be discussed in detail in chapter 9. For example, in order
to end up after 30 months with data on four informants per source-target-
language pair, we will have to start with more than four informants in
order to ensure against "dropping out". These practical considerations
hold to a lesser extent for other types of informant within the project.

These forty learners will be under regular observation over two and
a half years. This means that a great deal of their social contacts with
the host population will consist of contacts with the researchers. Moreover, it is most likely that their language learning propensity will be
influenced by their participation in the project. We will therefore have
considerable control effects. We see no way to avoid them, but we should
have some information about their extent and about the direction in
which they lead. To this end, six of the ten groups will be compared to
a group of six informants whose language acquisition is not so frequently observed but who have similar biographical characteristics to the
main sample. On three occasions, data about these control groups will be
collected: at the outset, after about one year and a half, and at the
end of the 30 months (these time spans are approximate). The same methods of data collection as used for the longitudinal informants will be
applied. We will call these control groups the "initial learner groups".

Six groups of the main sample will be compared with informants of a
different population - the "long residence groups" - whose inclusion in
the project was discussed in 1.4. These groups will consist of six informants. Data will be collected from them six times during phase A of
the project.

We also need some information about the language, language use and
cultural background assumptions of the target population. It will be
sufficient to collect data from a group of four native speakers of

the target language who will be interviewed once, and participate in one film-watching "session" (cf. 8.2.). These native speakers should belong to the immediate social environment of the foreign informants.

To sum up, we have four kinds of informants:

(1) Main group: 40 adult foreign workers, 8 per target language, 4 per source-target-language pair. They will be regularly observed over 30 months.

(2) Initial learner group: 36 adult foreign workers with similar biographical characteristics to those in the main group. 12 per target language (Dutch, French, Swedish), 6 per source-target-language pair. Data will be collected from them three times during the longitudinal study.

(3) Long residence group: 36 adult foreign workers with at least five years residence in the target community. 12 per target language (English, German, Swedish), 6 per source-target-language pair. Data will be collected from them six times during the longitudinal study.

(4) Native speaker group: 20 adult members of the target communities, 4 per target language. They should belong to the social environment of the other informants. Data will be collected from them twice during the longitudinal study, and in participant observation (cf. 2.5.2).

Ideally, it would be desirable for all teams to study all types of informant, but given the manpower and facilities available, only the Swedish team feels that it is in a position to do this. It is expected, however, that the insights into the control effect obtained from a comparison of the main and initial learner groups in three countries (France, Holland, Sweden), and the broader study of language use and communicative difficulties in three countries (England, Germany, Sweden), will give results that can be generalized.

We discuss in chapter 9 how these informants can be found and how they can be motivated to take part in the study. Similar methods of data collection will be used for all informants. For the main sample, each informant is interviewed once a month, the interview being video-recorded at least once every three months, and audio-recorded otherwise.

Other techniques will be used, and all methods will be discussed in detail in chapter 8. We will simply give in 2.5 below some general considerations motivating our choice of these methods and a brief description of each. For reasons of space, both are highly simplified here, and will be elaborated upon in chapters 4 - 8.

2.4 Summary

The following table summarizes the practical organization of the project by country, language and type of informant.

Read table 1 (page 35) here

2.5 Data Collection

2.5.1 General considerations

(a) We are studying acquisition. At a given time we wish therefore to know, in respect to the domains of investigation described in chapters 4 - 7, what an informant has acquired, what he has not acquired and what he is acquiring. We also wish to know why. That is, what factors (cf. 1.3.3) can explain this state?

(b) It was stated in 1.3.2 that the type of learner we are studying acquires the TL essentially in communication with TL speakers who belong to his everyday environment. Obtaining data representative of this communication is therefore highly important. These data will allow us to make inferences about (a).

(c) These inferences result from the examination of a text - the recorded (transcribed) data - and have to be verified as:
   - the text will not reveal all that the informant does know, i.e. what he could have used, but did not. Words or structures relevant for us may not be needed in communication, and not appear;
   - the text will not reveal what the informant does not know, or is "not yet sure of". In the latter case, he may avoid using a word or structure; the former case constitutes of course an alternative reason for the non-appearance of a word or structure

- Table 1 -

EUROPEAN SCIENCE FOUNDATION PROJECT: ECOLOGY OF ADULT LANGUAGE ACQUISITION (EALA) 1982-1986

Project directors: Wolfgang Klein and Jens Allwood.

Central co-ordination: Clive Perdue.

ESF co-ordination: Jostein Mykletun.

		Great Britain	Germany	Netherlands	France	Sweden
ORGANIZATIONS	Affiliations	NCILT Southall	Heidelberg University	Tilburg Kath. Hogeschool	Université de Paris-Vincennes	University of Göteborg
	Local Co-ordinators	Margaret Simonot	Rainer Dietrich	Guus Extra	Colette Noyau	Jens Allwood
LANGUAGES	Target Languages	English	German	Dutch	French	Swedish
	Source Languages	Punjabi / Italian	Italian / Turkish	Turkish / Arabic	Arabic / Spanish	Spanish / Finnish
INFORMANTS	Longitudinal Group 4 per SL	x x	x	x	x	x
	Initial Learner (Control) Group 6 per SL		x	x	x	x
	Long Residence Group 6 per SL	x x	x		x	x
	Native Speaker Group: 4 per TL	x	x	x	x	x

in the text;

- the text is a product. It has often been pointed out that it is as difficult to infer from this product what an informant intended to say as it is to infer what he understood in an interaction. For this latter case, an inappropriate response, for example, may lead us to infer that the informant did not understand the preceding utterance, but it will not necessarily tell us <u>what</u> he did not understand;

- if the text is representative of everyday verbal interaction, it will be possible to gain an idea of what the informant's exposure to language is. However, information about the two other sets of determining factors - cognitive/perceptual and propensity factors - will only emerge indirectly, and incompletely, from the text.

Thus, it is necessary for us to have the <u>informant's account</u> of what was meant, or what was understood, in respect of phenomena relevant to us, and to elicit linguistic phenomena which are absent from the text, if this is possible for the informant. It is also necessary to obtain the informant's account of what he was feeling during the interaction, his attitudes to the interlocutor(s), etc.

(d) The elicitation - or introspection - tasks necessary for (c) are not representative of an informant's normal use of the TL for at least three reasons:

- they are guided, or semi-guided. In such a situation, an informant is likely to have his attention drawn more to the <u>form</u> of what is being said/listened to than would otherwise be the case. This may result in an informant's becoming more aware of (aspects of) linguistic communication, which will contribute to the control effect mentioned in 2.3;

- the people giving such tasks are researchers, with whom the informant would probably not have had contact had he not been taking part in a project where such tasks are necessary (cf. again 2.3);

- there is nothing at stake for the informant. By this we mean that much of his everyday use of the TL may, if unsuccessful, lead to disadvantage (cf. 4.2), ranging from mutual frustration with neighbours to loss of a residence permit. We will call everyday interactions (where something is, at least, potentially, at stake) "authentic interactions". Authentic interactions are thus, at least potentially, stressful for someone whose command of the TL is not perfect. Although interactions with researchers whose interest lies in maintaining good relations with informants may also be stressful, they are not so for the same reason (see below). We will call interactions with researchers and where nothing is at stake: "project specific interactions". Thus "authentic" is used here in the sense of "everyday life", in contradistinction to "project specific". The distinction is not meant to imply that interactions with researchers are not also authentic.

(e)   For researchers, the clearest data come from situations where it is possible to make good quality recordings (i.e. in a place with no noise) and to have accurate knowledge (i.e. by being present) of the contextual conditions under which they were obtained. These conditions are not met when obtaining data representative of an informant's interactions with TL speakers of his everyday environment. ("Representative" has to be defined, of course, cf. 2.5.2.) (e) and, partially, (d) represent of course Labov's "observer's paradox" as applied to acquisition studies.

(f)   A speaker's performance when communicating is influenced by many factors. Some are beyond our control: we cannot for example arrange for someone to be tired, or relaxed. Some of the factors evoked in (a) to (e) which, however, can be controlled, and varied, and which must be taken into account in each data collection method are the following: the setting, the type of interlocutor(s), the attitude of the interlocutor(s), the type of interaction (is anything at stake?), the attention paid to speech (Labov) that the combination of the previous factors induces in the informant. (It may turn out, as the French pilot study indicated, that Labovian distinctions such as casual vs spontaneous vs formal speech will have some descriptive utility in the latter stages of the longitudinal study, and for the long residence and native

speaker groups. In what follows, we will however restrict ourselves to less sophisticated distinctions - namely unguided, semi-
guided and guided speech - as these will be of more practical use,
especially in the early stages of the longitudinal study. ("Spontaneous speech" will be occasionally used, but in a non-technical
sense.) Further relevant factors are: the type of activity - production, comprehension, introspection - a given method allows us
to examine, and to what degree; and the relevance, for the chosen
topics of investigation, of the data obtained by means of a given
method.

(g)   The idea of control and variation of the factors mentioned in (f)
is important (cf. 2.5.2). If some of these factors can be kept
constant, and others varied, over two or more data collection
methods, we may achieve some idea of the extent to which the variation influences the type of data obtained.

2.5.2 Data Collection Techniques

There follows a brief description of the methods chosen. Returning
to (b) above, we need to obtain some idea of what an informant's "typical" everyday TL contacts are. Three techniques will be used for this
(cf. also "accompanying observation" below): participant observation
(cf. 8.5), involving the researcher working, or otherwise participating,
in the TL milieu of the informants, and recording his observations in
the form of field notes; neutral observation (cf. 8.8), which involves
the audio-recording of interactions where the researcher is not present,
on the initiative either of the informant or the TL-speaker, and with
the (prior) agreement of both - The small amount of data obtained from this
technique in the pilot year was very informative (see, for example,
Becker & Perdue, 1982) - however, the practical difficulties encountered in obtaining permission indicate that it simply may not be possible to rely on this method in all countries, and it is therefore
optional; a recorded diary (cf. 8.2), where the informant keeps a
"log" of his TL encounters during one week, and talks about them at a
later meeting with researchers. This technique will essentially make
use of the informant's SL.

The situations where the informant would not use the TL if he were not participating in the project are, essentially, <u>monthly encounters with researchers</u> (cf. 8.3 and 8.4). These encounters will be motivated by proposing some activity (cf. 8.2) and at least one out of three will be video-recorded (cf. 8.4). They will take place where it is feasible for them to take place - the informant's home, the recording studio,etc. - but will generally be held in places where good quality recording is possible (cf. (e) of 2.5.1). They will vary in length between one to two hours. The linguistic activities planned for these encounters are voluntarily varied and therefore, we hope, interesting (cf. 8.1). Some time will be devoted to <u>unguided conversation</u>, which should allow us to obtain data on "small talk", and in particular phatics, question-answer sequences, general opinions, comparisons and narratives. Certain <u>themes</u> will be introduced into conversation, essentially in relation to the vocabulary studies planned (cf. chapter 6), to other phenomena studied which may not appear spontaneously (e.g., reference to future time, cf. chapter 7), to the informant's life in the target country and his attitudes to TL speakers. If these themes are introduced unobtrusively, the conversation should continue to be spontaneous, and yield argumentative sequences and narratives as well as specific linguistic phenomena. Small, guided, <u>ad hoc experiments</u> (repetition and translation tasks, descriptions of pictures or picture sequences, cf.8.3.4) will also be integrated into the conversation. In the video-recorded encounters, <u>prepared guided experiments</u> (apartment descriptions, stage- and route-directions, cf. 8.4.3) will also be attempted. These encounters will also be used for <u>play acting</u> (see below) and <u>self-confrontation</u> (see below).

In the methods outlined above, we may therefore draw a gross distinction between "authentic" interactions in everyday places, on the one hand, and "project specific" interactions on the other. This distinction is obviously not watertight, nor would we wish it to be. Our relationships with informants (cf. 9.3: essentially, researchers will endeavour to become enablers and confidants) will extend beyond the monthly encounters: it may happen that researchers and informants go on excursions together, or have parties, where recording may prove difficult, both for acoustic and inter-personal reasons. It may also prove

feasible to bring into a monthly encounter a representative of the TL
community with whom the informant is in everyday contact, in order to
simulate some everyday interaction (simulation, cf. below: play acting).
More particularly, one planned activity - accompanying observation -
will serve the special purpose of providing, if needed, concrete help
for informants. Here, the researcher accompanies the informant to the
post office, to appointments with authorities, etc., in order both to
record the interaction and to provide whatever assistance the informant
may need.

The attitudes of the interlocutors (cf. (f) of 2.5.1) in TL interactions are generally speaking as follows: the researcher is on the
whole co-operative, the non-researcher is not necessarily co-operative.

In the methods of simulation and accompanying observation, the
setting and the type of interlocutor do in fact cut across the "authentic vs project specific" distinction. The crucial difference is, however, that in the former, nothing is at stake, whilst in the latter,
something may well be at stake. The informant may feel some stress in
both situations: in the former because of the unusual activity of simulating an interaction in front of a video-camera (this is also true of
play acting and role play), in the latter because the "gate keepers"
(cf. 4.2) he is talking to have, in a broad sense, power. The speech obtained in both situations may be (at least in parts, and for different
reasons) unguided, and give instances of what N. Dittmar (personal communication) has called counselling, negotiative, bargaining and bureau-
cratic discourse.

There remain to be described the techniques of play acting and confrontation.

Play acting (cf. 8.4) is intended to simulate, with the assistance
of the researcher rather than of an outside person as is the case with
simulation, some interaction in the TL in which the informant partici-
pated, in order to tap, indirectly, both (the informant's account of)
the nature and structure of the interaction, and his reactions to it,
and to other participants. (Role play, cf. 8.8.3, an optional technique
used by some teams, is a more elaborated form of play acting which sets
out, using an adaptation of Morino's psycho-analytic techniques, to
make the informant recall - or imagine - vividly, some event experienced

or to be expected in the TL environment. Its main aim is to explore the motivational, attitudinal and emotional factors at play in the experienced or imagined event.) The text obtained in these techniques is broadly speaking similar to that obtained from simulation.

We will give one example of variation and control (cf. (g) of 2.5.1), which gives an idea of the approach we take whenever possible in evaluating data obtained by different techniques. If it were possible to record the same type of event - say a visit to the social security office - by observation (neutral or accompanying) and then in the studio (simulating or play acting) with the same informant and within a short space of time, we would have some yardstick by which to measure the variation of setting and interlocutor on the informant's use of the TL in this type of interaction (cf. in this context, 4.3.2: Conflict, co-operation and analysing the speech stream).

The technique of confrontation is the clearest introspection task that we are using. Here informants are confronted with either (a) a film clip of "typical" TL life (cf. 8.2.3) or (b) audio- or video-recordings of themselves (cf. 8.4.4):

(a)   aims to elicit the informant's comprehension of various aspects of the interaction, from single utterances to cultural presuppositions, and to evaluate the role of the informant's own cultural background in his interpretation;

(b)   is used to elicit the information described in (c) of 2.5.1, in as systematic a way as necessary.

(a) and (b) will be conducted chiefly in the SL at the beginning of the data-collection period, with the TL playing a progressively larger role. The informant's use of this latter will be constrained to some extent by the precise nature of the researcher's questions, that is, semi-guided.

2.5.3 Summary

There follows a recapitulative list of the data collection techniques giving - in relation to the above descriptions - the main characteristics of each, and broad indications of the type of data we expect to obtain. Unless otherwise specified, the data are in the TL and audio-recorded.[] indicates that the technique is optional.

- Table 2 -

Data Collection Techniques

technique	interlocutor	setting	type of interaction	type of activity which can be investigated	type of speech	other charac-teristics	determining factors (cf.1.3.3)	type of data
diary	informant only				unguided	SL	exposure (propensity)	(narrative)
participant observation	non-researchers	everyday	recurrent authentic	(production) (comprehension)	unguided	field notes	exposure	(vocabulary) (see accompanying observation)
[neutral observation]	informant, non-researcher(s)	everyday	authentic	production (comprehension)	unguided		exposure	see accompanying observation
accompanying observation	informant, non-researcher(s), (researchers)	everyday	authentic	production (comprehension)	unguided		exposure	counselling argumentation negotiation, bargaining, administrative
simulation	informant, non-researcher(s)	studio	pseudo-authentic	production (comprehension)	unguided	video	(exposure) (propensity)	see accompanying observation
play acting	informant, researchers	studio	pseudo-authentic	production (comprehension	unguided	video	(exposure) (propensity)	see accompanying observation
[role play]	informant, researchers	studio	pseudo-authentic	production, comprehension introspection	unguided semi-guided	video	propensity (exposure) perceptual	unlimited
conversation	informant, researchers	preferably no noise	project specific	production comprehension	unguided (semi-guided)		propensity (exposure) perceptual	unlimited
ad hoc experiments	informant, researchers	preferably no noise	project specific	production, comprehension introspection	semi-guided, guided		essentially cognitive/ perceptual	specifically elicited forms
technique	interlocutor	setting	type of interaction	type of activity which can be investigated	type of speech	other charac-teristics	determining factors	type of data
prepared experiments	informant, researchers	studio	project specific	production, comprehension introspection	semi-guided, guided	video	essentially cognitive/ perceptual	specifically elicited forms
con-frontation: film-watching	informant, researchers	studio	project specific	production, comprehension	semi-guided, guided	(SL)	cognitive/ perceptual, propensity	interpretations, opinions, definitions, specifically elicited forms
self-con-frontation	informant, researchers	studio	project specific	production, comprehension	semi-guided, guided	(SL)	cognitive/ perceptual	interpretations, opinions, definitions, specifically elicited forms

3. Previous Work

This account of previous work in SSLA is designed primarily to help the different teams in the E.S.F. project to become acquainted with work undertaken in each of the five countries which may prove relevant to this project.

It is therefore selective, and should not be interpreted as an account of the "state of the art" in SLA. For research on SLA in a broader context, see Wode (1981) and Felix (1982). Specifically, this account has been restricted to the untutored second language acquisition of adults in the five target countries, when such research exists. The criterion for the inclusion of related work which does not meet this definition is the relevance it is felt to have for the project by the various local teams.

3.1 France

3.1.1 There has been relatively little research in this field undertaken in France, and most work has concentrated more on children than adults. The first comprehensive description of SLA by immigrants in France appeared in Gardin (Ed.), 1976: cf. especially Noyau in this volume.

Broadly speaking, two traditions are represented in existing studies on SSLA by adults: the "contrastive analysis-interference" tradition (cf. 3.1.2) and the "interlanguage studies" tradition (cf. 3.1.3). Some attempt has also been made (cf. 3.1.4) to apply certain results to language pedagogy for adult immigrants.

3.1.2 Contrastive and interference studies. Morsly (1976), Pichel (1980) and Santos Pereira (1981) studied the spoken French of, respectively, Arabic-, Spanish- and Portugese-speaking adult immigrants. All three studies are based on a contrastive analysis of the linguistic systems of the relevant language pairs, and an error analysis is undertaken in order to ascertain the relative weight of the SL system, and of linguistic complexities of the TL system, in linguistic forms produced which deviate from the TL norm. Morsly does observe a certain variability in the production of her three informants both with respect to each other, and to the data obtained by different techniques, but does not pursue this question systematically.

It is also worth mentioning here the studies of de Oliveira (1974, 1975), which constitute the first attempt in France to describe the reciprocal effect that a bilingual's language systems have on each other.

3.1.3 Interlanguage studies.

Morsly and Vasseur (1976) re-trace the path from "classical" error analysis to the analysis of the learner's variety as a system in its own right and attempt to show, from data obtained from Arabic- and Portugese-speaking workers, that the explanatory power of the contrastive-interference approach may be less than had been supposed, and furthermore that the persistent linguistic problems evidenced by these informants should be related to psychological, social and economic aspects of their lives as immigrant workers.

The main body of work on SLA in France has come from the Groupe de Recherches sur l'Acquisition des Langues (GRAL: University of Paris VIII). A complete bibliography for 1976-1978 can be found in Perdue and Porquier (Eds.), 1979, and for 1979-1982 in Trêvise (Ed.), 1982. Perdue and Porquier (Eds.), 1980, give a fairly complete idea of the "state of the art" in SLA in France at that time.

This group has produced a number of articles dealing with general questions such as whether learner varieties have a specific status amongst natural languages (Arditty and Perdue, 1979; Frauenfelder, Noyau, Perdue and Porquier, 1980); the relationship between learner varieties and regional dialect (Deulofeu, 1980; Véronique, 1980); variation in learner varieties (Véronique, 1980; Véronique and Stoffel, 1979); the nature of the adult immigrant's linguistic knowledge (Noyau, 1980) and awareness (Mittner and Kahn, 1982). Empirical work has concentrated on the use of French under different conditions (that is, differences both in the social context of an interaction and in the methods used to collect data) by Arabic- and Spanish-speaking adult immigrants, with particular reference to (variation in) certain sociolinguistic variables: (ne)-pas and other realisations of negation (Dubois, Noyau, Perdue and Porquier, 1981; Trêvise, 1981); y avoir vs y en avoir, qu'est-ce que vs ce que (Véronique and Faïta, 1982), and others. The data collection techniques used were primarily the linguistic interview and self-confrontation.

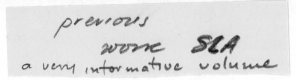

Véronique and his collaborators also accomplished some participant observation, and simulated a type of interaction between the French and Arabic
communities which is relatively recurrent, where a "spokesman" acts as
an interpreter for a countryman whose knowledge of the TL is limited.

Aspects of this research which concern the areas of investigation
of the E.S.F. project, and its data collection techniques, are mentioned
in the appropriate chapters of this field manual.

3.1.4 Pedagogy. Various articles have appeared in journals edited by the
different organizations concerned with adult immigrant education, which
take account to a certain extent of the research mentioned in 3.1.2 and
3.1.3. A complete bibliography may be obtained from: Bureau Documentation
Migrants du C.N.D.P., 91, rue Gabriel Péri, 92120 Montrouge, France.
Cf. also Porcher (ed.), 1978.

3.2 Germany

3.2.1 In Germany, systematic research on SLA of migrant workers began
about ten years ago (with one remarkable forerunner: Clyne, 1968). In
what follows, we shall concentrate upon two larger projects dealing with
untutored acquisition of adult migrant workers: the Wuppertal project
"Zweitspracherwerb italienischer und spanischer Arbeiter" (ZISA) directed by Jürgen M. Meisel, and the Heidelberg research project "Pidgin-
Deutsch spanischer und italienischer Arbeiter in der BRD" (HPD) directed
by Wolfgang Klein. Smaller studies on untutored acquisition as well as
studies on tutored acquisition and on children will be briefly mentioned
at the end. For a more comprehensive survey of the field, cf. Pfaff (1981);
for an annotated bibliography cf. Gutfleisch et al. (1979).

3.2.2 ZISA. The project comprised a cross-sectional study (1977-1978)
and a longitudinal study (1978-1982); pilot work had already started in
1974. Members of the group were W.-M. Ahnen, H. Clahsen, G. Jaehnicke, K.
Kennecke, M. Pienemann, U. Rohde (cross-sectional study); W.-M. Ahnen,
H. Clahsen, U. Kennecke, R.A. Mester, G. Neis, F. Struwe.

3.2.2.1 Aim. The project's aim was to describe and explain the untutored
acquisition of German by Italian, Spanish and Portuguese adults in a na-

tural setting and to determine the influence of social environment, attitudes and motivation in order to answer the question:"which elements constitute an 'interlanguage' and which factors determine an 'interlanguage'?"
(Clahsen,1980:55).

3.2.2.2 <u>Informants and data collection</u>. In the cross-sectional study, in-
depth interviews were conducted with 45 Italian, Spanish and Portuguese
workers, male and female, aged from 15-65, with a duration of stay ranging
from 1 to 17 years. These interviews provided linguistic data as well as
information on the socio-psychological background of informants (e.g. origin, education, job, contact with Germans). In the longitudinal study, 13
migrants (8 Italians, 3 Portuguese, 2 Spaniards) were interviewed every
second to third week over about two years; whenever possible, observation
started as soon as possible after the learner's arrival.

3.2.2.3 <u>Theoretical background</u>. The central idea is that second language acquisition is not a linear process leading from zero to target
variety but a multidimensional process: from the analyst's point of view,
it is a sequence of ordered developmental stages, but within each stage
there is variation which is to be explained by the existence of different
types of learners. The differences evidenced by learners are due to socio-
psychological factors, especially motivation and attitude. Thus, socio-
psychological factors determine not only the degree of language acquisition but also the kind of transitional system (cf. 9.1). Different transitional
systems are characterized by different strategies of simplification:
elaborative simplification (in order to further develop the acquired system)
and restrictive simplification (in order to facilitate the use of the
acquired system).

The important criterion for establishing developmental stages is the
ordering of acquired features on an implicational scale: "... if we find
that all learners of L2 who have acquired rule R_3 also possess rules R_2
and R_1, but those who do not yet have R_2 do not use R_3 either, then we
may assume that the three rules are ordered as $R_3 \supset R_2 \supset R_1$, and we can
furthermore hypothesize that each of these rules marks a new developmental stage" (Meisel et al., 1981:33).

3.2.2.4 <u>Areas of analysis and results</u>. In the publications available so far, only smaller selections of the total data have been analyzed. A detailed presentation of analyses and results of the study has recently been published (Clahsen et al.), discussion of which cannot be included here.

(a) Linguistic analysis. Analysis focusses on syntax, more specifically on the deletion of elements, the position of negation, and word order. In the following, we shall briefly sketch the results for word order.

The following implicational scale of five basic word order rules was established, where the rules are considered to define different acquisition stages (cf. Meisel,1982).

V → END ⊃ ADV-VP ⊃ INVERSION ⊃ PARTICLE ⊃ ADV-FRONTING

ADV-FRONTING: moves an adverbial into sentence initial position

PARTICLE: all non-finite verbal elements are moved into sentence-final position

INVERSION: subject and verb are inverted

ADV-VP: the adverbial is placed after the finite verb

V → END: finite verb moves to final position in embedded clauses

This acquisition order is then explained by psycholinguistic principles, e.g. by Slobin's (1973) "operating principles". An additional step consists in accounting for variation within the developmental stages thus defined by identifying different learner types: some learners acquire a rule perfectly and apply it in all appropriate contexts, others do not.

(b) The role of socio-psychological factors. In order to explain the differences between learner types the grouping of the learners on the basis of linguistic criteria was matched against a grouping on the basis of socio-psychological factors. Thirty-five variables per person were chosen which were felt to be the most relevant for the forming of attitudes and motivations. (For the computerized methods applied and the detailed results, cf. Meisel,1982). The preliminary results support the claim:"that the kind of interlanguage variety a learner uses within one stage of an ordered sequence of developmental stages

does, in fact, depend on the social setting and on resulting attitudes and motivations" (Meisel,1982).
(c) Practical applications. The study is considered to be helpful for an
evaluation of the learner's knowledge upon entering a language course,
and for establishing a psychologically plausible learning progression
(cf. ZISA,1979).

3.2.2.5 Additional information. The project intensively dealt with more
general aspects of SLA, foreigner talk and pidginization (Meisel, 1975,
1977). For more detailed information on methods and results, cf. Clahsen
and Meisel (1980), Meisel (1977, 1982), Meisel et al. (1981).

3.2.3 HPD. The project was run at the University of Heidelberg between
1974 and 1979; pilot work began in 1972. Members of the group were A.
Becker, N. Dittmar, I. Gutfleisch, M. Gutmann, G. Meyer, B.-O. Rieck, G.
Senft, W. Steckner, E. Thielicke, W. Wildgen, P. Ziegler.

3.2.3.1 Aims. HPD was designed as a cross-sectional study dealing with
the untutored SLA of adult Spanish and Italian workers. Its objectives
were:

- to describe the linguistic structure and development of learner varieties;
- to analyze how the learner's social and psychological background influences the acquisition process;
- to contribute to a better foundation of language teaching.

3.2.3.2 Informants and data collection. The sample consisted of a learner
group of 48 adult manual workers and a target language group of 12 Heidelberg dialect speakers. The learner sample was stratified as follows:

Duration of stay	Italian		Spanish		
	Male	Female	Male	Female	
up to 2.7 years	4	2	4	2	12
2.8 - 4.3 years	4	2	4	2	12
4.4 - 7.0 years	4	2	4	2	12
7.1 years and more	4	2	4	2	12
	16	8	16	8	48
	24		24		

The target language sample consisted of speakers belonging to the social environment of the migrant workers.

Two complementary data collection techniques were used:

(a) Participant observation, i.e. several researchers worked for two to four weeks in typical contact fields: in factories, in a pub, and at an immigration office.

(b) In-depth interviews. With each informant, a cautiously guided conversation (1-3 hours) was held at his home and tape-recorded. It provided both linguistic data and background information (origin, individual and social situation in home country, circumstances of immigration, situation at work and at home, contact with Germans, etc.) From these interviews, selections of 15-30 minutes per informant were phonetically transcribed for further analysis; most results are based on this corpus. Similar interviews were made with the Heidelberg speakers.

With 18 out of the 24 Spanish informants, a second series of interviews was carried out two years later; it also included small tests, such as oral ad-hoc translations and repetition tasks. (For details, cf. Dittmar and Klein, 1974; HPD,1975, 1976 ch. 4; Klein and Dittmar,1979).

3.2.3.3 Theoretical background. HPD can be characterized as a sociolinguistic empirical analysis of the form, function and development of the German of migrant workers within the framework of the interlanguage approach, which was then still in its infancy. The main theoretical assumptions and analytic principles were:

- second language acquisition is conceived of as a process of language change - a passing through a series of intermediate varieties leading (with possible detours) towards the target variety; this process contains certain regularities;
- it is assumed that the course and tempo of this process is essentially determined by social(and socio-psychological) factors;
- the descriptive framework applied to the analysis of variation should not fall behind the standards of explicitness and precision attained at that time in theoretical linguistics. Thus, for the study of syntactic and phonological variation, the descriptive tool of variety grammar (Klein, 1974) was used; a variety grammar is a probabilistically

weighted (transformational) generative grammar which allows the pro-
jection of extra-linguistic factors (social or psychological) onto
linguistic rules.

3.2.3.4 <u>Areas of analysis and results</u>. Over the first three years, the
analysis concentrated on grammar: mainly syntax, and, to a lesser extent,
phonology (Rieck, 1975; Tropf, 1982) and morphology (HPD, 1976: 240-281).
In its last two years, the project mainly dealt with lexical development.
and communicative behaviour. In what follows, only some aspects will be
highlighted.

(a) Syntax. An attempt was made to give a complete formal syntax for
each learner; all of the 48 learner syntaxes were integrated into
a variety grammar which was used to describe the overall development of sentence structure. Those rules which proved to be particularly sensitive to variation were used to compute a "syntactic index" (HPD, 1976, ch. 6) characterizing the informant's overall state
of syntactic elaboration and its distance from the target variety;
this index, rather than individual rules, was used to relate grammatical performance to social and other extra-linguistic factors.
(For details of syntactic analysis, cf. HPD, 1976, ch. 6, 1978;
Klein and Dittmar, 1979).

(b) Lexicon. The analysis of lexical development included selected closed
word classes, on the one hand, and various semantic fields, on the
other. More specifically, the following domains were investigated:
- modal verbs (HPD, 1978, ch. 4.2; Dittmar, 1979);
- verbs of motion, verbs of visual perception (HPD, 1978, ch. 4.1;
HPD, 1979, ch. I.1);
- the expression of locality and temporality (HPD, 1979, ch. II;
Klein, 1981a, 1982; Dittmar, 1981);
- negation (HPD, 1978, ch. 4.4);
- preposition (HPD, 1978, ch. 4.3);
- personal pronouns (HPD, 1979, ch. I.2; Klein, 1981b; Klein and
Rieck, 1982).

(c) Communicative behaviour. Several analyses have been made of how
foreign workers, with a very limited linguistic repertoire but often
highly developed communicative skills, organize narratives of per-

sonal experiences (cf. Dittmar and Thielicke,1979; Wildgen,1978;
Becker et al.,1978). Attempts were also made to apply methods of
conversational analysis to a longer piece of discourse with a
foreign worker (HPD,1979, ch. III).

(d) Social correlates of the acquisition process. In order to determine
the impact of social factors on the acquisition process, various
extra-linguistic variables were quantified and statistically related to the syntactic indices of informants. It was shown that for
example duration of stay is soon over-ruled by factors such as contact intensity or age at time of immigration; contact with Germans
in leisure time proved to be more important than contact at the
work place (HPD,1976, ch. 7).

3.2.3.5 Additional information. While most of the syntactic analysis
was based on variety grammar, some other methods have been applied as
well, for example implicational scaling (Dittmar,1978) or analysis of
theme-rheme structure (HPD,1979, ch. III; Klein,1981a).

According to the third objective mentioned in 3.2.3, attempts were
made to apply some results to a better foundation of language courses,
cf. HPD,1979, ch. IV).

3.2.4 Other projects dealing with untutored acquisition of adult workers.

(1) I. Keim, P. Nikitopoulos and M. Repp (Institut für deutsche Sprache,
Mannheim) did an exploratory study on Greek learners based on participant observation and interviews with a small number of informants.
Analysis was carried out on two levels: (a) morpho-syntactic structures with special emphasis on interference and pidgin features; (b)
discourse structure. To some extent, this project will be continued
within the framework of a larger project on "communication in urban
centres" (directed by W. Kallmeyer, Institut für deutsche Sprache),
in which communication with foreign workers is one specific aspect.
For details, cf. Keim et al. (1978).

(2) M. Orlović-Schwarzwald (1978) has studied 18 Yugoslavian workers.
The analysis concentrates on morphology; it is based on taped interviews (cf. also Gilbert and Orlovič, 1975).

(3) A.Yakut (1981) has studied language and communication problems
of Turkish families from a broad sociological point of view.
(4) W. Stölting (1975), Y. Bodemann and R. Ostow (1975) and H. Barkowski et al. (1980) include case studies of communication and
more specifically of communicative problems of migrant workers and
their families.

3.2.5 Related projects. There were and still are numerous smaller projects on the tutored language acquisition of migrant workers and their
children and language teaching to these populations; many of them also
include samples of linguistic analysis. Reports on experiences as well
as results are to be found in two periodicals: "Deutsch lernen" (ed. by
Sprachverband Deutsch für ausländische Arbeiter e.V., Mainz) and "Ziel-
sprache Deutsch" (Hueber, München).

Finally, three major projects on the acquisition of German by the
children of migrant workers should be mentioned:

(a) "Die Zweisprachigkeit jugoslawischer Schüler in der Bundesrepublik",
directed by W. Stölting and K.D. Bünting (University of Essen);
researchers were D. Delić, M. Orlović, K. Rausch and E. Sausner (for
details, cf. Stölting et al., 1980).
(b) "Das bilinguale Sprachverhalten türkischer Schüler an Essener Schu-
len", directed by I. Meyer-Ingwersen and K.D. Bünting (University
of Essen); researchers were R. Neumann and M. Kummer (for details,
cf. Meyer-Ingwersen et al., 1977).
(c) "Muttersprache italienischer Gastarbeiterkinder", directed by Aldo
di Luzio (University of Konstanz); researchers are D. d'Angelo,
P. Auer, R. Behrens, M. Etterich, J. Gumperz, K. Pirrwitz, M. Ries,
M. Roßteuscher (for details, cf. di Luzio, 1982).

3.3 The Netherlands

3.3.1 Most of the research on SSLA in Holland has dealt with the use of
Dutch by foreigners (cf. 3.3.2). Some studies have focussed on the use of
Dutch by natives towards foreigners (cf. 3.3.3); on relations between language attitudes and L2 proficiency (cf. 3.3.4); and on comprehensibility
of L2 use of Dutch (cf. 3.3.5).

3.3.2 <u>Use of Dutch by foreigners</u>. Research in this area has been mostly oriented towards syntax, with most attention being paid to word order.

Jansen and Lalleman (1980a; 1980b) and Jansen et al. (1981) treat the placement of pre- and postpositions and the placement of the verb in the Dutch of 8 Turkish and 8 Moroccan men who vary by age (21-48 years old), length of stay in the Netherlands (1-15 years),profession, type of contact with native Dutch speakers, and L2 proficiency. The main question in their research is to what degree features of word order are influenced by structural features of the respective source languages. They made transcriptions of single, pre-structured interviews lasting 30-45 minutes in the informants' homes and from these selected 100 successive utterances per informant for further analysis (cf. Jansen and Lalleman 1980a:48 ff. for the full content of one of these interviews).

In contrast to both Moroccan Arabic and Turkish, Dutch has special alternation rules in the following two cases:

	Verb-Position	Pre/Postposition
Turkish	V-final	Postposition
Moroccan	V1/V2	Preposition
Dutch	V2 in declarative main clause V-final in subordinate clause	Preposition Postposition

In declarative main clauses, the verb in Dutch usually appears in second position. Compare:

- non-topicalized: S-V-O: <u>ik ken hem niet</u>   (I don't know him)

                  S-V-Adv: <u>ik liep gisteren buiten</u> (I ran outside yesterday)

- topicalized: O-V-S: <u>hem ken ik niet</u>   (Him I don't know)

                  Adv-V-S: <u>gisteren liep ik buiten</u> (Yesterday I ran outside)

In spoken form, the finite verb frequently appears in Dutch in first position, for example, <u>lust ik niet</u> (I don't care for it); <u>heb ik al</u> (I already have it); <u>heb ik hem gisteren al gezegd</u> (I already told him yesterday). In subordinate clauses the verb appears finally, as in <u>omdat ik hem niet ken</u> (because I don't know him); <u>omdat ik gisteren buiten liep</u> (because

I ran outside yesterday). Furthermore, Dutch allows both pre- and post-positions, for respectively location: op de weg (on the road), in de kamer (in the room); and direction: de weg op (up the street), de kamer in (into the room).

That Turkish and Moroccan Arabic do not have these alternation rules mentioned above leads to the following predictions for Turkish and Moroccan learners of Dutch:

- Turkish speakers of Dutch will prefer verb-final position in main clauses: ik veel geld verdien (I a lot of money earn); Moroccan speakers of Dutch will prefer verb second position in subordinate clauses: omdat ik verdien veel geld (because I earn a lot of money);
- Turkish speakers of Dutch will prefer postposition; Moroccan speakers of Dutch will prefer preposition.

So few subordinate clauses were observed that verb placement analysis for Turkish and Moroccan speakers of Dutch had to focus on main clauses. The following positions could be distinguished: V1 lust ik niet (I don't care for it); V2 gisteren liep ik buiten (Yesterday I ran outside); V3 gisteren ik liep buiten; V-final gisteren ik buiten liep. The distribution of verb placement (by percentages) was as follows:

	V1	V2	V3	V-final
Turks	7.6	57.8	10.8	24.0
Moroccans	10.5	77.1	8.7	4.0

Both groups of informants use all verb positions distinguished, but noticeable differences can be seen in their scores for use of V2 and verb-final position. The difference regarding verb-final position is significant, and is interpreted as interference from Turkish by the Turkish speakers of Dutch.

On the basis of a syntactic index, the sixteen informants were divided into three levels of proficiency. The syntactic index was determined by the following four criteria: average sentence length, person/number agreement between subject and predicate, presence of subject pronoun, and presence of article/demonstrative/possessive pronoun.

For the Turkish speakers it appears that the higher the syntactic level, the more V2 structures and the fewer V-final structures they use. Interference, therefore, appears to manifest itself mainly in the early phase of second language acquisition.

Regarding the use of pre- and postposition: both Turkish and Moroccan informants used both positions, but both preferred preposition. A more detailed analysis of the use of prepositions yields the following distribution (in percentages) of errors and omissions (cf. Jansen et al., 1981: 324):

	Moroccans	Turks
Preposition errors:	10.6	7.5
. Selection errors	75.5	61.1
. Prep. before Subject/Object	14.9	16.7
. Prep. before Inf. complement	9.6	22.2
Preposition omissions	6.6	19.0

The difference in distribution between Turks and Moroccans is especially noticeable with the omissions of prepositions (mainly the preposition in). The omission ("avoidance") of prepositions by Turkish speakers of Dutch is interpreted as interference.

Hulstijn (1982; pilot study 1979) has also done research on how adult learners of Dutch handle subject/verb inversion (INV) in declarative main clauses and final placement of the verb (VF) in subordinate clauses. His research focused however on the question of how speech monitoring is influenced by the following four factors: time pressure, attention, degree of explicit knowledge of rules, and degree of impulsivity. The latter two factors were studied by means of a metalinguistic interview and a "matching familiar figures test" respectively.

The degree of monitoring was operationally derived from the degree of correct use of INV and VF. The results were obtained in strictly experimental ways by means of specially-constructed story repetition and completion tasks. These tasks were completed under four different conditions:

Attention focused on

Time pressure:	Information	Grammar
present	1	3
absent	2	4

The informants consisted of 32 foreigners (16 with English as their first language and 16 others with a wide range of first-language backgrounds), all of whom were selected on their degree of proficiency with respect to Dutch INV and VF.

In all of the experimental conditions, a significant difference was found in the accuracy of INV and FV; the average correct scores were 83% and 47% respectively. The English speakers of Dutch performed much more poorly in VF, but somewhat better in INV than did the non-English subjects. A satisfactory explanation for these phenomena was not offered.

On the four factors influencing speech monitoring which Hulstijn studied in his experiments, only the factor "attention" showed a significant influence on the degree of monitoring: attention to grammar is paired with strong monitoring. The remaining three factors (time pressure, degree of explicit knowledge of rules, and degree of impulsivity) appeared to have no affect on the degree of monitoring.

In a further analysis of the same data, Hulstijn discussed the following word order phenomena in second-language speakers of Dutch:

- discontinuity of verb constructions in subordinate clauses, e.g., _... dat hij heeft een appel gegeten_ (that he has eaten an apple) instead of _dat hij een appel gegeten heeft_;
- adverb preposing in subordinate clauses, e.g., _... dat vandaag hij thuis-blijft_ (that he's staying home today) instead of _... dat hij vandaag thuisblijft_;
- inversion after adverb preposing in subordinate clauses, e.g., _... dat vandaag blijft hij thuis_ instead of _... dat hij vandaag thuisblijft_;
- V-final in main clauses, e.g., _deze winkels oude meubelen hebben_ (these stores have old furniture), instead of _deze winkels hebben oude meubelen_;
- V1 in main clauses, e.g., _speelt zij in de tuin; en moet hij om acht uur werken_ (plays she in the garden, and must he work at eight o'clock).

The final study we report on here regarding word order by adult learners of Dutch is that of de Vries (1981), whose observations are from a functional perspective. Following his discussion of some communicative problems in a transcribed and annotated interview of a Dutchman with two Turkish men (18 and 27 years old; both 1 1/2 years in the Netherlands), he deals with the thematic structure (order of old and new information) in the Dutch of the two Turkish informants. A text of 363 words from each informant was analyzed. The types of thematic structure occuring in these texts were as follows, by number of sentences of each type (de Vries, 1981:112):

	Informant 1	Informant 2
Type 1: old-new	30	35
Type 2: new-old	4	3
Type 3: new	79	65
Total	113	103

In both case studies a comparable pattern is shown. Both informants prefer Type-3-sentences, e.g., vijf jaar moet zijn (must be five years), beetje verzinnen (somewhat fabricate), tien jaar zoiets (approximately ten years), beetje drinken zo (drink somewhat like this).

Besides the word order studies discussed here, Belder et al. (1980) have attempted to develop a probability grammar for nominal clusters (NC) in the Dutch of foreigners. Their data corpus is based on interviews with three Turks (two of these informants appear also in de Vries,1981). As control data, they use data collected earlier from conversations with five Dutchmen of comparable socio-economic class living in Leiden.

Some observations are:

- the Turks use a NC consisting exclusively of a noun more frequently than do the Dutchmen from Leiden;
- the Dutchmen use a NC with (pre-)determiners and/or post-determiners more frequently than do the Turks;
- if the Turks use (pre-)determiners, then adjectives or quantifiers are used more frequently than are articles or demonstratives.

Belder et al. summarize their presentation of probability grammars with a discussion of three general problems in this regard: the degree of representativity of the corpus, the degree of context independence of the grammar, and the calculation of chance occurrence.

3.3.3 Use of Dutch by native speakers towards foreigners. The Werkgroep Taal Buitenlandse Werknemers (1978; hereafter WTBW, "Group for the Study of the Language of Foreign Workers") has done four studies in a project on foreign talk (FT):

1. What stereotypes are found in books for youth (e.g., Robinson Crusoe) and comic books (e.g., Kuifje) of the Dutch used by foreigners?
2. What intuitions do Dutch people have regarding FT?
3. What does FT sound like in actual speech on the street with passers-by?
4. What does the FT of counter clerks sound like who have regular contact with foreigners?

The results of the research were also reported by the WTBW (1980a) and in Snow et al. (1981).

For the second of these four studies (on intuitions of Dutch people), two groups of students were given a list of 13 Dutch sentences. Group 1 was asked to write down how the average Dutchman would say each sentence to a foreigner (resulting in foreigner talk); and Group 2 was asked how a foreigner who barely talked Dutch would say the same sentences (resulting in Dutch by Foreigners, Buitenlands Nederlands - BN). In the third study (speech on the street with passers-by) three foreigners (provided with hidden cassette recorders) asked passers-by for directions to the post office in broken Dutch. And finally, in the fourth study, speech was recorded (after obtaining permission) between foreigners (almost all of them Turks and Moroccans) and counter clerks at the Central Housing Office (CHO) and at the Residence Registration Office (RRO).

The results of the four studies were subjected to a comparative, mostly syntactical analysis; the main conclusions were:

- FT cannot be considered a homogeneous or stable register, but is qualitatively influenced by the level of L2 proficiency of the person being spoken to and the nature/length of the conversation. (Especially in the 4th study, high correlations were shown between a low level of L2 proficiency and a high degree of FT.)

- Some features of FT appear in all of the studies (especially deletion
  of article); others do not.
- The degree of presence of FT-features varies tremendously between the
  four studies (e.g., the use of the infinitive in place of the finite
  form of the verb varies from 49% in study 1 to 0% in study 3).
- The second study shows noticeable overlap in native intuitions about
  FT and BN.

Snow et al. (1981) went into further detail in the analysis of the
results of the third and fourth study, including (cor)relations found
between the degree of L2 proficiency and the degree of FT. Not only does
there appear to be a great degree of agreement between the two studies
regarding the sort of deviation from the standard language, but also regarding the frequency of these deviations. Native speakers as well as
non-native speakers show a strong tendency towards deleting determiners,
a mild tendency to delete subject pronouns, auxiliary verbs and copulas,
and the least tendency to use infinitives instead of conjugated verb forms.
Furthermore, on the basis of different measures of average utterance
length it appears that:

- long sentences of native speakers are coupled with long sentences of
  non-native speakers; similarly, short sentences are coupled with short
  sentences;
- longer utterances of native speakers are coupled with more FT features.

Different sorts of comparisons between L2 use and FT make it clear that
there is interaction between the two phenomena. FT can be shown to be an
attempt to foster communication effectiveness by variable accommodation
to the language use of the L2 speaker.

3.3.4 Language attitude and L2 proficiency. In one extensive (1980b) and
two summary publications (1980c; 1979), WTBW (cf. 3.3.3) reported on research on the language attitudes and language proficiency of 20 Moroccan
men (17-39 years old; 2-11 years in the Netherlands). Interviews in Dutch
were held with these 20 informants, based on a pre-structured questionnaire.
This questionnaire (cf. WTBW 1980b: 68-69 for a complete version) consisted of 3 parts:

- questions about social position, schooling, housing, etc.;

- questions about attitudes to the Netherlands, Dutch people and the Dutch language;
- judgements about speakers (with a stimulus tape of fragments of Dutch speech of 30-40 seconds in duration, spoken by 3 Turks, 3 Moroccans and 2 Dutchmen).

On the basis of the interviews, 6 indices were developed:

- a social index (SOI), based on the following 9 variables: age, marital status, length of stay in the Netherlands, kind of job, schooling in Morocco/Holland, whether formal Dutch training was followed, housing situation, and contact with Dutch people;
- a syntactic index (SYI), based on 4 criteria (cf. the studies of Jansen and Lalleman referred to in 3.3.2);
- a general attitude index (GAI), based on answers to the questions re-ferred to above (a high GAI indicates positive attitudes);
- a stimulus attitude index (SAI), based on the judgements about the stim-ulus tape (a high SAI indicates positive evaluation of the stimulus voices);
- a judgement index (JI) of the Dutch used by the 20 Moroccans, based on evaluations (scale 1-10) by 48 students of linguistics;
- a self-judgement index (SJI), based on a comparison by the Moroccan in-formants of their own L2 proficiency with the Dutch spoken on the stim-ulus tape.

These 6 indices yield the following correlation matrix (cf. WTBW 1980c: 157):

JI	SAI	GAI	SOI	SJI	r
.82	.63	.64	.74	.08	SYI
	.44	.30	.43	.36	JI
		.46	.47	.06	SAI
			.59	.12	GAI
				.14	SOI

The main conclusions drawn were:
- the high correlation between JI and SYI points to reliability of the

criteria used for the SYI;
- the fairly high correlation of SAI and GAI with the SYI indicates a connection between language attitudes and language proficiency level;
- the high correlation between SYI and SOI is remarkable: the Moroccans
appear to speak better Dutch the younger they are, the shorter the length
of stay in the Netherlands, the more schooled work they do, they less
formal L2 training they have had, and the more Dutch friends they have;
- the very low correlations between SJI and SYI is remarkable and difficult to explain.

Finally, WTBW discusses some limitations of their research. In particular, the fact that the interviews were held in Dutch led to difficulties
for the informants in understanding the questions and formulating their responses.

3.3.5 <u>Comprehensibility of L2 use of Dutch</u>. Van Heuven et al. (1981) presented to 53 Dutch pupils audio-recordings of 21 speech fragments, each of
20 seconds' duration. Sixteen of these fragments were of Dutch spoken by
Turkish, Moroccan or Yugoslavian workers; and for contrast, 5 fragments were
of Dutch spoken by Dutchmen (the latter "to stabilize the judgement norm").
The pupils were asked to judge these speech fragments (on a 5-point scale) on
9 factors: foreignness, comprehensibility, understandability, fluency, intonation, word stress, pronunciation, word order and morpho-syntactic correctness. Using a regression-analysis, Van Heuven et al. tried to predict the
factors "foreignness" and "comprehensibility" from linear combinations of the
other factors. The degree of foreignness appeared to be determined mainly
by fluency, morpho-syntactic correctness, pronunciation and word order, while
the degree of comprehensibility appeared to be determined mainly by intonation, fluency and word stress. For the factor comprehensibility, priority
is noticeable for prosodic (phonetic) features rather than for non-phonetic
features (morpho-syntactic correctness and word order).

These results were used by Van Heuven and de Vries (1981) for further
examination of the role that phonetic (F) factors (sentence intonation, fluency and word stress) in contrast with non-phonic (NF) factors (word order,
word choice and morphological marking) plays in the comprehensibility of L2
use. Eight primitive non-verbal actions (e.g. someone turning a plate over)
were shown to a Turkish informant who had to give a verbal description of

these actions. The 8 elicited descriptions were "normalized" in different ways.

- Type 1 utterances: with F- and NF-deviations from standard Dutch (the original version was spoken by the Turkish informant);
- type 2 utterances: with NF-deviations and F-normalizations (rephrased by a Dutchman);
- type 3 utterances: with F-deviations and NF-normalizations (rephrased by the same Turkish informant);
- type 4 utterances: with F- and NF-normalizations (rephrased by the same Dutchman).

These 4x8 utterances were offered under non-ideal listening conditions (i.e. with added noise) to 64 Dutchmen whose task was to act out the described actions. It appeared that F-normalizations had a much greater effect (both in terms of correct scores and reaction times) on the comprehensibility of performed speech than NF-normalizations.

In another task 145 Dutchmen were asked to judge the comprehensibility of the 4x8 utterances on a 10-point scale. In this task it also appeared that phonic factors determine comprehensibility more than non-phonic factors do, although to a lesser degree.

3.4 Sweden

3.4.1 Migrant workers are entitled to regular language tuition in Sweden. SLA outside the classroom is therefore not the most important phenomenon in this country, and has received little attention from researchers. As far as we know, there is almost no research dealing specifically with un-tutored acquisition (cf. however Kotsinas, 1980). In what follows, we will mention three studies whose concerns are related to some extent, although not entirely, to those of this project: Svenska som målspråk (cf. 3.4.2); Optimering av svensk uttalsundervisning (cf. 3.4.3), and that of Hyltenstam (cf. 3.4.4). Kotsinas' study is described in 3.4.5.

3.4.2 Svenska som målspråk (Swedish as a TL. Department of Linguistics, University of Stockholm, S-106 91 Stockholm) ran from 1973 to 1980, and was concerned with aspects of language structure and language use that represent learning problems for adult immigrants who study Swedish as a second language. Aspects of lexical structure, morphology and basic syntax were studied in a functional perspective.

Combining error-analysis with typological studies, this project has established a typological profile of Swedish and has related it to the major immigrant languages in Sweden. The project has also produced a systematized collection of examples of authentic errors. The input to the error analyses were mainly compositions written by adult students in Swedish classes at various levels of proficiency.

A complete list of reports may be obtained from the above address. Hammarberg and Viberg (1977), Hammarberg and Viberg (1979) and Åslund (1976) are more relevant to the concerns of the E.S.F. project.

3.4.3 <u>Optimering av svensk uttalsundervisning</u> (Optimal teaching of Swedish pronunciation. Department of Linguistics, University of Lund, Helgonabacken 12, S-223 62 Lund) ran from 1976 to 1979. Its aim was to improve the teaching of Swedish pronunciation to adult immigrants, to suggest pedagogical priorities, and to specify a basic prosody (i.e. rhythmic and prosodic patterns) as well as a basic pronunciation of segmental features. Special attention was given to prosody. In a broader perspective, the project contributed to the integration of a theory of (foreign) accent within a theory of linguistic variation in general.

Some specific questions of this project were:

- What are the most important features in an acceptable Swedish pronunciation?
- What constitutes interference from the SL, not only from the point of view of speech sounds but also of syllabic structure and prosodic features?
- How do these SL features impair understanding?
- How are these features avoided?
- What are the causal relations between different features of a foreign accent?

The project has established comprehensive accent archives containing samples of foreign accents from 25 languages. These samples were elicited by asking immigrants who were judged to have a typical Polish, Arabic, etc. accent, to read a piece of Swedish prose and describe a series of pictures. Error analyses in terms of variations from target vowels and consonants as well as from target components of the prosodic system have been carried out. These analyses underlie (a) an evaluation of the errors; (b) experiments, in which the parameters that were hypothesized to be crucial were manipulated through analysis by synthesis, and (c) practice in a "pronunciation clinic".

Reports on this project may be found in Gårding and Bannert (1979), Bannert (1979) and Bannert (1980).

3.4.4 Hyltenstam (1977) deals with the acquisition of Swedish negation by adult second language learners. He finds that the variety of Swedish, or "interim language", spoken by his subjects is characterized by many variable rules. For example, some learners variably place the negation before and after the finite verb (and this variation is not random in Swedish). Hyltenstam also found that his 160 adult subjects showed a similar, regular route of acquisition, independently of differences in background such as knowledge of other foreign languages or, to some extent, differences in SL. (The only significant background variable was length of education.)

His subjects proceeded from the structurally simple to the structurally more complex, where the simple was characterized by unmarked categories and the complex by marked categories. Hyltenstam also did a minor study on those learners who regressed, and concluded that what was acquired last was also the first to be lost.

Hyltenstam also deals with the acquisitional route towards interrogative structures, and of subject-verb inversion in declaratives after sentence-initial non-subjects. The results from this study are consistent with the generalizations above.

These studies were combined into a Ph.D. dissertation (Department of Linguistics, University of Lund, 1978) where he claims that whereas lectal continua have the same degree of structural complexity at any point, interlanguage continua have different degrees of structural complexity at their polar points.

The data underlying all these studies were elicited by means of cloze tests.

3.4.5 Kotsinas (1980) discusses varieties of Swedish spoken by adult Greek immigrants who have acquired Swedish outside the classroom. The data consist of samples of spoken language.

A comprehensive description of linguistic features of these learner varieties will appear in a forthcoming dissertation. The main feature

described in the 1980 study is the extension of the verb <u>kommer</u> (come)
to fill many different functions, a phenomenon which may be compared to
the overgeneralization of the German verb <u>kommen</u> by Spanish and Italian
learners, which was discussed in 1.5.4.

3.5 Great Britain

There has been considerable research effort into the acquisition of
English as a second language in the United States, Britain and other
English-speaking countries, although most of this research has been directed
at second language acquisition within tutored contexts. There has, however,
been very little study of the acquisition of English by adult immigrants in
Britain and, to our knowledge, there are no published accounts of the spontaneous language acquisition of English by Punjabi or Italian adult immigrants. But there are a few British empirical studies of language use by
adult immigrants, rather than language acquisition, which are relevant to
the ESF project:

1. The National Centre for Industrial Language Training (NCILT)
   has published (from 1976) pedagogical material which is aimed at
   increasing awareness of English first and second language speakers
   of the difficulties of inter-ethnic communication. The empirical
   research into interaction between English native speakers and South
   Asian English speakers was undertaken in collaboration with J.J.
   Gumperz and is described in Gumperz and Roberts (1978), Gumperz, Jupp
   and Roberts (1979) and Gumperz (Ed.) 1982: 22-56, 57-72, 232-256. This
   research is directly responsible for some of the issues that are raised
   in chapter 4 of this manual.
   Another related project co-ordinated by NCILT formed part of the Council
   of Europe Modern Languages Project: "Teaching the language of the host
   country to adult migrants".
   The aim of the project was to develop student autonomy. This included
   an extensive needs analysis with second language speakers, including
   logs of language use, and examining preferred learning strategies.
   The work is described in NCILT working papers (Gumperz, Jupp and
   Roberts 1980).
2. The Linguistic Minorities Project (Institute of Education, University
   of London) has researched the changing patterns of bilingualism in

several regions in England. Included in the data are Punjabi and
Italian speakers and adults who are not receiving regular language
tuition. A short summary report was published in September 1983.
See also Saifullah Kahn (1980).

3. Research has been carried out on the needs and expectations of
   Asian redundant workers. The Commission for Racial Equality has
   published the results: Redundant Asian Textile Workers (1983) and
   further case studies are described in Furnborough, Jupp, Munns and
   Roberts (1982).

4. Finally, the project on Doctor-Patient Communication skills at the
   University of Lancaster examined the discourse of second language
   speaking doctors and the data and analysis was used as the basis
   of pedagogical materials. The project is described in Candlin, Leather
   and Bruton (1974).

References for 3.5

Candlin, C.N., J. Leather, and C. Bruton: English language skills for
overseas doctors and medical staff. Work in progress I-IV. Mimeo,
University of Lancaster. April-June 1974.

Furnborough, P., T. Jupp, R. Munns, and C. Roberts: Language, disadvantage
and discrimination: breaking the cycle of minority group perception.
Journal of Multilingual and Multicultural Development 3 (3), 247-266 (1982).

Gumperz, J.J. (Ed.): Discourse Strategies: Studies in Interactional
Sociolinguistics 1. Cambridge University Press, Cambridge 1982.

Gumperz, J.J. (Ed.): Language and Social Identity: Studies in Interactional
Sociolinguistics 2. Cambridge University Press, Cambridge 1982.

Gumperz, J.J. and C. Roberts: Developing awareness skills for inter-ethnic
communication. National Centre for Industrial Language Training,
Southall 1978.

Gumperz,J.J.,T. Jupp and C. Roberts: Crosstalk. The National Centre for
Industrial Language Training, Southall 1979.

Gumperz, J.J.,T.Jupp and C. Roberts: Crosstalk - the wider perspective.
National Council for Industrial Language Training, Southall 1980.

Saifullah Khan, V.: The "mother-tongue" of linguistic minorities in
multi-cultural England. Journal of Multilingual and Multicultural
Development 1, 71-88 (1980).

Conclusion

In conclusion, it is clear that except in the case of Germany, SSLA by adults is a relatively recent area of research, and still limited in scope. There have only been two major projects carried out to date (ZISA and HDP), and these projects have had a certain influence on some of the other work discussed (in Holland especially), as regards both data collection methods and the (primarily syntactic) areas of investigation. Almost all the studies discussed have adopted a cross-sectional approach.

4. Understanding, Misunderstanding and Breakdown

4.1 Introduction

In this chapter, we will examine the role of understanding and misunderstanding in SSLA. We will be particularly interested in the effects
on acquisition of social and cultural factors and the potential for misunderstanding contained in them. These factors concern the immediate social
context in which the TL is encountered, the cultural background expectations and assumptions acquired in primary socialization, and their signalling by both parties in an inter-ethnic encounter. Of the groups of
factors determining the acquisition process which were mentioned in 1.3.3,
this area of investigation is therefore concerned firstly with the learner's
cognitive/perceptual disposition and his exposure to the TL, and then with
the effect that understandings and misunderstandings during contacts with
TL speakers has on his propensity to learn.

4.2 Inter-ethnic communication and spontaneous second language acquisi-
tion

4.2.1 The social and cultural context of second language acquisition. We
said in 1.3.2 that an adult learner has, paradoxically, to learn in order
to communicate, and to communicate in order to learn. The implications of
this statement are far-reaching for the acquisition process both in terms
of the attitudes displayed by the TL community, and in terms of the learner's motivation and awareness in learning. We must particularly bear in
mind that our informants come from a group that has fulfilled roles in
western European society as an unskilled labour force, and has come to be
one of its most socially disadvantaged groups. Their position in the social structure compounds any predisposition within the TL community towards
racist and social or cultural stereotyping. In addition, any lack of competence in the TL, and any differences in social and linguistic behaviour,
further reinforce the negative expectations of the TL community. The cumu-

lative effect of these factors frequently gives rise to the image of immigrants as persons of poor communicative ability, social inadequacy and low intelligence. In this context, continued misunderstandings in inter-ethnic communication further reinforce such stereotypes, so that such encounters can aggravate the hostility of the host community. This in turn becomes a demotivation for the L2 learner to engage in such encounters, and "communicate in order to learn".

While the factors outlined above provide the context in which the TL is encountered, and may in themselves fuel misunderstandings between the participants, there is a further important contributory factor to misunderstanding in inter-ethnic encounters which affects acquisition. This is the effect of bringing together in such encounters two different sets of primary socialization. We take as our starting point in examining this effect, the view that the use of language reflects and reproduces social systems, thus representing in its patterns of variation much of the variation that characterizes human cultures. In other words, we take it that when we speak, we encode and transmit social and cultural values and assumptions. The process of L1 acquisition is inseparable from the cultural and social context through which it is acquired. Societies (and groups within societies) have differing views of reality and of appropriate behaviour within situations; they also have different conventions within conversations for establishing shared meaning and for managing the conversation.

Therefore, not only conventions such as these, but general background assumptions of participants must be taken into account.

We suggest that while the learner is also acquiring the TL through exposure to language in use, and the social and cultural reality transmitted by that language, he also brings to any interaction the cultural values and conventions gained in primary socialization, and these are likely initially to remain dominant. If these differ markedly from those of the TL, the differences are likely to affect adversely the mutual negotiation of meaning in inter-ethnic encounters. These misunderstandings, occurring in the hostile social context outline above, will often be negative experiences for the participants, with consequent effects on the process of acquisition and the development of inter-ethnic relationships. Thus, in any investigation of adult L2 acquisition, the factors of the social context of TL encounters, of the primary socialization of the participants, and of the interrelation between these two phenomena, must be examined.

The initial encounter with the TL often occurs in situations in which the TL speaker is in a gate-keeping position (cf. Erickson, 1976). By this we mean that the balance of power is tipped firmly in favour of the TL speaker, whereas the learner is from the outset in a position of having to appeal for his rights.

For the learner, this means (cf. 1.3.3) that he is frequently in a situation in which it is the other interactant who holds the major right to speak, and so the possibilities of communication with the other may be severely curtailed. Similarly, the attitude of the TL interactant will be an important factor in determining the kind of input from which he is expected to extract meaning.

In addition, and in contrast to the process of L1 acquisition, where misunderstandings take place in a supportive environment, any failure to communicate one's needs on the part of an adult acquiring a second language constitutes a double frustration: firstly, the adult experiences the self-frustration contained in being unable to present the same self-image that he presents in his SL, and secondly, any misunderstandings may have grave consequences - one may lose one's livelihood, one's right to financial support, or even the right to remain in the country in which one has lived for years and built a life for oneself and one's family.

Finally, the experience of repeated misunderstandings and break-down - where the learner's signals are not interpreted as intended, or where he is unable to interpret the TL participant's meaning - may lead to a low motivation to engage in interaction at all, because the stress involved is so high. Thus the learner may enter a cycle in which he will avoid exposure to the TL, and thereby lessen his chances of acquisition (cf. 4.5).

For the TL speaker, emotions and attitudes towards a learner can vary from a positive appraisal of the language produced as "exotic and charmingly foreign" to a negative assessment of the learner as an ignorant and parasitical member of society. We suggest that stereotypes of the latter kind are more prevalent among "gate-keepers" (and it is mainly in gate-keeping encounters that an immigrant is first exposed to the

TL) for the following reasons:

- when the TL is initially used by a learner (at least in countries where there is no early language training) it is used out of necessity to acquire certain rights or vital pieces of information concerned with survival, such as acquiring a job, a residence permit, a roof over one's head. The instrumentality of these requirements is evident. There may indeed be no other motivation on the part of the learner to speak at all in these initial encounters;
- the gate-keepers themselves are accustomed to view the learner from this instrumental perspective and from this perspective alone. They do not expect to be able to indulge in phatics, or communication about the difficulties experienced on the basis of repeated previous experience. Rightly or wrongly, on the basis of this experience, the learner appears to the native speaker as being motivated by exclusively materialistic ends;
- any difficulty in communication is seen as a factor that hinders the achievement of the gate-keeper's job, rather than as a charming feature of a foreigner. Thus the more time the gate-keeper has to spend with the learner in order to achieve mutual understanding, the more frustrated he may become;
- a low level of ability in the TL may be interpreted by the gate-keeper as ignorance or stupidity;
- different cultural norms and modes of signalling may be misinterpreted: for example, an omission such as that of introducing oneself (superfluous for a Punjabi for example, and probably for immigrants from rural backgrounds in other countries, who are completely unused to defining themselves in terms of a proper name) may well be interpreted by the TL speaker as downright rudeness.

The cumulative effect then, of such interactions for the TL speaker, may be to develop or reinforce negative stereotyping of the SL culture and of individuals from it. This effect may vary between groups of informants in different countries, depending on the role that racism plays in each country; one would expect for example Finns in Sweden to encounter less racism than Turks in Germany, Arabs in France, or Punjabis in Britain.

In conclusion then, in early contact with the TL the learner will often be in stressful situations, both by virtue of his lack of the TL, and because of the gate-keeping nature of initial encounters. He will be extracting meaning on the basis of his own cultural expectations, interposing gestures, tone of voice, etc. in accordance with these. The TL speaker will in all likelihood be judging the learner according to his own cultural expectations, and the stereotypes built up from previous encounters. The occurrences of frustration, misunderstanding and breakdown in inter-ethnic encounters may act as a demotivation for the learner, and impede both the process of acquisition and the development of social relationships with the target community.

4.2.2 Background assumptions, immediate context and conceptual organization. The way in which any one speaker will interpret or express meaning depends to a great extent on the signalling systems, both verbal and non-verbal, of his own culture. Individuals in any given situation act in accordance with culturally determined assumptions of at least the following types:

(a) the expectations of what is likely to happen in a given situation;
(b) the way in which information is signalled linguistically;
(c) the ways in which the sympathy of the other participants can be engaged, and to what degree one can expect to engage it.

Each of these aspects of the interaction will be interpreted by participants on the basis of their own cultural assumptions and will form a "style" of communication. Any analysis should include among its aims, not only a description of linguistic terms used in an interaction, but also a search for ways of signalling meaning that may be common to members of a SL group but may differ from means of signalling used by native speakers of the TL.

We posit that negotiation between speakers is a result of interaction at three separate levels. The broadest of these levels, and hence the most difficult to define, is the conceptual level. Here, information received from the interactant's preconceived ideas about the situation is organized. We term this level the "schema".

Schemata form mediating links between the body of cultural assumptions and experience, and the language in which these assumptions are actualised. As a result of continued reception of information within an interaction, the conceptual sketch of what is happening shifts in both speakers and it is thus that meaning is negotiated. (For an example of shifts in schemata, cf. 4.2.4: Goal switching.) Linguistic items are signposts both to and from the conceptual sketch that the speaker or hearer forms.

Since, however, in inter-ethnic communication, the interactants may share neither cultural assumptions nor the same linguistic tools for expressing their intended meaning, it is likely that they will overlook clues in each other's speech to a considerable extent, or misinterpret them. For example, well-known cultural differences exist between how much a speaker thinks he has to justify a point in conversation, and what types of justification are perceived as relevant, or acceptable.

Finally, misunderstandings may occur in inter-ethnic communication as a result of differences in the organization of information at this level, regardless of the differences in linguistic strategies used to signal and display them.[1]

4.2.3 <u>Goals and intended meaning</u>. The second of the levels at which meaning is both inferred and expressed concerns the goals underlying an utterance. These goals will be determined by the participants' conceptual interpretation of what is happening, and by what they expect of each other (i.e. their schemata). These goals may change during the course of an interaction.

There are at least two important aspects of intentional goals: the emotional/attitudinal, e.g. pleasant, angry, apologetic; the cognitive, e.g. a piece of information, an opinion. These aspects can occur independently but mostly they are simultaneous and mixed, for example, a favour, a dressing down. Both types may be shared by the participants or may conflict violently. Goals that are more instrumental and cognitive will

---

[1] Linearization problems such as those discussed in 5.1.1 can be assimilated to this level. In chapter 5, however, our interest is precisely on the linguistic means the learner uses to structure information in his utterances.

be comparatively easy to analyse from the context, but it will be important to define to what aspects of a situation the attitudinal goals are related, e.g. the situation itself, whether they are role-related, etc. We may illustrate this by an example:

Situation I	Situation II
A: What is it, Ashraf?	C: What do you want, Chaim?
B: My sister is coming.	D: My sister is coming.
I need day off.	I need day off.
A: Well, now, let's have a look	C: Not bloody likely. What ...etc.
Speaker A's goal is to be collaborative	Speaker C's goals: not to make concessions and not to collaborate

Situation I looks as if it is a collaborative situation where B's goal is achievable because A's attitude is helpful and A does not try to block B's request from the outset. The fact that B's goal of politeness is not realised in TL terms is immaterial in this particular context.

Situation II is an antagonistic one where D's instrumental goal is unlikely to be achieved because C's goal of blocking any request from D turns the request into a confrontation. D's failure to achieve his attitudinal goal of politeness probably only makes matters worse. As this example shows, there can be situations in which the goal of one participant can be to express rage, anger or rudeness towards the other, which means that successful communication need not always result in positive emotional experience for both sides.

On the other hand, we are aware that in Situation II, C's seemingly antagonistic reply may amount to no more than abusive language being used as a sign of familiarity between members of the same work-force. This point underlines the necessity of having access to both participants' views of their own and the other's behaviour in any given piece of communication.

Hence, the example above illustrates that ascription of intentions and goals is difficult. Our ascriptions depend to a large extent on assumptions we make about the relationship between speaker or hearer's overt behaviour and motives, and the desires or needs we assume them to have. This is true of us both as participants in and as analysts of conversation.

The desires and needs we have assumed above are of a social nature. They are simply a social version of the maxim that individuals strive for pleasure and try to escape pain, i.e. in this case that they want respect and recognition - social pleasure - and that they want to avoid shame and disgrace - social pain   (cf. Allwood, 1976).

Another way to say this is that they wish to preserve their positive face, i.e. to gain social approbation, and that they also wish to preserve negative face, i.e. they wish to be unimpeded autonomous members of society (cf. Brown & Levinson, 1978).

In the achievement of these two ends, speakers make use of their rationality and consequently select a strategy ranging from extreme directness that threatens either one's own positive or negative face or that of the hearer, to indirect insinuations of attitude that are far less face-threatening to either participant. Between these two extremes there exists a variety of strategies that, although potentially face-threatening, include redressive action.

The strategy finally chosen by an interactant will depend on the norms and beliefs of his culture as it applies to such variables of importance for the relationship as the relative power distribution and social distance between the participants and the weight of the imposition as viewed through the norms and beliefs of their respective cultures. These variables are treated in more detail in 4.2.7. As their perception by informants is an important factor in ascertaining understanding and misunderstanding, they form part of our investigation, cf. 4.3.2.

4.2.4 <u>Goal switching</u>. The interaction between expectation and information from the ongoing situation may result in participants switching goals according to the interpretation they make of the input from their fellow interactant.

Let us consider the following interchange that took place at the outset of a telephone conversation:

A: Hallo, Mr. Smith, you're the Personnel Manager, I believe.

B: No, I'm the General Manager.

We can all infer that A now has to make some sort of retrieval. We do this on the basis of our cultural experience which is actualised at the level of language. So we would expect A now to respond with something like:

> A: Oh, I'm terribly sorry, I must have been given the wrong infor-
> mation.

The native speaker observing this interaction is able to predict this
shift, in general terms, as a result of stored knowledge (the schemata).
In fact, we predict the switching of A's goals on the basis of the assumption that B's response will have shifted A's schemata to include
embarrassment and retrieval of a faux pas over and above the already
existing schema of management hierarchy. A has scanned the various
schematic options, and the chosen schemata determine the goals and language through which they are expressed. Here, the relationship between
A and B has changed, and so A will have different goals from those originally intended. Throughout the conversation, the necessity to switch
goals arises repeatedly as we:

(a)   establish what is happening;
(b)   are constrained as a result of (a) and reformulate the next action;
(c)   have to effect changes in (a).

Thus we can observe how the switching of goals arises. In the above example, this is what happened:

Planned goals	Actualised goals
Greeting	Greeting
Introduction	Retrieval of faux pas
Establish relationship	Establish goodwill to enable
	making an appointment

Make an appointment

In this example, the planned goal of introduction has been actualised
as a faux pas, so that A has to take some redressive action to preserve
B's positive face in order to achieve ultimately the final instrumental goal of the interaction (to make an appointment). The negotiation
at this point thus involves a switching of both attitudinal and instrumental components of the goal of the next utterance. The necessary ad-
justments will find their actualisation in the language produced. We
turn to this now.

4.2.5 <u>The relationship between context, goals, speaker perspective and the formal properties of language</u>. In assessing misunderstanding and breakdown, formal linguistic items serve the hearer and analyst as a check on the assumptions made about the various components of an interaction (cf. the analysis proposed in the Appendix).

Let us recall briefly the points made in 4.2.2; cultural and social experience will determine expectations as to:

(a) what is likely to happen in any given situation;
(b) the way in which information is signalled linguistically;
(c) how best to engage the sympathy of the other participant and to what degree one can expect to engage it.

If the participants in an interaction have differing cultural backgrounds and are, as a result, working on different assumptions, the greater the difference between these assumptions, the greater the amount of language needed to establish common ground and achieve satisfactory negotiation of meaning. But let us look at an example where the participants do not achieve this end.

The interviewee in this example is a young Asian, role-playing an interview with a prospective employer at the end of a retraining course in English with Engineering Skills.[1]

<blockquote>
A: ?Can you tell me about the welding that you learnt?
B: yes there is a/ acetylene welding acetylene gas welding and electronic welding
A: hm sorry and what
005 B: electronic arc welding
A: electric arc welding
B: yes
A: right yes
</blockquote>

---

[1] Transcription conventions are given in 8.7. In the illustrative examples of chapters 4 - 7, use of these conventions is however kept to the minimum compatible with the point to be made. Here, for example, pauses + and unclear sequences ( ) are marked, as it is significant that speaker B is hesitant and unforthcoming.

```
      B: yes and er + gas welding
010   A: ?and you did some gas welding right?+?can you tell me about
      B: (yes)
      A: the gas welding you did?
      B: ( it was it ) ++ one is oxygen gas and the other one is acety-
         lene + is both working with copper rod + there
015   A: hm + hm
      B: I work
      A: yes ?what sort of things did you do what sort of things did you
         weld?
      B: is make some ++ angle you know just practise our welding + is
020      roughly made job there ( not proper )
      A: hm well the welding we do here as you know is erm + mig welding
         + ? dyou know what mig welding means?
      B: yeh +++ no
      A: well it's er ++ it's welding with a gas flux ++ right
025   B: (yeh)
      A: we did
      B: yes they ( they is ) I think ++ production work
```

(From Thorpe, 1981)

The excerpt has to be considered in the context of the whole interview,
in which, out of a total of 70 questions, the interviewee gave a one-
word answer to 27 of them; another 14 of his replies consisted of four
words or less.

In this particular excerpt, the interviewer attempts in the very
first question to find out what the candidate has learnt from the course.
He receives the answer:

there is a/ acetylene welding and electronic welding

which does not explain what the candidate has learnt personally. Instead,
the impersonal form there is leaves the interviewer in some doubt as to
whether the candidate has had practical experience of these types of
welding. In lines 10 and 12 the interviewer tries to reiterate his question, but again is diverted by the impersonal form of the reply:

one is oxygen gas ...

The interviewer makes a final attempt in lines 17 and 18 to get the candidate to define his own practical experience. The repeated use of an impersonal form:

is make some angle

leads the interviewer to the conclusion that the candidate has no practical experience of these types of welding.

This misunderstanding is partly caused by the candidate's assumptions about appropriate behaviour in this context: they did not include the awareness of having to sell oneself. This conflicted strongly with the expectations of the interviewer, who as a result of the Asian's taciturn behaviour, concluded that he was unco-operative and evasive. In a subsequent discussion with the candidate, it emerged that his command of English was far higher than that produced in the interview context would lead one to believe.

The candidate's speaker perspective of using the minimal response strategy to avoid exposing inaccuracies in his production of English was at odds with the interviewer's. The latter was trying to give the candidate as much opportunity as possible to exhibit his knowledge of welding, whereas the candidate later revealed that he thought the interviewer was asking so many questions in order to find a reason for rejecting him. Thus the interviewer was left, as a result of this conflict of perspective, with the opinion that the candidate knew little about welding, let alone mig welding, which was the most important type of welding in that factory.

As an analyst, one might well reach the same conclusions as the interviewer. This example highlights the importance of being able to check back on the veracity of the hypotheses made by the researcher that are bound to be limited by one's own cultural subjectivity (cf. 4.2.6). The example acts also as an indicator of the need to compare and contrast an informant's use of language in situations of stress and in those where the stress is removed. We will return to this in 4.3.2.

The example also serves to illustrate that the participants' respective expectations and interpretations of the situational setting, their roles and status, and the means through which their goals are attained are severely at odds with each other's. Individual goals, speaker perspective and assumptions about the context are actualized through language and it is thus that, as analysts, we will be able to ascertain whether our initial assumptions about what is happening were correct or not. This will lead us to outline a general approach to the analysis of understanding and misunderstanding in inter-ethnic discourse, which will be described in the Appendix. Some of the dangers involved in the interpretation of inter-ethnic communication are discussed below.

4.2.6 <u>Caveats in the analysis of misunderstandings</u>. An analysis of inter-ethnic discourse begins with the formulation of a hypothesis about the overall interaction, in other words, working from the top down.

The native speaker analyst makes intuitive assumptions about what is happening in the conversation and then uses the analysis of prosody, syntax and lexicon as a reality check for this hypothesis; in other words, works from the bottom up.

As individuals from a specific European cultural background we may well be in danger of imposing our own cultural assumptions onto the discourse of a speaker from a different background and attributing meaning and intent to him that are not at all his own.

For example, in an authentic counselling session recorded by the English team, a Punjabi speaker appeared to be making unusually lengthy and awkward pauses, although his language seemed to be fairly fluent. This feature called into question the original hypothesis that he was attempting, as client, to give a concise account of a problem. After closer examination of the way in which he was using pauses, it became clear that his purpose was to allow the counsellor, or even to compel the counsellor to name the precise nature of the problem for him. This proved, after checking back with the client, to be the case, since the client felt that directness on his own part would be a violation of the rules of respect for a counsellor and appear to be too demanding. The pauses were an expression of the client's cultural assumptions about personal boundaries and consequent appropriacy of behaviour in this situation, and amounted to an expression of his attitudinal goal.

To avoid attributing meaning incorrectly, the initial hypotheses formulated about an interaction should be left as broad as possible and then checked against the detail of prosody, syntax and lexis to see if other patterns and rules are emerging as discourse conventions/features, aris-

ing from differences of conceptualisation and of the linguistic means
for expressing meaning.

In other words, speech constantly triggers assumptions, expectations and connotations in the hearer about the speaker's intended meaning. As analysts, it is only when some aspect jars on our perception
that we look at the bottom level of detail of linguistic items to give
us clues for the re-interpretation of our "top" hypothesis about the interaction.

4.2.7 Variables of the interaction. As we have said, the process of analysis to investigate misunderstanding or breakdown begins by the researcher making a hypothesis about the interaction, starting from the
general (top down) and proceeding to the particular (bottom up). In making the hypothesis, the analyst is in a different position from the interactants in that the whole interaction can be observed and listened to,
before any hypothesis is made.

In forming hypotheses, and in the later reality check carried out
through the analysis, we suggest that the following variables should be
borne in mind since they will influence the negotiation of meaning between the participants.

These variables concern cultural assumptions and their signalling
through language. The success of the interaction will depend on the ability of the participants to establish or negotiate these variables in
such a way that they are mutually compatible.

(a) Ethnic identity. The degree of ethnicity, ethnocentricity and rac-
     ism present in the individuals, and the degree to which language is
     used to establish or maintain a self/group identity, whether volun-
     tarily or involuntarily, which is different from that of the other
     participant. We distinguish here between: ethnicity - a sense of be-
     longing to a culture; ethnocentricity - a rigid acceptation of
     one's own culture and a rigid rejection of other cultures; racism
     - an antipathy based on unfounded or inflexible generalizations.
     These positions may find expression in linguistic and behavioural
     modes such as dialect, register, "foreign" linguistic features,
     "foreigner talk", attitude, eye-contact. We should consider the de-
     gree to which cultural mobility is demonstrated in such areas;

whether, for example, there is evidence of a lack of ability to code-switch or a lack of desire to do so. A learner may wish to limit this mobility in order to maintain identity and/or resist acculturation.

(b) Attitudes and emotion. The way in which attitude and emotion are signalled by verbal and non-verbal means. These may be displayed involuntarily (e.g. blushing), indicated through verbal behaviour (e.g. accent, pitch or loudness) or signalled in speech (e.g. statements about emotional state), cf. Allwood (1978).

(c) Perception of the other. It is important to attempt to define what each participant attributes to the other in terms of attitudes, motives, intentions and rationality: to look at how he is interpreting the other person in terms of his own assumptions and expectations. The following factors are likely to influence this process:

The ethnic factor. The degree to which ethnicity, ethnocentricity or racism affects the participant's view of the other, or of the topics or goals of an interaction.

We suggest that ethnicity should not prove a barrier to the successful negotiation of meaning, except in as far as it might impede the recognition of other views of reality, appropriacy and signalling conventions.

Ethnocentricity, with its high correlation to personality characteristics such as difficulty in coping with ambiguity will result in increased difficulty in negotiation.

Racism will increase this difficulty further.

Co-membership. The degree to which co-membership is present or negotiable in the course of the interaction, and the degree of ability or desire to recognize and respond to linguistic and behavioural overtures made in this area.

Erickson (1976) has demonstrated the importance of establishing co-membership in gate-keeping encounters. While ethnic or pan-ethnic co-membership is important, particularistic co-membership (e.g. shared work-place, shared interest in football) is also significant. The more various co-memberships can be established and recognized as such, the more likely it is that sympathy and goodwill can be established between participants.

In analysing the data, it is of interest to discover the extent of
co-membership and the weight this is given in shaping the attitudes of the participants to one another in the interaction. For
example, a participant expressing a strongly ethnocentric identity
may not in fact be moved by the evidence of a particularistic co-
membership with the other participants. Equally, the same co-membership factor may carry different weights in different contexts.
For example, having a work place in common is likely to be more significant in situations where a "team" identity is fostered, as in
the public transport industry, than in situations where people are
fairly much on their own, as in most noisy factory environments.
Role, status, power. The perception of role, status and power in
the interaction, the degree to which signalling devices for these
are mutually interpretable, and the potential mobility, in relation
to these factors, of the participants.
As we observed in 4.2.1, many naturally occurring encounters between TL and L2 speakers will be in gate-keeping situations, where
the TL speaker holds power and is evaluating the other in order to
grant, or not to grant, access or privilege. How this situation is
perceived by either side, and whether the modes of signalling relative status, etc., are recognized, will play a part in the success
or otherwise of the interaction.
Ascribed attitudes and emotions. The extent to which the modes of
expressing emotion and attitudes (see above) are mutually interpretable.
A participant interpreting another's behaviour through his own
norms and expectations may ascribe attitudes and emotions that are
not in fact present in the other. Equally, he may fail to interpret
emotions that are present. For example Punjabi speakers will tend
to describe emotional feelings in terms of physical symptoms, and
this may not be understood by native speakers of British English.

(d) Perceptions and assumptions about the interaction. The variables
listed above will clearly affect how the interaction is perceived,
and how expectations are negotiated within the course of the encounter. In addition, however, there are some factors which are specific
to the interaction, although the variables mentioned play a part in

shaping them.

Goals. The extent to which the goals of the participants, both instrumental and attitudinal (cf. 4.2.3) are compatible.
The extent to which the achievement of goals is dependent on such factors as: accurate negotiation of facts; conveying attitudes; a high or low level of verbal interaction. The way in which these goals are presented or negotiated, and the extent to which these are understood by each participant. For example, different ways of structuring an argument in relation to instrumental goals may act to obscure the goal, or promote irritation.

Expectations of success. The extent to which participants expect the interaction to be successful in relation to their goals.
The learner who has repeatedly failed to negotiate his intended meaning successfully may have very low expectations of success in communication with members of the indigenous population in certain situations.

The nature of the interaction. The extent to which the interaction is perceived as face-threatening by the learner in particular, and the ways in which this is handled. Assumptions about behaviour in conventional settings; in an interview, for example (cf. 4.2.5).

Awareness. The extent to which participants are aware of the factors which can cause misunderstanding in interaction.
These factors include recognition of when a misunderstanding or breakdown has taken place and the implementation of appropriate strategies for repair; the management of "uncomfortable moments" in the interaction; awareness on the part of the participants of their own language behaviour and its intended meaning and of the same elements in the hearer.

Having formed a hypothesis, taking account of the above variables, about context, purpose, speaker perspectives and schemata in the interaction, the rest of the analysis has as its aim to investigate the text in depth as a reality check on the hypothesis made, and to modify/change the hypothesis in the light of the findings. The various steps of the "top-down" and "bottom-up" approach outlined in 4.2.6 are given in the Appendix.

4.3 Processing the input

4.3.1 General questions. The immigrant is faced at the outset with accomplishing, under conditions that can be difficult (cf. 4.2.1), the
task that faces any language learner: changing his perception of the
streams of sounds he encounters from a meaningless babble to a perception of these sounds as meaningful utterances expressing the thoughts
and feelings of his interlocutors. The possibilities open to the learner of effecting such a change are dependent on factors of the following
type:

(a) Are certain segments of what he hears more salient than others?
     Such salience could be produced by stress and prosody or by a seg-
     ment being at the end or the beginning of an utterance. Similarly:

(b) Are there formal surface similarities between what he hears in the
     TL and the SL?

(c) Are certain segments of what he hears connected with clear contex-
     tual features such as non-verbal gestures or salient objects in the
     immediate setting?

(d) Is there a "motivated" connection between what he hears and fea-
     tures of the context? Such motivation exists for example for icons
     and indices, i.e. sounds that are connected by similarity or conti-
     guity to their function or meaning.

(e) Are there certain expressions he hears very frequently? Here the
     role of the mass media may be important. But it is perhaps even
     more important to try to determine what type of everyday uses of
     language he is exposed to initially, as a bystander in various
     types of linguistic interaction. For example, a special case of
     language that he might be exposed to is the use of the TL by other,
     more proficient SL speakers. Study of the TL varieties of the long
     resident informants (cf. 2.3) may give us some idea of the impact
     of such exposure on the acquisition process.

(f) Other important factors are: the language learner's opportunities
     to produce, i.e. to practice and to act in the target language;
     the types of language at all relevant for him to use given the
     particular social environment of his daily life; his motivation to
     learn (e.g. certain key expressions) through need or desire; and

his linguistic awareness in general.

Although this list is in no way exhaustive, it gives an indication of the complexity of the factors. Some of the factors will be important all through acquisition, while others will only be important initially, or else in later stages of acquisition. Among the factors that will be important could be operating principles of the type formulated by Slobin (1973). Others which probably play a role almost continuously are the tendency to judge what is happening in terms of cognitive and emotive schemata which have been learned earlier on in life. In other words, the learner draws on earlier background assumptions to make sense of behaviour and events currently facing him, which, in the case where differences exist between source and target culture, means that misunderstandings can arise.

The learner's problem-solving ability will not only be apparent in his use of operating principles: it may also be used in his attempts to understand compound words - a task which is complicated by phenomena like idiomaticity and non-transparent connections in expressions like hot dog.

What has been said so far can be seen as a specific illustration of the overall factors determining language acquisition mentioned in 1.3.3. Since obviously only a small part of what has been mentioned can be studied in the project, we have selected below some areas that seem interesting and possible to investigate.

4.3.2 Areas of investigation

4.3.2.1 Cultural background and understanding. As we said above, the learner of a new language uses assumptions and interpretative strategies acquired in his primary socialization in order to make sense of the target language input that he encounters. This applies to his understanding of both verbal and non-verbal events. In the early stages of acquisition the universal aspects of gesture and body language will serve as important aids for him. The idea of the study proposed here is to examine the role of cultural preconceptions for the informant's understanding of TL interaction. This will be done by showing him selected videotaped "typical" spoken interactions between TL speakers (cf. 8.2.3) and subsequent-

ly questioning him in (initially) the SL on his understanding and awareness of what he has seen. In particular, it seems important to determine
his understanding of the following parameters of linguistic communication:

(a) What was the overall purpose of the interaction?
(b) What is the setting of the interaction?
(c) What is the role identity of the interacting speakers; in particular,
     what power and status relations are of interest here?
(d) What is the topic being talked about?
(e) What are the emotions and attitudes of the speakers and listeners?
(f) Is the interaction being carried on successfully or unsuccessfully?
(g) What are the purposes of speakers in specific utterances?
(h) How are particular utterances understood both with regard to more
     cognitive content and emotional tone?

Questions such as these would reveal a great deal about the cultural assumptions that the informants bring to the learning situation with regard to: appropriate ways of behaving; the ways in which status, role
and power is expressed in the target language culture; the ways in which
emotions and attitudes are understood to be expressed in the target language; what are taken to be significant signs of conflict or co-operation between speakers; comprehension ability in general.

Obviously, some of the factors mentioned above will be more relevant in the early stages of acquisition and others, such as comprehension
of complete utterances, only later. Here we have tried to give a general
presentation of factors of interest during the whole period of the longitudinal study.

4.3.2.2 <u>Conflict, co-operation and analysing the speech stream</u>. In this
paragraph, we will examine the conditions under which the learner has
to analyse the speech stream. Here he draws upon what we termed in 1.3.3
his cognitive/perceptual disposition: the ability to break up sequences
of sounds into smaller units, to identify recurring elements and to associate them with particular meanings, etc.

We can hypothesize that this task is easier for the learner under
certain conditions: when there is a <u>consensus</u> between him and his inter-

locutor on the activity they are engaged in, and when the subject-matter of the interaction is immediately present, as when, for example, participants co-operate in accomplishing a concrete task and when the situation is not stressful. This type of situation provides the learner with a large number of contextual clues to the meaning of utterances, and his comprehension is immediately checked against the reality of the task to be accomplished. Furthermore, co-operative face-to-face interaction will provide gestural and prosodic indications to enable him to decompose the speech stream and to assign meaning to its component parts, and sympathetic feedback.

(This is in fact a well-tried hypothesis, for Berlitz, in elaborating his "direct method" of language teaching, was not unaware of the pedagogic advantage to be drawn from such situations.)

The less the situation corresponds to that described above, the harder the task is for the learner. Thus if for a given type of interaction, it proved possible to obtain and compare data from accompanying observation and data from play acting, the informant's relative comprehension in each situation will allow us to check both the hypothesis expressed here and the extent to which play acting approximates "authentic" interaction.

4.3.2.3 Looking for important words. One particular strategy for achieving some understanding of a message may be to look for important words. What clues are available to help the learner identify the important words in a given situation?

(a) One clue may be the extra-linguistic context in which the message is uttered. A spoken form can be associated with an entity by gesture: in the work-place, for example, objects which serve in the accomplishment of the work may be named with an accompanying gesture, and these names/gestures will occur frequently in the early stages. The informant, recognizing the objects and the order in which they are named, can then rely on his knowledge of the world to infer the semantic relationships holding between the names. An experimental example of what we mean is given by the "stage directions" experiments (cf. 8.4.3). Imagine a situation where there are an ashtray (Aschenbecher) and a shopping bag (Tasche) visible to a

learner, and where the learner knows he is about to receive an instruction. If he identifies in the utterance the word <u>Aschenbecher</u>,
followed by the word <u>Tasche</u>, he can interpret the utterance, given
his knowledge of the respective sizes and shapes of these objects,
as an instruction to put the ashtray in the bag. This particular
experiment is described in detail in 7.3.2.2.

This strategy may prove particularly relevant in interpreting reference to people in the immediate situation, and constitute the
basis for constructing an initial pronoun system.

If this hypothesis turns out to constitute an important factor in
an informant's attempt to understand utterances, then we may expect
some reflection of it in the informant's production, which would
then consist of essentially <u>noun based utterances</u> where the nouns
would refer to persons, place and to items in specific discourse
domains. Examination of the whole of an informant's vocabulary in
the early stages (cf. 6.3) provides us with means of checking this.

(b) The previous example suggests that in a given utterance, in a given
context, certain words are essential if (partial) comprehension is
to be achieved. This is also true of certain expressions whose form
is invariant and which are used to fulfill certain important functions in TL communication: phatic - "how are you", "excuse me", ...;
conative - "would you mind", "could you...", etc. Certain set
phrases may be perceived by the informant as fulfilling important
functions for him (cultural assumptions may, of course, make this
perception different from that of TL-speakers), and they may be acquired as unanalysed wholes (cf. 6.2.5: Formulaic Expressions),
i.e. as a memorized sequence of sounds with a specific intonation
contour. Subsequent production of these expressions, as wholes,
may give TL-speakers a superficial impression that informants are
<u>at ease</u> in the TL, which is not consistently apparent on closer ex-
amination, and which will, of course, further contribute to mutual
misunderstanding.

(c) Prosody, in particular emphatic stress and tone of voice, may well
serve generally as clues to the importance of words in utterances
and specifically (cf. 5.1.4) to signal new information. Intonation-
al conventions not shared by SL and TL are on the other hand like-

ly to make comprehension generally more difficult.

(d) Finally, the input may simply consist of what the TL speaker considers to be important words ("foreigner talk"): the emotional and attitudinal connotations of the use of foreigner talk are, however, unlikely to facilitate comprehension on the part of the informant.

4.4 Feedback processes

4.4.1 General questions. If communicative interaction is to be effective, i.e. if the speaker is to convey information to the listener and the listener to grasp the information conveyed by the speaker, they both have to have means to check the effectiveness of conveying and understanding the information, respectively.

Feedback mechanisms become important very early in the acquisition of spoken language. If feedback mechanisms are not mastered by either speaker or listener there will be problems in spoken discourse and acquisition will prove to be extremely difficult, if not impossible. In fact it could be claimed that feedback is a necessary requirement for learning.

There are two main aspects of the feedback process which have to be mastered by our informants both as speakers and as listeners:

(a) Eliciting feedback. This can be done by feedback elicitators such as tag questions and particles such as eh or right in English. Feedback can also be elicited non-verbally, e.g. by a certain type of head nod.

(b) Giving feedback. This can be done with the help of small feedback-giving particles specific to different languages. English examples are umhm, yeah, yes, mm. Feedback is also given non-verbally, primarily through head movements.

The functions of feedback include indicating whether one has heard what has been said, indicating whether one has understood what has been said, and last but not least whether one has accepted what has been said, i.e. one indicates one's emotional and cognitive appraisal or attitudes to what has been said. This last function is very important since languages differ conventionally in the way feedback particles carry additional attitudinal content. A positive umhm does not sound the same in Swedish and Spanish, for example, and might therefore easily be misinterpreted.

What has been said holds for both speaker and listener, with the difference that the speaker is interested in whether his message has been heard, understood and accepted while the hearer is primarily interested only in hearing and understanding; whether he is also interested in accepting depends on his attitudinal and emotional goals.

Foreign workers will, in general, learn spoken language. They will therefore very quickly have to learn some way of coping with feedback processes in the TL. In the beginning this will probably be done mostly by non-verbal means but after having acquired a small amount of the TL they will use this - in addition to non-verbal signalling - to interact. For example, they might use this language simply to signal a willingness to participate using yes to indicate "I hear you". This might cause frustation on the part of the TL participant, who expects yes to indicate agreement with a proposition, and lead to the attitude (familiar from observations in Britain) of "they understand when they want to".

However, feedback processes also include more than the so-called backchannel signals discussed above. Corrections, repeats and repairs from both speaker and hearer are important elements of feedback. In normal spoken interaction both speaker and hearer constantly correct themselves and others. The speaker corrects himself when he, on the basis of his auditory feedback, notices that something has gone wrong, phonologically, lexically, syntactically or pragmatically. And if the setting permits, the hearer will also correct and repair the speaker on the same grounds. The hearer, furthermore, corrects his own understanding in addition to his own mental work by eliciting feedback on his understanding by asking metalinguistic questions such as: "Do you mean x?".

We may imagine that a learner whose linguistic awareness is high will use such metalinguistic questions more often, and to greater effect, than an informant who is less linguistically aware. Such repairs play an important role in guiding the acquisition process. The learner receives feedback on his progress and can also elicit feedback when he needs it. It is also, as we have said, one of the main ways in which a learner will manifest his own awareness in acquiring the language. His corrections and repairs manifest his own ideas of what his language should be like. It is expected that he will develop in acquiring the TL a metalinguistic vocabulary which will make it easier for him to signal his linguistic awareness (cf. 6.2.3).

4.4.2 Areas of investigation. In order to get a picture of the role of feedback processes in spontaneous language acquisition by adults the following areas could perhaps prove to be fruitful for further investigation:

(a) A study of early feedback elicitation and giving. How does the learner manage feedback during his first year of language acquisition? On what aspects of the TL does he elicit feedback and in which areas does he give feedback? Does he, for example, restrict himself only to backchannel signals or does he also use types of repair and correction? When does he first show signs of developing a metalinguistic vocabulary?

(b) A study of early feedback comprehension. Is the learner at all aware of feedback signals and how does he understand them? How does he interpret their cognitive and emotive content? This study could most easily be carried out through film-watching and/or self confrontation (cf. 8.2.3 and 8.4.4).

(c) A study of the development of strategies for repair and correction. The second language learner's set of repair strategies serves as a potential for coping with problems concerning comprehension and production of the TL. It is a search potential which can be used either for detecting trouble sources or as a heuristic for learning more of the TL. A development pattern can be conceived of in terms of: what aspects of linguistic communication these repairs are directed towards; what form the repairs take; what social features (e.g. power relations) the occurrence of the different repair strategies are contingent upon.
The form of repair can be described in terms of various distinctions developed in previous sections, e.g. in terms of whether the repair is carried out by self or other; whether it is spontaneous or elicited by a request for repair; whether it occurs in the same turn as the trouble source or in some of the following turns. Fur-

thermore, in case of a self repair, we can ask to what extent and
in what way self indicates to other how the repair is supposed to
be understood. And in case of a repair made by other, we can ask to
what extent and in what way other indicates how the repair is supposed to be carried out.

4.5 Misunderstanding and breakdown

4.5.1 <u>General questions</u>. In 4.3 and 4.4, we were concerned with studying
the development of comprehension and understanding in spoken interaction,
focussing especially on some of the factors that influence early comprehension processes and on the development of feedback processes, including
repair and correction. In this paragraph, we return to the effect that
misunderstandings and (in extreme cases) breakdowns in communication may
have on the acquisition process.

In 4.2.1, we suggested that if a learner is misunderstood or misun-
derstands in an emotionally upsetting way, and if the misunderstanding
is not taken care of, one consequence may be that the learner will try
to avoid communicative situations in the TL that he feels to be stressful, threatening, or in any way upsetting. This avoidance will provoke
fossilization at a low level of TL competence. On the other hand, such
painful experiences could also be seen as a challenge which has to be
overcome and might therefore instead act as a spur on the acquisition
process. Both possibilities imply however that we attempt to examine the
effect that misunderstandings have on our informants' propensity to
learn.

4.5.2 <u>Areas of investigation</u>

4.5.2.1. <u>Understanding and misunderstanding of attitude and emotion</u>. We
said in 4.2.7 that mutual (mis)interpretation of attitudes and emotions
is an important variable in inter-ethnic encounters. It is also a crucial factor in influencing the informant's motivation to learn.

Attitudes and emotions may be displayed, indicated or signalled
(cf. 4.2.7). Although authentic encounters are what interest us most
here, it may prove difficult to infer with accuracy how these aspects
are interpreted by the participants. It will therefore be necessary to

obtain supplementary information by confronting the participants (informant and TL speaker(s)) with recordings of these encounters, if this is
at all possible. An alternative source of information is the speaker
perspective phase of play acting (cf. 8.4.2), and more particularly if
the informant's interlocutor is a TL speaker whom he may meet in everyday encounters outside the project. It is also important in confrontation to establish the intended meaning of informant's utterances, and
to compare this intended meaning with the effect of the utterance on the
TL speaker, as the informant may well be imposing linguistic discourse
devices from the SL on to the TL.

4.5.2.2 <u>Attitude, emotion, avoidance and fossilization</u>. We have said
that the factors which might lead to avoidance and/or fossilization are
found in situations which have been painful or in some way negatively
emotionally charged for the language learner. We therefore propose to investigate some such situations through play acting and, optionally, role
play by action interview (cf. 8.8.3). In particular, role play conducted
from the point of view of the language learner himself provides a way to
let him select and present problematic episodes. This in turn enables
the researcher to follow up with questions about the informant's reactions, e.g. with regard to avoidance, which in turn provides data on the
informant's awareness of factors influencing the acquisition process.
This approach should therefore give us insights into the relationship
between attitudes and emotions, the informant's awareness of these, and
the acquisition process.

Putting it a slightly different way (cf. Schumann,1978), we are investigating the way in which contact with TL-speakers affects the psychological distance learners have in relationship to the TL, and the effect
of this distance on fossilization.

4.6 <u>Suggestions for data collection</u>

4.6.1 <u>General remarks</u>. In this section we briefly describe data collection techniques that seem to us to be useful for the areas of study suggested above.

All techniques which give us information about the language learner's everyday situation, i.e. self-recordings, diaries, observation and

to some extent interviews and role play are relevant for the section as
a whole.

Since in the initial stages of language acquisition our informants,
although verbally passive in the TL, will be interpreting TL data, it
will perhaps be more fruitful to collect data with regard to comprehension
than to production. For this, film watching with subsequent questioning
in the SL should prove to be a productive technique.

4.6.2 Specific studies

4.6.2.1 Processing the input. For the studies presented in 4.3 we make
the following suggestions·

(a) cultural background and understanding: film watching combined with
     interview in source language;
(b) conflict, co-operation and analyzing the speech stream: events of
     spoken target language interaction involving the informant should be
     recorded, if at all possible. This could optimally be done through
     some sort of accompanying observation. The same event should also be
     played during a play scene, drawing on the informant's instructions.
     The play scene should also preferably be video recorded. The two
     recordings can then be compared;
(c) looking for important words. The data obtained in (a) and (b) could
     also be used in self-confrontation, where the informant can be asked
     to identify words he recognizes, and, if possible, explain what they
     mean and why they are used. The end result of the process of looking
     for important words will presumably be their intake and subsequent
     production by the learner: here, what is needed is a count of the total
     number of word tokens of different word types. We return to this word
     count in 6.3.

4.6.2.2 Feedback processes

(a) Early feedback elicitation and giving. Since this is a descriptive
     study, what is needed are data from the informant in a variety of
     different types of linguistic interaction, which would enable us to
     get an idea of the determining conditions of feedback giving and elici-
     tation. Thus, all the types of observation, in addition to self-

recording and conversation will be of value. What is then needed is an analysis of the occurrence restrictions on the different types of feedback and a count of the number of tokens per type of feedback expression.

(b) Early feedback comprehension. Here film watching is suggested, i.e. asking the informant about what different feedback expressions occurring in the film mean and why they are used. Also self-confrontation can be used; interviewing the informant about feedback expressions he himself or his interaction partners have used on a videotaped interaction played back to him. In both cases the interviews should be in the SL and concern both the comprehension and awareness of the informant by using questions such as: "what is meant by x", "why is x used", "when and where is x used", "how should x be used?"

(c) Development of repair strategies. Here it is desirable to scan selections from data collected for occurrences of repairs, since the amount and kind or repairs are to a great extent dependent on situational parameters.

In order to get more detailed data on repair strategies, these can be brought into focus in play acting for example. Another possibility would be to design part of a self- or other-confrontation session as an editing game, where the informant is encouraged to make repairs directed towards the behaviour on the screen. It should be stressed, however, that the significant data for this study are first and foremost repairs made during more authentic interaction.

4.6.2.3 Misunderstanding and breakdown

(a) Understanding and misunderstanding of attitude and emotion. Data can be collected in interviews using film watching or self-confrontation as a stimulus. Insight can be gained by asking the informant to describe attitudes as expressed by varying prosody in examples of the same sentence, and by asking him to listen to an utterance and to pick out words that the speaker attaches specific emotions to. Film watching can be used by asking the informant about what the emotional and attitudinal content is of specific utterances, expressions and types of non-verbal behaviour. Self-confrontation can be used in a similar manner. In both types of interview questions of what, why, where, when and how as applied to what is being investigated are of interest both for assessing the informant's comprehension and his awareness.

(b) Attitude, emotion, avoidance and fossilization. Since what we are investigating here are informants' own impressions of problematic encounters in the target language, the two best methods are probably conversation and play acting or role play. Of these, play acting or role play are preferable since they not only involve talking about an event but also in some sense acting it out, which engages the informant's participation to a larger extent.

Not only the play itself but the speaker perspective analysis at its end can be expected to yield valuable insights into the informant's feelings about the critical event. Self-confrontation could also be used with data from accompanying observation, role play or conversation; the aim of this will be to discover to what extent stress (both situation and role related), and the low expectations of the L2 speaker in an authentic situation contribute to loss of understanding and language when compared with use of language on the same topic with an "enabling" researcher.

5. Thematic Structure of Utterances

<u>Introduction</u>

We will be concerned in this chapter with two related questions:
- how is a syntax built up by a learner of a L2?
- how does a learner, at a given moment, use the syntax he has to structure information in utterances?

These questions bear respectively on the second and third aim of this project (cf. 1.3). We will also examine, in relation to these questions, the problem of language-specific vs generalizable factors (cf. 1.5) in the acquisition process.

If a speaker wishes to express an amount of complex information, he is faced with what Levelt (1981; 1982) calls the "linearization problem", that of arranging the information in temporal order. Within the utterance, options have to be taken as to which item to place in utterance-initial position, utterance-second position, and so on. Utterances also have to be placed in temporal order with respect to each other.

What are the principles which govern these choices? Previous work suggests that, both at utterance- and at discourse-level, there are language-independent and language- (and culture-) specific factors at work.

Before making hypotheses about the interaction of these factors with the learner's developing syntax in the thematic structuring of the utterance, we will give a brief and - of necessity - simplified account of some relevant previous work, which will attempt to give some indication of the learner's problem.

5.1 The problem

5.1.1 <u>Arrangement of information in discourse</u>. Linde & Labov (1975), Klein (1981c), Levelt (1981; 1982) and Ullmer-Ehrich & Koster (1981) have investigated the problem of linearization in certain discourse domains (and particularly the expression of spatial relationships: apartment or living-room descriptions, route directions, spatial networks).

Levelt (1982a:201), following Kempen (1977) distinguishes, for a possible theory of the speaker, between "the processes involved in the genesis of the ideas underlying speech" (conceptualizing), and "the processes involved in the choice of linguistic forms for their expression" (formulating). The development of communicative intentions, selection of information from the speaker's knowledge, and linearization of this information, belong to the former.

For the particular domain of spatial relationships, the process of linearization is apparently extremely regular. Linde & Labov found that the physical space of an apartment was linearized, for purposes of verbal description, into a temporal "guided tour", in which the speaker started at the door and "guided" the interlocutor through the apartment, room after (connected) room: in the case of branching - i.e. disconnectivity - one branch was described in full, then the speaker jumped back to the point of departure in order to describe the remaining branch(es).

For living-room descriptions, Ullmer-Ehrich and Koster found that speakers chose a gaze "tour" round the room from left to right, or from right to left, and interrupted the tour, under certain conditions, to describe sub-areas of the room.

Levelt attempts to systematize these findings, and those of his own experiments on more abstract spatial networks, by the following principles: the speaker will adopt maximal connectivity; if total connectivity in the description is not possible - as in the case of two branches to be described - the speaker will minimize the size of return jumps, i.e. will describe shorter branches before longer branches and, in the case of multiple branching, will take branch nodes on a first-in-last-out basis.

Another type of discourse domain where the linearization process can clearly be seen to be at work is the narrative, in which events are described. This is discussed in 7.4.2.3. Here too, the principles suggested by Levelt can be seen to be operating: examples in 7.4.2.3 are taken from the discourse of a learner of German. Maximal temporal connectivity is the rule in this learner's narratives, and both temporal jumps and a return to the original temporal framework are explicitly marked.

To the extent that processes of conceptualizing such as linearization

are concerned with the efficient retrieval of information on the part of
the speaker, and with his facilitating comprehension for the listener,
they may be seen as independent of particular cultures and languages.
However, as Levelt points out, linearization in discourse depends also in
part on the (assumed) mutual knowledge[1] of speaker and hearer, and this
knowledge can be culturally dependent. Thus, when cultural assumptions
about the "normal" ordering of phenomena in discourse differ (that is,
when speaker and hearer do not know that these assumptions are not mutual)
misunderstandings can arise leading, as we suggested in 4.2, to possible
frustration and resentment.

5.1.2 <u>Arrangement of information within the utterance</u>. The learner will
bring such cognitive/perceptual prerequisites as those mentioned in 5.1.1
to his acquisition of an L2. Clearly, this is an important area for tracing
the influence of language- and culture-specific vs generalizable factors
in SSLA, and as such forms part of the problems evoked in chapter 4.

In this chapter, however, we are only concerned with these phenomena
to the extent that they govern <u>the thematic structure of utterances</u>. That
they do so has been clearly shown by Ullmer-Ehrich and Koster (1981), and
by Karmiloff-Smith (1980). The former authors link discourse principles
such as connectivity to the notion of "topicality". Their account of topicality - which we will adopt here - attempts to explain why topicality,
although not in itself a syntactic function, is usually signalled by the
initial position of an utterance (in the TLs, at least: cf. 5.1.4). Topicality is governed by pragmatic constraints, such as the givenness/new-
ness of information in an utterance, or what the utterance is "about".
As - in either account - topicality can apply to various syntactic cate-

---

[1] Clark and Marshall (1981) use the term "mutual knowledge" to describe
the way people make or interpret definite reference: "They search memory
for evidence that they, their listeners, and the object they are referring
to have been 'openly present together' physically, linguistically, or indirectly. Or they search memory for evidence that the object is universal-
ly known within a community they and their listeners mutually know they belong to. With such evidence they can infer mutual knowledge directly by
means of an induction schema." Thus (cf. 5.1.2 and 5.2.2) mutual knowledge is a necessary, but not a sufficient condition for a referent to be
considered as "given information" in discourse.
In this paragraph, however, "mutual knowledge" is used more loosely, to
include not only referents that can be assumed by speaker and hearer to
be mutually known, but also mutual expectations about appropriate ways of
expressing oneself in general (cf. the "schemata" of 4.2.2).

gories, position is a clear linguistic means to signal it. The initial position in an utterance can therefore be reserved for an item of given information, or the item that the utterance is "about".

What is "given" in an utterance, or what an utterance is "about", depends, at least to a certain extent, on the type of discourse, and on the type of speaker.

Ullmer-Ehrich and Koster found that in living-room descriptions, subjects overwhelmingly produced utterances of the type: spatial adverb + subject ..., whether they were given instructions to describe the room <u>or</u> to describe the pieces of furniture in the room. They concluded that their subjects conceptualized these descriptions as being "about" spaces, and formulated their utterances accordingly, with the space in topic position.

Karmiloff-Smith found, in a picture-describing task given to English and French children of 6 - 9 years old, that these subjects "massively" adopted the following linearization strategy: find a main protagonist in the series of pictures, introduce him (with an existential expression or definite referring expression), then reserve utterance-initial position for expressions (pronouns, zero anaphora) referring to him. This strategy was systematic enough to provoke repairs (N_1 gives N_2 to $N_3 \rightarrow N_3$ has N_2 from N_1) if N_3 refers to the main protagonist. Notice that this strategy was used by both French- and English-speaking children.

A final example comes from the Heidelberg pilot study. In an experiment designed to elicit spatial prepositions, the experimenter pretended it was Easter, and hid an egg. The informant then had to instruct a subject (who was out of the room while the experimenter was hiding the egg) to hide the egg in the same way.

The experimenter took the egg out of her pocket, went to the wall on which the blackboard was, stood on a chair next to the blackboard, looked at the top edge of the blackboard but decided not to hide it there. She got down from the chair, pushed a table against the wall under the blackboard, stood two books upright (with a space of about four inches between them) in the right-angle made by the table-top and the wall. She placed the egg between the books in the space provided, and placed a shopping-bag in front of the books to close the space, thus hiding the egg.

Everything was put back into its original position, the subject was summoned in and given the experimenter's jacket with the egg in the pocket.

The writer of this section of the field manual decided to make this description of this episode "about" the experimenter, thus achieving (he hopes) both connectivity and economy - given information is systematically in topic position, zero anaphora abounds. The informant, however, was not describing, but giving instructions to the subject about finding an egg, moving the egg (and therefore the subject) in space, and manipulating other objects in order to hide the egg. This is how he did it:

1. Kommen Sie
   (Come   you)

2. Halt
   (Stop)

3. Dein äh Jacke die Tasche Ei   nehmen Sie
   (your   jacket the pocket egg take you)

4. Die Tafel   bei   gehen Sie
   (The blackboard near to go   you)

5. Oder die Tafel   oben äh   oben sehen Sie   (subject stands on the chair
   (Or   the blackboard above above look you)   and looks)

6. Oder auf nehmen Sie   (subject moves to put egg on top of blackboard)
   (Or on   take you)

7. Nee!   (informant gestures to subject to get down from chair, which
   (No!)   he does)
   (XXX)   (inaudible: interruptions from other people present)

8. Die Tisch auf ++   die Tafel   bei   Tafel   nehmen Sie
   (The table on   the blackboard near to blackboard take you)

9. Weiter ++ weiter   (table is now against wall)
   (Further further)

10. Die Bücher   (sundry gestures, interrupted by experimenter)
    (The books)

11. Das Buch äh   nehmen Sie
    (The book   take   you)

12. Oder bei   Hand äh + Wand   äh Wand
    (Or near to hand   wall   wall)

13. Die Bücher äh bei Wand äh
    (The books   near to wall)

14. Eier zwischen + Eier zwischen + Eier zwischen + das Buch +
    (Eggs between   eggs between   eggs between   the book
    (xxx) (inaudible: interruptions from other people present)
    Zwischen zwei Buch
    (between two book)

The informant first makes reference to the subject (1, 2), then lo-
cates the egg, going from the general, given context to the specific location Dein → Jacke → die Tasche → Ei, and tells the subject what to do:
nehmen Sie. 4, 5, 6 involve the subject's movements in space: the subject
being established, the utterances are therefore "about" space - die Tafel
bei, die Tafel oben, auf - and it is these expressions that receive strong
stress/intonation (Sie in utterance - final position is a weak form [zə];
oder (or), which appears to the left of utterances 5, 6, 12, has the function of connecting two utterances or parts of utterances, and will not concern us here).

Utterances 8, 12, 14 are "about" moving new objects in space by the
subject: in 8, the object (table) is first established, then its goal
(blackboard), and then the instruction is given. The instruction being,
in context, redundant, it is omitted in 13, 14. This same process can be
seen in two stages in 11, 12: object + (redundant) instruction + goal. In
all utterances from 8 - 14, it is the objects, and their goals, which receive strong stress/intonation.

The relationship object + direction + goal is realized as NP_1 + prep
+ NP_2. If the "object" is given (as in the case for the experimental subject in 4, 5, 6: "move yourself to the blackboard"), the surface realiza-
tion is goal + direction + "object": NP_2 + prep + verb + NP_1.

There are some similarities between this example and Ullmer-Ehrich's
and Koster's findings. There is connectivity: the instructions are to perform successive manipulations, although here, of course, the successive
manipulations were imposed on the informant by the nature of the task. Within each utterance - or sequence of utterances - it is the pragmatic consideration of what the utterance is felt to be "about" which decides in the
majority of cases which element is in topic position.

5.1.3 <u>Summary</u>. The work described here seems to indicate that certain domains of discourse have their own "natural order" (Levelt, 1981). In discourse, spatial relationships are described connectively, as are event descriptions or instructions to perform actions, which follow the temporal sequence of the events described, or the actions to be performed. The "natural order" phenomenon can also be observed between clauses, where, for example, a condition is normally expressed before the conclusion, causes are generally stated before results, etc., and within the utterance, where speakers tend to place an expression referring to a human actor in utterance-initial position, or to place together in an utterance items that "belong together" semantically. One well-discussed phenomenon in respect of this latter tendency is the verb-object "Gestalt", to which we return in 5.2.2.

These "natural orders" interact with pragmatic constraints (what information is given at a certain point, what the discourse is about) and govern the thematic structure of individual utterances.

The learner will bring to the L2 acquisition task a fully-developed discourse competence, and will therefore be able to rely successfully on those processes shared by speakers of his SL and TL speakers. This will not be the case for SL-specific processes.

As we said in 5.1.1, we will assume that processes which facilitate memory load are, largely speaking, not language-specific. Furthermore, pragmatic constraints as they affect word order such as information given at a point in discourse, or what a discourse is about, although obviously discourse-dependent, are generally speaking not specific to a given language. The qualification "generally speaking" is necessary, as Thompson (1978:24-25) points out, since the grammatical properties of certain languages may partially or totally override pragmatic word order possibilities (cf. 5.2.1).

However, in a given language the linguistic devices available to indicate the thematic structure of an utterance, and the relative freedom of use of these devices are by definition specific to that language. These phenomena constitute a large part of the analytic problem the learner is faced with in acquiring a specific language, and have to be inferred from the input, as we saw in chapter 4.

5.1.4 <u>Input</u>. The preceding discussion has highlighted three devices for signalling the thematic structure of utterances: word order, anaphoric linkage and stress/intonation. We will briefly comment on each.

We wish to trace the acquisition of the linguistic means of structuring information in <u>utterances in context</u>. We are therefore by definition dealing with spoken language, and this fact may pose a descriptive problem from the point of view of the input.

<u>Word order</u>. The TLs show more diversity in the means used to structure information in spoken discourse than can be seen from grammars of the standard languages which describe basic word order, as these grammars are not primarily concerned with variations from the norm. Here, the canonical declarative written sentence is subject-verb-object.

Spoken English perhaps keeps closest to the SVO-order, relying more on stress as a suppletive device. Spoken French relies less on stress and more on syntactic devices such as clefting and detachment (compare English: <u>did you do that</u>? and French: <u>c'est (bien) toi qui a fait ça</u>?). Dutch, German and Swedish are often referred to as "verb second" languages, giving relatively free word order possibilities in relation to spoken English, with Swedish having virtually no syntactic constraints on topicalization (cf. the <u>satsflätor</u> discussed by Allwood, 1974).

Thompson (1978) suggests a typological continuum along which natural languages may be situated, which ranges from languages where pragmatic considerations govern word order to languages where grammatical relations govern word order. She speaks of "pragmatic word order" languages (PWO) and "grammatical word order" languages (GWO). English is situated at the GWO end of the continuum; its fundamental word order constraint is "the constraint against moving elements in such a way as to create a sentence in which an unmarked NP precedes a verb of which it is not the subject" (p. 32). The general syntactic picture for the TLs would seem to be one of relatively freer word order possibilities as one goes from English to Swedish: one might therefore equally expect pragmatic considerations to play a progressively greater part in determining word order.

As most of the studies on word order in the TLs have been concerned with the written language, and as this general preoccupation is reflected in the small (and unreliable) amount of information available on intonation (see below), much work (especially in participant obser- vation and interviews with the TL groups, cf. 2.3) will be needed to complete this picture, and in particular to discover word order pheno- mena more specific to the native speakers with whom the informants come into contact.[1] For example, HPD (1978) found in their study of the Heidelberg dialect a stylistic, discourse-dependent device of topicali- zing the main verb of an utterance.

This problem (and the problem of anaphoric linkage below) is further compounded by Bates' (1981:14) contention that "not all rules are created equal". Even if two languages share similar topicalization rules (or have comparable pronoun systems), this does not mean that their speakers attach the same weight to these phenomena in production and comprehension. Semantic and pragmatic factors can lead speakers of each language to use a rule more, or less.

Anaphoric linkage. Once a referent has been introduced into a discourse by a speaker (a typical example is an indefinite NP) it may be taken up again in subsequent utterances[2] by a more "economical" marker, for example a noun preceded by a definite article, a pronoun, or indeed no form at all. The previous sentence may serve as an illustrative example: a referent taken up again by it, zero anaphora for by the speaker. The "egg-hiding description" of 5.1.2 is another possible example.

"Taking up a referent again" means that in an utterance in which an anaphoric marker occurs, the marker will represent given information, and will frequently occur, in the TLs, in utterance-initial position.

Case-/number-marking, strong and weak forms, alternative sub-sys- tems of pronouns in the TLs and the internal development of the NP are discussed in 7.2: we will merely refer the reader to this section.

---

[1] R. Le Page (personal communication) suggests that the TL variety spoken by immigrants belonging to a relatively homogeneous SL community established in the target country may provide crucial input for learners with the same SL. This would constitute a further justification for the inclusion of "long resident" informants in this project. Cf. also 4.3.1.

[2] For reasons of space, we will not discuss cataphoric reference here.

Stress/intonation. In all the TLs - although to a lesser extent in French - stress/intonation can serve to indicate which elements in an utterance are more prominent, or noteworthy (typically, those elements representing new information).

Quirk et al. (1972) link the nucleus of a tone-unit to the distinction between given/new information: "The focus, signalled by the nucleus, indicates where the new information lies" (p. 940). Givón (1979:98) also sees this principle at work in both the pragmatic and (to a lesser extent) the syntactic mode of communication (for this distinction, cf. 5.2.1). Ullmer-Ehrich and Koster (1981) further suggest that stronger stress/intonation serves to distinguish information that is given in an utterance by virtue of the mutual knowledge of speaker and hearer, from information given by the context of discourse, which receives less marked stress/intonation.

Quirk et al. link given/new information, anaphoric linkage and stress/intonation in terms of two principles: the principle of "end-focus" and the principle of "end-weight". The first concerns the tendency speakers (of English) have to place new information at the end of utterances, the second, their tendency to place more complex structures at the end of utterances: "Since it is natural to express given information in few words (e.g., by pronoun substitution), these principles work together, rather than against one another" (p. 943).

5.2 Questions

5.2.1 Two main questions. The two main questions we are asking in relation to 5.1 are the following:

(a) How are our informants' utterances structured, and how does this structuring develop? (And what is the interplay, in the acquisition process, of syntactic, pragmatic and semantic factors?)

In order to answer (a), we will have to take into consideration a related question:

(b) How does a learner, at a given moment, use the word order, morphology and intonation he has, to structure information in utterances?

Let us consider first the learner's early utterances. If he can combine two or more words in making complete utterances[1], how does he combine them? One possibility open to the learner is to adopt general principles such as those mentioned in 5.1: go from given to new information; state what the utterance is about, then comment on it; place context before entity, etc. Another possibility is to rely on the grammatical devices used for structuring information in SL utterances (these two possibilities are not mutually exclusive, of course).

Generally speaking, whatever possibilities learners use, we expect their early utterances to be, in some intuitive sense, syntactically elementary (cf. Schumann, 1978).

Whereas Thompson (cf. 5.1.4) uses the notions of PWO and GWO to characterize language systems, Givón (1979:97), in suggesting that there exist "two extreme poles of communicative mode, the pragmatic mode and the syntactic mode", is chiefly concerned (as we are) with types of language change. Progress along the continuum from the pragmatic mode to the syntactic mode characterizes certain diachronic processes, the development of pidgins into creoles, of child language into adult language, and the shift from informal to formal style in adult language. Slobin (1977) studies the same type of language change as Givón (as well as "changes occurring in one language as a result of contact with another in the minds of bilingual speakers"). Of his four "charges" to Language: be clear, be processible, be quick and easy, be expressive, the first two "strive toward segmentalization" while the second two "strive toward synthesis"; the first two characterize pidgins and child language, the latter two characterize fully developed adult speech.

In both Givón's and Slobin's accounts, the developmental process is from simple, analytical and transparent language to complex, synthetic and opaque language. By "transparent" vs "opaque" is meant the lesser or greater "distance" that separates the surface form of a message from its content, cf. for example, Kay & Sankoff, 1974.

---

[1] In other words, we assume the beginner's words roughly to correspond to the major constituents of a TL utterance.

Transparency, in Slobin's framework, is an "answer" of Language to
the charge "be clear" (1977:186): "there is a tendency for Language
to strive to maintain a one-to-one mapping between underlying semantic
structures and surface forms, with the goal of making messages easily
retrievable for listeners. To be "clear" ... is to strive for semantic
transparency".

We are also investigating development, but of a different type
than those cases discussed by Givón and Slobin. It will be fruitful,
for a general account of language development, to enquire to what
extent the adult L2 learner follows the pattern suggested by these authors
for other types of development.

Givón sees the exclusive use of the pragmatic mode in pidgins as
being dependent on three parameters: communicative stress, lack of
common pragmatic background, and immediately obvious context. These
three parameters are more or less true of the communicative situation
in the TL community of the type of learner whose acquisition we are
studying.

Communicative stress: he has to communicate in the TL in order to get
things done; lack of common pragmatic background: he does not entirely
share the background assumptions of the TL community, cf. chapter 4;
immediately obvious context: it is often the case that the tasks or
topics to be negotiated by linguistic communication are instrumental,
and immediately dependent on the situation of communication (as in the
work-place, for example, cf. 4.3.2 and 6.2.1). These conditions were
implicit in the discussion of the learner's early comprehension of TL
utterances in 4.3.

As a working hypothesis, then, we will suggest that the learner's
early utterances share to a certain extent the characteristics of the
pragmatic mode. The characteristics that are directly relevant here are:
topic-comment structure; word order can be governed by the pragmatic
principle that old information goes first, new information follows;
prominent intonation marks the focus of new information, intonation
on old information is less prominent; no use of grammatical morphology;
loose conjunction. These characteristics will gradually give way to:
subject-predicate structure, subordination, use of grammatical morphology, etc.

This working hypothesis is SL- and TL-independent, and is likely
not to correspond completely to the facts in the ten linguistic cases
of acquisition that we are studying. The Spanish learner of French may
be able to draw more successfully than the Spanish learner of Swedish
on his previous linguistic knowledge, as French and Spanish are
linguistically more related than Spanish and Swedish. English and German
are both Germanic languages: the Italian learner of German may, however, be able to draw more successfully than the Italian learner of
English on the pragmatic word order possibilities of Italian when
communicating in the TL (cf. Bates, 1981:10). However, it will be most
interesting to see how closely the hypothesis corresponds to all cases
of acquisition in the project. The hypothesis, stated in this fashion,
will allow us therefore to compare, albeit indirectly, the overall
course of language development in the type of learner we are studying
with that postulated for other types of learner, while at the same time
addressing a problem fundamental to this project: that of language-
specific vs generalizable phenomena (cf. 1.3.1).

The learner's early utterances will therefore, we hypothesize, be
structured essentially along pragmatic principles and the semantics
of these utterances will be vague. Later on, as the semantics become
more precise and syntactic phenomena play a greater part, the learner's
utterances will become less transparent.

One example of early transparency here would be the one-to-one
mapping between semantic concepts such as temporality, modality,
conditionality, negation, quantification, and open class words having
some, not necessarily obvious, link to TL nouns, adverbs, etc. (cf.
Dittmar, 1982). "Vague" in the previous paragraph means that the semantic relationships between items in an utterance will not be explicitly
marked: the hearer will have to infer, for example, whether the
relationship between item 1 and item 2 in a 2-place utterance like
Father - Rome is locative, directional, or whatever. This is the re-
verse case of the learner's analytical problem discussed in 4.3.
These concepts and relationships will gradually become more precise and
less transparent as they become more grammaticized.

As an illustrative example, an adult speaker of German L2 with
Spanish L1 studied by Becker and Klein (1979) used a basic 2-place

structure in his utterances, where the first place was used to pose
a subject (this term is not technical and includes "new" and "old"
subjects) about which he was going to speak:

autonomo + nicht viel Geld
(independent worker + not much money)

or to give a spatio-temporal "context" for the second-place notion:

fünfundsechzig Jahre + Pension
(sixty-five years   + pension)

These are statements, whose intonation contour is: place 1: rising,
pause, place 2: falling. The informant could add further modality to
this structure by prefixing it with modal adverbs:

normal vielleicht august + nicht urlaub ++ dezember + alles in Urlaub

This utterance is analytical, and consists of a modalized sequence
of two simple utterances, corresponding to the standard English "idea":
"it is usually the case that if there is no holiday in August, everybody goes on holiday in December".

5.2.2 <u>More specific questions</u>. Building on the general - and hypothetical - ideas of 5.2.1, we may ask more specific questions:
I.a. Let us imagine a basic word order system, say:
(Place 1) (Place 2)   Place 3
- where the brackets indicate that one, both or none of the
  positions can be filled (under certain conditions, see below);
- where statements and questions are indicated by intonation;
- where place 3 receives more prominent stress/intonation;
- where negation occurs immediately next to the element to be
  negated;
etc.
b. What are the pragmatic factors that govern the use of this system?
Is place 1 used to provide a "context" for the utterance (time,
place, modality)? Is place 2 filled by given information - and
this would include zero anaphora - place 3 by new information?
Are there other, discourse-specific (or speech act specific) constraints which govern the ordering of elements (what a type of

discourse is "about", for example)?

c. What are the semantic relationships that hold between each element of the basic utterance? (Some possible candidates are: possession, attribution, determination, modal and spatio-temporal contextualization, identification, see below.)

II. How will this system evolve?

Verbs. For Becker & Klein's informant of 5.2.1, and for informants in other studies (v. Stutterheim's, 1982, Turkish-speaking learners of German are a very clear example), it is difficult, and sometimes impossible, to assign syntactic distinctions such as N vs V to items in utterances. "Verbs" appear in "infinitive" or "root" form - versteh, lernen, mach, etc. - in what we have called place 2 or place 3 of a basic utterance (cf. 4.3.2.3, the "noun-based language" of the learner). An important question we may ask is therefore: when do recognizable verbs appear and how? Is the first step to reserve place 3 for a verb and its complement? Do conjugated forms first appear in place 3?

In particular, what semantic relationships - such as those in I(c) which we may infer - are made explicit by verbs, and to what extent is this explicitation dependent on the SL, or on the TL?[1]

Noun phrases. How does the internal development of the NP (cf. 7.2.2.3) interact with the structuring of information in utterances?

Firstly, how does the development of a pronoun system including anaphoric pronouns intervene? Is there a progression from simple ellipsis of an NP, through an overgeneralized use of a basic anaphoric pronoun (das, ça), to more correct use of TL possibilities?

Work on acquisition in children (cf. Karmiloff-Smith, 5.1.2) has shown that when the first type of anaphora appears, it occurs

---

[1] In Dutch, for example, the verb hebben (have) is implicit in many utterances where it would be obligatory in the other TLs, e.g.: Mag ik nog een pils? (May I another beer?)

systematically in topic position. In what position of an utterance do our informants indicate anaphoric relations? Can we trace a progression here?

Secondly, is the internal development of NP more apparent in some positions of an utterance than in others? Is it, for example, the case that definiteness is first marked explicitly when it is not predictable from word order? Given our general hypothesis that early word ordering is governed by pragmatic principles, a noun (phrase) in place 2 of our hypothetical basic word order system represents given information, i.e., information mutually known to the speaker and hearer. One would therefore expect definitely referring N(P)s, but not indefinitely referring N(P)s to occur in this position. Data from one informant in the German pilot study (discussed by Dietrich, 1982) is interesting in this respect. The informant uses nouns with and without the definite article: Hund (dog), der Hund, to express definite reference, and nouns with and without the indefinite article: Hund, ein Hund, to express indefinite reference. The rule for marking the kind of reference is:

(a) Definitely referring Ns occur in pre-verbal position, indefinitely referring Ns occur in post-verbal position.

(b) If a definitely referring N occurs in post-verbal position, or an indefinitely referring N in pre-verbal position, then its reference must be explicitly marked by the appropriate article - der, ein - or by some other linguistic means.

Dietrich concludes (p. 17): "As definiteness is a property which depends on the hearer's knowledge, or more exactly on what the speaker assumes the hearer's knowledge to be, and, seen from this perspective, is dependent on the thematic structure of utterances, it is possible that a general principle governing the thematic structure of learners' utterances can be seen to be at work behind the regularities described in this paper".

Movements of items. Amongst possible "movements" (permutations, frontings, endings), are those which carry meaning (e.g., subject-auxiliary inversion in questions) acquired before those that are less semantically expressive (e.g., verb to the end in German

subordinate clauses)? Does topicalization of the verb complement appear late, as previous work (Meisel, Clahsen, Pienemann,
1981) suggests?

5.3 Data collection

(a) As we said in 5.1.4, data from the group of TL native speakers
(and, possibly, from the "long residence" groups) will be important if we are to evaluate the similarities and differences between informants' production and input: for example, we said that
some TLs had a freer word order than others in spoken language,
and we have to be sure that this tendency is reflected in the
specific varieties of the TL that informants are exposed to.

(b) Word order, anaphoric linkage and intonation, as means of formulating messages, are dependent on the linguistic and extra-
linguistic context. In order to take the context into account,
we will have to work with stretches of discourse of variable
length: from a simple question-answer sequence to a long narrative.
It may prove necessary to select rather severely the type of discourse to be analysed - perhaps only question-answer sequences
(concentrating on intonation, ellipsis and givenness/newness),
narratives (anaphoric linkage), instructions (see below) and
"guided tours" (see below) - since a study of intonation involves
narrow and time-consuming transcription, and since it will be
necessary to analyse regularly the same type of discourse phenomena.

It is proposed to select these stretches of discourse essentially
from the interview, firstly because this takes place once a month, and
secondly because criteria for measuring the "naturalness" of speech
obtained by this technique have been well studied (Labov, 1972a).

For question-answer sequences, it may prove possible to supplement the data from the interview from two other sources:
- play scenes: a relatively high incidence of question-answer
   sequences is to be expected, the more so as it should be possible
   for the investigator to provoke them;
- experimental data: one of the ad hoc experiments envisaged is the

game of "twenty questions" (cf. 8.3.4), which is specifically designed to elicit questions from the informant. If he enters into
the spirit of the game, the questions will be authentic in that
they are genuine requests for information.
Three other techniques which should prove fruitful in ascertaining how
a learner uses the syntax he has at a given moment to structure information in utterances, are (a) the grounding phase of play scenes, (b)
the "preposition" experiment and (c) apartment descriptions and route
directions[1]:

(a) grounding in play scenes is one of the rare situations we have
    where it is natural for the informant to give instructions. These
    instructions often involve the movement of people and objects
    (by people) from a source to a goal. We therefore have a natural
    situation which involves orders, deixis and events which can be
    structured in a "natural" way (agent-object-source-goal), i.e.,
    three phenomena which are important for this chapter;
(b) the preposition experiment (cf. 5.1.2): (a) can be contrasted
    with the "preposition" experiment which is less "natural" in the
    sense that the informant has been specifically told to give orders,
    but which involves the same type of event. We therefore have a
    larger data-base and the possibility of controlling, by comparison,
    possible differences in the two situations;
(c) apartment descriptions and route directions. We are planning to in-
    corporate into the interview variants of "apartment descriptions"
    and "route directions". Another source for "apartment descriptions"
    may be the grounding phase of play-scenes.
         It will in practice not prove feasible to ask informants to
    give a description of their apartment, as we will very probably
    be acquainted with its lay-out ourselves early on in the project.
    Thus the question would be perceived as artificial. However, it
    is much less likely that we will know the lay-out of the informants'

---

[1] Film-watching may also be valuable, as the theme of the discussion
is normally particularly clear.

work-place, or of all the administrative buildings they may visit.
It will therefore be natural, in the interview or in the grounding
phase of a play scene which would happen in a relevant place, to
ask informants to describe that place. Similarly, it will be
natural, in the interview, to ask an informant how he gets to a
certain place (e.g., to work from home). It may also prove possible to simulate route directions in a play scene.

These methods of elicitation may prove particularly fruitful, for three reasons:

(a) for apartment descriptions, we are dealing with what Linde & Labov
(1975) term a "natural experiment": it is motivating, it is
reproducible, it is objective (one can check the description
against reality afterwards), it is more conversation-like
than experiment-like, and it elicits (here in TL) a well-
practised linguistic skill (here in SL);

(b) we will be using parallel procedures to those used in experiments with adult native speakers: for English, Dutch and
German at least, we will therefore be able to compare the
performance of our informants with the results of existing
and well-documented experiments;

(c) audio- and video-techniques should allow us to compare
similar tasks performed respectively in absentia and in
praesentia (even if the latter case is symbolic). A comparison of the data obtained from each situation should
allow us to ascertain which devices are used, and to what
extent, to structure information: how are the deictics of
the videoed experiments dealt with in the interview? what
links (temporal, spatial, conditional, etc.) do we find
between utterances? is connectivity signalled by the same
devices in both situations? etc.

6. Processes in the Developing Vocabulary

6.1 Introduction

6.1.1 The semantics of the growing vocabulary. Building up a vocabulary is one aspect of adult SSLA which has received relatively little attention hitherto. This is surprising in view of the fact that the learner's first attempts at making himself understood in a foreign language usually involve the acquisition of a few standard (unanalyzed) expressions and some words of basic communicative importance (cf. 4.3.2).

In particular, the concept of "formulaic" speech has been relatively neglected (cf. however, the studies of Hakuta, 1974; Huang, 1971; Wong-Fillmore, 1976), because the central focus of interest in the study of language acquisition has been in the past years on the creative application of grammatical rules.

This area of investigation is also of interest in that it is one where marked differences in the acquisition process may be observed between tutored acquisition (in general), and untutored acquisition (in general).

In the former case, vocabulary and syntax are taught concurrently, but separately (thus a language learner receives "grammar lessons" and "vocabulary lessons"). In the latter case, the learner is acquiring an elementary syntax and an elementary vocabulary in the same communicative activities and has to draw on both - as well as on non-linguistic communication strategies - in order to communicate.

6.1.2 Production and perception. The emphasis in this section will be on informants' production, as the general problem of perception has been dealt with in chapter 4, cf. especially 4.3: Processing the Input.

In that section, we said that in the process of understanding utterances, use is made of all available information including contextual clues and general knowledge of the word; thus it is often the case that a learner understands an utterance in situation without necessarily taking in the specific lexical items in it. The main pre-occupation of this section is, however, with lexical items in use, and the main data base will therefore be the learner's utterances, com-pleted by self-confrontation, where informants will be asked to make explicit their use of certain lexical items (cf. 6.3).

6.1.3 <u>Outline of the section</u>. In 6.1.4, we will briefly discuss the general questions that interest us here. In 6.2, we will describe in more detail the five types of lexical field chosen and the specific questions we will be asking of each. In 6.3, guidelines will be given of the type of data to be collected, and of methods of analysis.

6.1.4 <u>General questions</u>. The lexical fields are chosen as they are likely to provide us with at least partial answers to a major question (a), and a minor question (b).

For a given lexical field:

(a) What semantic processes are at work as it is built up?
(b) What are the strategies a learner uses in situation to express meaning in this field?

(a) Here, the TL lexical field is intuitively presupposed - "movement verbs", "time", "person", etc. - and we trace the way in which it is progressively filled, or its items differentiated. In saying that a field is "filled", we could imagine an incremental process, whereby one specific <u>signifié</u> of the field was assigned a specific <u>signifiant</u>, then another <u>signifié</u> another <u>signifiant</u>, and so on. A different area where the same process could be observed is that where a specific communicative function was associated with one unanalyzed (or "formulaic") expression - <u>hellohowareyou</u> - then another function with another expression - <u>thanksverymuch</u> - and so on, until the "field" (here, of phatic expressions) was "filled".
     This "filling" process can take another form - as in the "cow" example of 1.5.4 - whereby a subordinate term which is cor-rectly used as a subordinate term, fulfills by extension a super-ordinate function - <u>cow</u> is used correctly to denote "cow", and

incorrectly, by extension, to denote "farm animal".

In saying that a field is "differentiated" we can take for illustrative purposes the "kommen" example of 1.5.4. A (perceived) field - abstract and concrete movement - is filled first of all with an overgeneralized term - kommen - and then progressively less general terms are acquired. These two processes can interact. Let us take two examples:

- The German personal pronoun system. Klein (1981b) has suggested that the learner can acquire from the set of features that constitute the pronoun system - person, number, deixis, etc. - those features that allow him to build a basic system of personal reference composed of TL pronouns functioning in an overgeneralized way: thus German das is assigned by the learner (amongst others) the feature [+ anaphoric] and is the general anaphoric marker for all person and number;

- Lexical innovation. This phenomenon has already been mentioned in connection with informants' perceptual ability in 4.3.1. Here, we will simply give an example. In German, as in the other TLs, there is a partially creative process for designating the rooms of a house: function + zimmer. The learner may identify this process and overgeneralize it, thus Schlafzimmer (bedroom), but *Küchenzimmer (*cookroom), etc.

Another process which may interact with the two already mentioned is the following: a lexical field may be filled or differentiated in the TL as it is in the SL (lexical transfer).

An important factor in determining which type of process is used by the learner in building up his lexicon is undoubtedly his communicative environment: if successful communication with native speakers of the TL involves recurrent use of specific expressions or lexical items in some environment, then we can hypothesize that the learner will recognize and understand, and consequently acquire those items. This elementary remark motivates the choice of the domains - "work", "home", "social relations" - described in 6.2.1.

Some systems of lexical items are not dependent on the environment. For example, whatever the environment, we can expect that the learner will have to make reference to people, places and

time. This fact, and the fact that plausible hypotheses abound as
to the semantic processes at work and the order of acquisition motivated our making a separate study of them (cf. chapter 7). Here,
we will take three further lexical fields which, in contrast to
those of 6.2.1, are somewhat less dependent on the communicative
environment: expressions of emotional attitude (6.2.2), metalinguistic vocabulary (6.2.3) and modality (6.2.4). Finally, we
will make a special study of formulaic expressions (6.2.5).

(b) Whatever the semantic field, the learner's lexical stock will
often not allow him to "get his message across" by precise
lexical means; he then has of necessity recourse to what have
come to be termed "lexical gap fillers" in the literature (cf.
for example, Faerch and Kasper, 1980).

In relation to each domain studied in 6.2.1 - 6.2.5, we shall
attempt to draw up as complete an inventory as possible of these
strategies. A preliminary analysis of the pilot-study data points
to the importance of the following strategies:

- various types of paraphrasing: for example immer nicht (always
  not) for nie (never), immer viel trinken (always much drink),
  for saufen (booze);

- gestures, of which the most frequently used were deictic gestures,
  iconic gestures used to represent or illustrate the objects or
  processes in question, conventional non-verbal communicative
  gestures such as nodding, shrugging one's shoulders, etc.

- code-switching: for example:

  toute cette chose je la comprends *intuitivamente* + et bon je
  (all this thing I understand it intuitivamente + and well I
  veux dire en en mon espagnol *un nebulosa* + ? comment [di]*nebulosa*?
  mean   in in my spanish un nebulosa + how say nebulosa?)

These strategies can be combined. In the following example, the
Spanish informant just cited uses code-switching and paraphrase:

je [ne] pas si vous a comprené je dis le mot en espagnol c'est +
(I not   if you have understood I say the word in Spanish it's +
un son *gangoso* + nous disons *gangoso* que c'est un chose *como* un
a sound gangoso + we say gangoso   like it's a thing como a

mélange + un mélange de sons
mixture + a mixture of sounds)

6.2 Areas of investigation

6.2.1 Home, work, social relations. Our informants' lexicons will
exhibit a concentration of items in some domains and paucity in others.
A preliminary analysis of pilot data from Heidelberg has shown that the
size of the vocabulary and the degree of differentiation is clearly
related to the area in which language contact takes place, and its
relevance to the speaker. Lexical fields of importance in the course of
a subject's work exhibit a higher degree of precise differentiation
than those also occurring in everyday life but which are not frequently
referred to in language contact. Thus whereas the field "home" was
poorly developed for most informants, this was not the case for lexical
fields covering the areas "work" and "social relations" (this general
term covers the informants' relationship to family, friends, authorities,
shopkeepers, etc.). Though Turkish workers in Germany quickly learned
to use words like Block (special sort of iron box), Winkeleisen (angle
iron), Gerüst (scaffold), Locheisen (hollow punch), Stabeisen (wrought
iron), Kranwagen (crane truck), words like Herd (cooker), Schrank
(cupboard), Fenster (window), Küche (kitchen), Wohnzimmer (living room),
Spülbecken (sink), Waschbecken (washing-basin), Sessel (arm chair) do
not occur in their active vocabulary. The assumption that communicative
factors, that is the content of language contact situations and their
relevance to the learner, shape the content of the lexicon will be
pursued systematically taking as an example some selected domains of
everyday life. The areas "work", "home" and "social relations" would
seem to be most promising since it is likely that the rate and degree
of development in all three areas will be directly dependent on the
situation of the individual learner.

In addition to this question, which encompasses the study of the
distribution of lexical items based on communicative requirements,
the structure of these fields will also be examined from the point of
view of other processes: lexical innovation, as in the function + zimmer

example of 6.1.4, and the possible influence of the SL on the structuring of these fields.

6.2.2 <u>Expressions of emotional attitude</u>. Another area of importance for
the language learner is the area of emotional attitude. In the course
of acquiring a new language, and culture, any language learner will
have experiences which will make him act strongly and emotionally - in
particular if he is an adult and if the acquisition of the new language is directly connected with the satisfaction of basic needs and
desires. He will express these reactions partly in his SL, and partly in
the TL.

In conjunction with the studies proposed in 4.5.2 on how emotion
and attitude affect the acquisition process and of how an understanding
of target expressions of emotions and attitudes are acquired, a study
will be made of how informants express emotional attitudes in the TL.

The term "emotional attitudes" is used in order to distinguish
a field of content distinct from, e.g., (narrowly) cognitive attitudes
of an epistemic or boulumaic[1] kind, which are discussed in the section
on modality (6.2.4). Emotional attitudes then include attitudes of the
following kind: joy, sorrow, anger, surprise, interest, fear, shyness,
contempt, frustration.

All of these attitudes can be expressed by several linguistic
means. Those of particular importance seem to be vocabulary, for
example adjectives like <u>angry</u>, <u>sad</u>, <u>happy</u>, <u>sorry</u>, and interjections
like <u>ouch</u>!, <u>wow</u>!, <u>hoorah</u>!; formulaic expressions like <u>nice meeting you</u>,
<u>lovely day</u>, etc.; syntactic patterning as in the use of exclamations:
<u>attaboy</u>!,<u>what a day</u>!, <u>will I go</u>?, <u>well, I never</u>!; and prosodic patterns
and bodily communication.

It is to be expected that prosody and body language will be predominant in the early stages of language acquisition, followed by
formulaic expressions, vocabulary and more syntactic means in later
stages. Thus a possible area of study is the expression of emotion by

---

[1] Wanting and wishing.

prosody and body language from material from the first year of observation. This should be supplemented by a study of the use and growth of vocabulary, formulaic expressions and syntactic patterns to express emotion during the whole period of data collection. This could be done simply by studies of the frequency and co-occurrence of the emotional expressions in the data. In other words, this would be one of the lexical fields we would continue to study after the systematic word count of the early stages (cf. 6.3).

6.2.3 <u>Metalinguistic vocabulary</u>. We said in 1.5.4 that we have chosen to study metalinguistic vocabulary as this vocabulary reflects the linguistic awareness of the learner, and that we consider linguistic awareness to be a possibly important propensity factor in acquisition. It is necessary, before turning to the questions we are asking about the acquisition of metalinguistic vocabulary, to examine briefly its relationship to linguistic awareness.

6.2.3.1 <u>Metalinguistic vocabulary and linguistic awareness</u>. To our knowledge, little attention has been paid in studies on SSLA to the nature of the learner's awareness of the language he is acquiring, and to the role this awareness may (or may not) play in the acquisition process. A study of linguistic awareness in this project should therefore serve two purposes: to explore relatively uncharted territory, and to provide data which may be compared with studies of linguistic awareness in other learner types, in particular, children acquiring an L1 or an L2 and students receiving formal training in L2.

Most of the work on the role of linguistic awareness in language acquisition has indeed concentrated on children (cf. for example, Sinclair, Jarvella and Levelt, 1978) or on formal schooling (cf. for example, Arditty & Mittner, 1980 and Trévise, 1982). In much of this work, we find that awareness and metalanguage are associated.

Boutet et al. (1982) found that children can verbalize their awareness of different aspects of an utterance: its enunciative properties, its stylistic level, its meaning and its form. Scholastic metalanguage concentrates on this latter aspect. However, children comment on the form of utterances before undergoing language training,

and continue to comment on aspects of utterances that are not taught,
even after some years of language training. Indeed, Berthoud (1980)
points out that even for a specific linguistic phenomenon that has
been taught, there is no necessary fit between the teacher's and the
pupil's description of the phenomenon: this underlines the importance
for the teacher/researcher of understanding the subject's metalinguistic discourse.

Jakobson (1960) describes the metalinguistic function of language
as discourse centred on the code. His illustrative examples are all
"direct" question-answer sequences, in the sense that the speaker, in
asking a question - "what do you mean by that?", "what is a sophomore?",
etc. - wants to obtain information on the code and expects his interlocutor to supply it. These "direct" metalinguistic questions provide
some subjects at least with an efficient means of learning a language:
D. Slobin's daughter Heida (Slobin, 1978) is a good example of what is
meant here.

Compare this type of metalinguistic question with a not infrequent
classroom sequence like:

Mary (on taperecorder): Mr Smith is ill today.
Teacher: Pierre, what did Mary say?
Pierre: Mary said that Mr Smith was ill that day.

The teacher's question is metalinguistic in Jakobson's sense,
but, unlike his examples, it is not "direct". Pierre (one assumes)
knows that the teacher has understood what Mary said and does not
require information from him, but rather a repetition, in indirect
speech, of what Mary said, with particular attention to tense and deictic adverbs (whether Pierre would use this metalanguage is beside the
point). In this type of exercise, the pupil manipulates the language-
object without, in the last resort, necessarily knowing what the forms
mean.

Thus we have two extremes of "discourse centred on the code": the
"direct" exchange of information between speaker and hearer, and manipulation of language without any necessary communicative intent. There
are metalinguistic activities which fall between these two extremes,
in particular certain of the data collection techniques being used

in this project, e.g., self- and other-confrontation (cf. 8.4.4, where the "control" or "awareness heightening" effect of these techniques is discussed).

For expository purposes (but keeping in mind that the exposition is highly simplified) we may say that many previous studies on linguistic awareness have distinguished between three types of linguistic activity in the speaker:

(a) unconscious mechanisms of production and perception;
(b) "unconscious awareness" which by definition cannot be verbalized;
(c) "conscious awareness" which may or may not be verbalizable.

(b) and (c) serve two functions. The first, in language use, serves to regulate utterances and to adapt them to the interlocutor: Labov's (1972a) style-shifting, and Marshall and Morton's (1978) fault-finders and fault-describers would be examples of this function. The second, in language acquisition, helps (or "drives" in Marshall and Morton's terminology) acquisition or learning, thus adding (selected) rules or items to (a). Metalinguistic vocabulary is from this point of view the reflection of part of one type of linguistic activity, namely (c).

Thus four points should be kept in mind when examining the acquisition of metalinguistic vocabulary:

-    there is a link between metalinguistic vocabulary and awareness. However, not all linguistic awareness can be verbalized and there is no necessary fit between what the learner verbalizes and what he does (Berthoud, 1980);
-    metalinguistic verbalizations can be naïve and are not necessarily linked to schooling. Everybody becomes aware of some linguistic facts, perhaps especially (cf. Slobin, 1978, and Oksaar, 1981) if he is exposed to more than one language. This is, of course, the case of our informants;
-    if language activity is seen as situation-dependent, metalinguistic verbalizations may be directed towards the enunciative properties of (part of) an utterance, its appropriateness, its semantic content, as well as its formal properties;
-    there are different kinds of metalinguistic activity, ranging from

manipulations of the language-object to the asking of direct questions about language. The data-collection techniques used in the project may provoke different types of metalinguistic activity.

6.2.3.2 Questions. The definition of metalinguistic vocabulary implicit in 6.2.3.1 is broad: that language which can be used to talk about a language. We will thus be looking at all words or expressions:

(a) which are used by informants to talk about language and language activity: sound, say, mean, and also fast, difficult, etc.

(b) which, while not normally referring to language, are mentioned to achieve such reference in a specific situation, as, for example, the word sesquipedalian in the sentence: "What is the meaning of sesquipedalian?" (Lyons, 1977:6).

In relation to the general questions of 6.1.4, we may hypothesize that, at least in the early stages, metalinguistic vocabulary will be acquired item by item to serve a specific communicative function (as indeed Jakobson's term suggests). Words, or formulaic expressions, will be acquired as they are required to ensure the exchange of messages (nicht verstehen, no understand ...; I say, je dis ...; was heißt, comment s'appelle ..., etc.). Moreover, we may hypothesize that for some learners at least, spontaneous metalinguistic questions constitute an efficient learning strategy as, of course, they do in child language acquisition.

At the same time, some words - e.g., say - may be used as superordinate terms which will later be differentiated: ask, tell, etc.

Studies in French (reported by Besse, 1980) have shown that metalinguistic vocabulary, taken as a whole, has a relatively high frequency overall in word frequency lists such as Le Français Fondamental. We will assume (although we cannot prove) that this is the case for the other TLs. If such is indeed the case, further questions may be asked:

- will the input to adult workers reflect this frequency? Here, a careful comparison of the longitudinal and initial learner groups will be important; for the former, the frequency of metalinguistic input may turn out to be an artefact of this project;

- what is the role of the source language/culture in the acquisition of metalanguage? Heeschen's (1978) work on Eipo metalinguistic vocabulary shows that it has terms referring to content and appropriateness, but shows little concern for structure: is this the case for the metalinguistic vocabulary of any of the SLs? If so, will it influence the type of vocabulary acquired?
- will the input to, and communicative needs of, adult workers result in a difference in the acquisition of metalinguistic vocabulary as compared with child learners of the same TL?

Answers to all these questions will give us, partially (cf. 6.2.3.1) an indication of the nature and degree of each informant's awareness of the TL. For comparative purposes, some data should also be obtained at the beginning of the longitudinal study, in the SL, to assess each informant's awareness of the SL.

That these questions may be interesting is illustrated by data from two of the informants of the French pilot study. These informants are both over 40 years old, had been in France for over three years at the time of the interviews, are workers, with minimal primary education and a few weeks' initial French training for Latin American refugees on arrival in France. They live primarily in a Latin American environment in Paris and (to paraphrase Schumann, 1978) their ego is highly impermeable to French life.

Both were asked a specific question on the formation of negative sentences in French during a self-confrontation interview. M 1 replied[1]:

dans la négation pour nous c'est tout le temps un seul mot *no*+ nous
(in the negation for   us   it's always   one single word no + us

c'est tout le temps *si* et *no* + *si* c'est oui et + mais pour c'est très
it's always   si and no + si it's yes and + but for it's very

difficile pour *no* + et je ne comprends bien encore qu'on fait la
difficult for no   and I   don't understand well yet that one uses

---

[1] Both informants have a strong Spanish accent which more or less "standard" orthography does not do justice to.

utilisation de ne pas quand le *verbo* je ne comprends le temps de le
uses   ne pas when the verb I don't understand the tense of the
verbo...
verb...

toute cette chose je la comprends *intuitivamente* + et bon je veux dire
 all this thing I understand it intuitivamente   + and well I mean
en en mon espagnol *un nebulosa* + ? comment [di] *nebulosa*?
in in my Spanish   un nebulosa + how say   nebulosa?)

M 2 replied:

en espagnol la négation c'est + c'est un seul + c'est c'est pas euh
(in Spanish the negation it's + it's one single + it's it's not er

utiliser la négation + *verbo* négation + et en espagnol (xx) c'est pas
to use the negation + verb negation + and in Spanish (xx) it's not

ça c'est + la négation c'est *no* et + c'est fini...
that it's + the negation it's no and + that's that...

... si vous dit *no* avant de *del verbo* oh oh ou après c'est la même
... if you say no before the   verb oh oh or after it's the same

chose en espagnol + c'est pas la même chose en français + c'est pas la
thing in Spanish + it's not the same thing in French   + it's not the

même chose
same thing)

These extracts may illustrate some general differences between
these informants' speech:

(a) cognate words - verbo, intuitivamente, etc. - often retain their
    "Spanish" form in both informants' speech. M 1, however, frequently
    and explicitly code-switches, signalling that he is about to use
    Spanish, and accompanying the Spanish word with a metalinguistic
    question, or a paraphrase (as in the example of gangoso given in
    6.1.4). M 2 very rarely does this. In other words, both use
    "Spanish" borrowings in their speech: only M 1, however, systema-
    tically mentions Spanish words with a metalinguistic intent;
(b) both M 1 and M 2 frequently self-correct. However, as far as one

can judge, M 2's self-correction is, typically, spontaneous,
whereas M 1 shows evidence both of spontaneous self-correction
and of a more reflective "thinking aloud" in French as in the
following remarkable example, where he is explaining that he and
his wife once lived with a French family:

[nusave vivi] vivre non [nusavõ nusavevivõ]?non? [nusave viv(r) õ]
euh dans famille de française;

(2) M 2's "technical" metalinguistic vocabulary is somewhat limited;
the example above constitutes a fairly full grammatical explanation for him. M 1 is grammatically more sophisticated, as the
above examples show.

Overall, M 1's verbalizations give the impression that he is more
aware of the form of utterances than M 2. This is not to say, however,
that M 2 is linguistically unaware. Both express a consistent awareness
of the target norm and make deprecating comments about their own speech.
Their awareness diverges, however, in M 1's emphasis on ways of speaking
(he relates that intercomprehension between himself and speakers from
the Midi of France is easier than with speakers from Paris) and M 2's
emphasis on ways to speak (he gives an extremely detailed account of why
he is not able to have a conversation with speakers of French, which contains marvellous insights on how to engage a conversation appropriately,
how to choose a topic, etc.).

Generally speaking, two different types of linguistic awareness
are evidenced in M 1's and M 2's speech by differences in the type
(and/or quantity) of code-switching, metalinguistic questions, self-
repairs and metalinguistic vocabulary. M 2's speech gives a general
impression of stability, M 1's speech gives an impression of relative
instability as his attention fluctuates between what he is saying and
how he is saying it. No firm conclusions for acquisition can be drawn
from a cross-sectional pilot study: the above examples do, however,
give some indication of the type of phenomenon we will be investigating
in the field of metalinguistic vocabulary, and of linguistic awareness
in general.

6.2.4 Modality. As a theoretical term in linguistics, modality has been used in many different ways. In view of the organization of the project, we will suggest here a use of the term based on semantic and pragmatic concerns. From this point of view, modality has usually been taken to concern either the relation between a speaker and a certain state of affairs, which we can call subjective modality, or the status of a state of affairs per se, which we can call objective modality.

Cognitive attitudes like believing, knowing, hoping, wishing, and their linguistic manifestations are examples of subjective modality, while statements about the possibility or necessity of a certain state of affairs are examples of objective modality. In natural language utterances, these two types of modality occur together and it is mostly very difficult to say that an utterance purely exemplifies one or the other type of modality. For example, a speaker says: "Perhaps it will rain tomorrow". This utterance is vague between an objective statement of possibility, a guess or a hope.

However, the fact that it is difficult to say in precise terms what type of modality has been expressed in a particular utterance does not detract from the importance of modality for a language learner. In particular, what has been called subjective modality here is essential in all communicative situations. It is hard to imagine communication that is not dependent on believing, desiring, wondering about, guessing, hoping for or commending, etc., on the one hand, and on the other hand, communication that does not aim to influence listeners' beliefs, desires, wonders, guesses or hopes. In some way or another, the language learner must acquire expressive linguistic means that allow him to perform these tasks.

As is the case with most other types of content, modality can be signalled linguistically in a variety of ways: lexically, for example, by auxiliary verbs like can, may, ought (the modal verbs), main verbs like believe, wish, wonder, adjectives like certain, good, possible, adverbs like perhaps and well. Often these lexical items occur in formulaic expressions like is it possible .. or most certainly .., etc.

Modal features are also indicated by syntactic pattern, as in our traditional distinctions between sentence moods: indicative, interrogative, imperative, exclamative. (The classification used here is based on morphological and syntactic features, as distinct from a more

classical taxonomy based purely on morphology.) As regards the latter
mood, modality overlaps with what we referred to earlier (cf. 6.2.2)
as the expression of emotional attitude. Finally, modality is indicated
through intonation and body language. For example, belief is in many
languages not only signalled by an indicative order of words, but also
by falling intonation. And similarly, wonder is often signalled by
rising intonation. Hand or facial gestures, or head movement can also
be used to indicate a questioning, wondering attitude or an affirmation
of belief.

In view of the ubiquity of modality, the language learner must,
right from the initial stages of language acquisition, find ways of
indicating it. It is probable that his first ways of doing so will be
through body language and intonation. But fairly rapidly, he will probably also learn to use some types of vocabulary, formulaic expressions
and syntactic patterning. In the beginning, there will probably be
overgeneralization so that words like perhaps might be used not only
to indicate possibility, but perhaps also for potentiality or counter-
factuality. Finer distinctions will be acquired gradually, for example,
wh-questions and different types of negatives (no, not, none); basic
dimensions in epistemic modality, i.e., not only perhaps, but also can,
must, and so on will appear.

As an illustrative example, Klein's (1981a) informant, who had been
in Germany for five years, signalled statements and questions by intonation, had acquired a differentiated negative marker (nicht, kein, nein),
one epistemic adverb (vielleicht), one appreciative adverb (normal),
and two overgeneralized modal verbs (muß, kann), used epistemically
and deontically, although infrequently and never in conjunction with
another verb. This minimal lexical/intonational system was (we saw in
5.2.1) sufficient to allow him to express such complex ideas as: "it
is normally the case that if there is no holiday in August, everybody
goes on holiday in December".

In tandem with the study of how emotional attitude is expressed,
a study of how intonation and (optionally) body language is used to
express modality will be carried out during the first year of observation. In conjunction with this, a study of the vocabulary, formulaic
expressions and syntactic patterns of modality should be carried out

for the whole period. We would thus have another type of analysis within the total account of how the earliest acquired linguistic items are used. This analysis can then be further related to background variables such as the SL, the informants' needs, or language-independent cognitive aspects of the organization of modality, allowing us in this way to relate the acquisition of modality to features in the informants' background.

6.2.5 <u>Formulaic expressions</u>. We have already mentioned formulaic expressions when their study was relevant to the areas of investigation discussed above. Here we will look at this aspect of language use from a more global point of view, and ask specific questions about its relationship to the acquisition process.

An early attempt to distinguish "formulaic" vs "free" expressions was made by Jespersen (1924). Following Jespersen, formulas are fixed expressions in which neither stress, rhythm nor words can be changed. Whereas free expressions are based on an innovative and propositional use of verbal means, formulaic speech is repetitive and memory based. Jespersen considers this distinction also as relevant from an acquisitional point of view: free speech is acquired on the basis of applying grammatical rules, whereas formulas are unanalyzed, invariant units.[1]

Jespersen's ideas have been taken up in studies on L2 acquisition in various ways. Huang (1971) found many "prefabricated" patterns in his subject's speech. This led him to postulate imitation as an acquisitional strategy independent of the process of rule-formation. Hakuta (1974) observed the same phenomenon of prefabricated utterances in Uguisu's speech (a five-year-old Japanese learner of English), particularly in the early stages. In these cases, learning seems to take place through rote memorization of segments of speech without knowledge of

---

[1] From the learner's point of view. In other words, the learner will acquire (we hypothesize) both expressions which from the point of view of the TL <u>are</u> formulaic, i.e., not decomposable, and expressions which he initially <u>perceives</u> as formulaic, and which he will subsequently decompose.

their internal structure. The learner "tunes in" on regular, patterned speech and these formulas are slowly broken down or "freed" from their invariability.

In the speech of Wong-Fillmore's (1976) subjects (5 Spanish speaking children learning English as L2), some formulaic expressions remained wholly formulaic through the nine month period of observation and perhaps afterwards. Other expressions began as formulas, but quickly loosened up as the learners ascertained which parts could be varied. Furthermore, some expressions were taken over correctly from the L2 input, whereas other expressions were completely idiosyncratic inter- pretations of what the child had heard. According to Wong-Fillmore, formulas are used and developed in the following way: firstly, the formula is used as an invariant form; further on, the formula functions as a basic frame to which other constituents like noun phrases or prepositional phrases may be attached; finally, the formula is broken down and new combinations may arise with elements taken from the former- ly "closed" basic frame. Wong-Fillmore's subject Nora passed through these stages with the formula how do you do dese:

(a) invariant, non-expansive form: how do you do dese?
(b) expansion of basic frame: how do you do dese flower power?; how do you do dese in English?
(c) breaking down of basic frame: how do you like to be a cookie cutter?; how did you make this?; how you make it?

Hakuta (1974) also points out that a pattern like do you becomes varied only gradually into segments like does he or did you. Initially, do you is used for expressing several intentions, e.g.: do you have coffee?; do you saw some star eye? (= did you see); what do you drinking, her? (= what does she drink?); what do you doing, this boy? (= what does this boy do?).

The use of formulaic expressions serves specific cognitive and social functions. From a cognitive perspective, formulaic expressions motivate the language learner to search for internal structure and by this analysis expand his verbal repertoire in a creative direction. From a social perspective, formulas offer the language learner an oppor- tunity to show verbality with very limited linguistic means. Their use can also lead to misunderstandings (cf. 4.3.2). If the language learner could communicate only by a creative application of grammatical rules, he would be able to say much less. Showing verbality is of great importance for establishing and maintaining verbal and social contact, and formulaic expressions can be an important means of doing so.

This motivates our inclusion of formulaic expressions, which will be studied systematically in the early stages, and then in relation to the other areas of investigation described in 6.2.1 - 6.2.5.

The two specific questions we are asking in this section have to do with (a) the communicative environment of the informants and (b) the general role in acquisition of formulaic expressions:

(a) we wish to know what formulaic expressions are acquired in what order, and to fulfill what communicative functions. These questions may be relevant to other questions, such as the acquisition of expressions of emotional attitude, of modality and of metalinguistic vocabulary.

(b) is segmenting frames a central learning strategy? Wong-Fillmore's work with children seems to indicate that this is the case. E. Clark (1978a:20) adopts much the same view in her discussion of linguistic awareness in children, where she cites "practising and playing with language" as one aspect of the child's developing awareness: "They repeat sentence frames, substituting one word for another; they try out different sentence types". One way of answering the above question would therefore be to examine whether the progressive decomposition and manipulation of formulaic expressions follows the same chronology, for their relevant parts, as the acquisition of these features as evidenced in non-formulaic utterances.

6.3 Suggestions for data collection

In order to obtain an adequate and reliable picture of the distribution of different types of linguistic expressions with respect to the various domains and their development over time, while also taking into consideration possible changes in living conditions, it will be necessary to document the number and degree of differentiation of the expres-

sions used by learners when speaking about everyday life in casual
conversations. This documentation must take place over the entire
period of observation and will mean that the domains "work", "home"
and "social relations" must be touched on regularly in conversation.
This specific elicitation will, however, not be necessary for the other
domains, as we are interested in how items from each of them are
acquired and used in order to fulfill communicative functions. It will
be worthwhile in this respect to examine field notes and recordings
from participant and accompanying observation.

For a number of reasons this data base will not be sufficient to
give precise information on the range of expressions covering each
domain and the way these develop during acquisition. If casual conversation is to be as natural as possible, it will for the greater part
take its own course, and though the scope for intervention is there
(in part, through our briefing of informants, cf. 8.2.3), it is nevertheless limited.

Conversations will not always provide an adequate number of statements relating to one domain which a detailed analysis of the pertinent
lexical repertoire would require. In addition to this the designation
of the exact meaning speakers associate with their words may be
difficult taking the interview material alone as a basis.

More accurate information can be obtained by asking the subjects
themselves to give the meanings of the words. They can be confronted
with their own utterances presented to them in the original context
where the meaning is either unclear or somehow specific to the learner's
language (these can be unsuccessful paraphrases or novel word-compounds)
and can be asked to translate or paraphrase as best they can. Thus,
self-confrontation will be an important technique for this area of
investigation. Experimental elicitation procedures will be required also
to supply supplementary data for specific semantic domains in the
lexicon. These will be elicited either during the video session (cf.
8.4: the apartment describing experiment is a clear example of the elicitation of the vocabulary of "home"), or else we can ask informants
to give oral descriptions of picture material which can take the form
of department-store catalogues, scenes from films or sketches (cf. 8.3).
The video-recorded material mentioned here will be further exploited

to examine the gestural communication strategies used by informants
(cf. question (b) of 6.1.4). Detour devices (such as paraphrasing) used
to fill lexical gaps will be identified in all the elicitation techniques.

To sum up the previous paragraph, all the elicitation techniques
can and will be exploited from different points of view. It follows
that all material transcribed in the project can and will serve for
analysis, at least in its early stages. Thus our approach will be
flexible at first, and more selective later in the light of first results.

The topics mentioned in this section will be analyzed from a
quantitative and from a structural point of view:

- Quantitatively. We are establishing for each SL-TL combination a
  computerized word-form lexicon containing specifications of the
  context (speaker, time, type of technique, line of text, etc.) in
  which each entry appears, and a derivational lexicon containing
  alternative morphological realizations of a given stem, accompanied
  by syntactic and semantic specifications, such as the thematic
  domain to which an item belongs. Programs which are either already
  in existence, or which are relatively straightforward to set up,
  will allow us to establish:
  - the size of a given informant's lexicon at a given time;
  - the distribution of its entries in respect to semantic domains;
  - absolute and relative frequency of occurrence of its entries in
    text (type-token ratio);
  - the linguistic context of its entries (concordance).
- Structurally. A complete model flexible enough to allow the description of structural changes of the vocabulary and the development of the meaning of specific lexical items cannot be proposed
  at this stage. An analysis of the data available so far has merely
  shown that it will be necessary to take the entire utterance into
  account in the analysis of lexical items. The early stages of
  second language acquisition seem to be characterized by utterances
  in which meanings, normally expressed by one word in standard speech,
  are spread piecemeal so to speak over the entire utterance, inclu-

ding nonverbal behaviour, as the following examples show:

machen + lassen = stellen, legen (put, lay):
<u>Mach</u> dem Tasche zwischen dem Stuhl <u>lassen</u>
(make the bag between the chair let = put the bag between the
chairs)

sitzen + gehen = setzen (sit down)
Dann <u>geh</u> Stuhl <u>sitzen</u>
(then go chair sit)

weg + mit + rein = stecken, tun in (put, place in)
...Aschenbecher <u>weg</u>, <u>mit</u> dem Tasche, Tasche <u>rein</u>.
(...ashtray away,   with the bag, bag into = put the ashtray
into the bag)

mit eine Bewegung schlagen = klopfen (tap, pat)
Jetzt müssen Sie ihn <u>mit eine Bewegung schlagen</u>
(now must you   him with a movement   hit = now you must tap him
on the shoulder)

For formulaic expressions, and for most aspects of modality and
emotional attitude, it will be necessary to analyse the stretches of
discourse in which they appear. For the studies of prosody and body
language suggested specifically for 6.2.2 and 6.2.4, and more generally
for lexical gap filler strategies, it will be necessary to establish
what types of prosody and gestures occur, what their distribution is,
and how this distribution can be explained.

7. Reference to People, Space and Time

7.1 Introduction

7.1.1 The problem. Successful communication requires reference to:

- persons, for example by expressions like you, Marilyn Monroe, the man who invented powder, or the Turks living in France;
- places, for example by expressions like here, behind the second door to the left, on earth, or deep in my heart;
- times, for example by expressions like yesterday, two months after my arrival, in 1984, or when the saints go marching in.

Such reference often includes the expression of spatial relations (below, in, behind, etc.), of temporal relations (before, ago, during, etc.), of distances (five meters, very far, etc.), and of durations (three minutes, half a life, etc.). Similarly it often indicates the social relationship between people, by politeness forms, for example.

All languages have numerous devices to express this reference, and since it is one of the most important components of any successful communication, a learner must necessarily learn the specific means developed for this purpose by the language he has to use. This immediately justifies the inclusion of reference to people, space, and time among the list of major research topics.

Now, the devices to express this reference share some properties across languages (though not across all languages), while in other respects, they differ from language to language. For successful communication, the learner can draw on what he assumes to be identical for source and target language, and he gradually has to complete it by what is different. Moreover, all languages offer a rich variety of possibilities for expressing this reference, some of which are practically equivalent in many contexts, but not all of these possible devices are equally important for daily interaction. An appropriate analysis of the acquisition process in this domain cannot therefore be limited to an investigation of how different expressions used for referring are learned, but rather it has to analyse how, at a given point in time, the learner tries to make optimal use of the devices he has at his disposal at that time. It is in this sense that the second objective of our project (an investigation of the acquisition process) cannot successfully be pursued without simultaneous consideration of the third objective (an investigation of language use, cf. 1.3.1). Approaching both objectives at the same time is also crucial for a deeper understanding of causal factors which determine the acquisition process and its tempo. For his immediate communicative needs, the learner has to acquire some means to refer to people, space, and time; thus propensity is high and so presumably is acquisition speed. He may then have learned only a small selection of the means the target language offers, but if optimally used, this selection may be sufficient for his immediate communicative needs; thus propensity and probably acquisition speed may dramatically decrease. That this is more than a speculation is clearly shown by previous research on the acquisition of temporality in SSLA (cf. Klein, 1981a and Dittmar, 1981).

7.1.2 Language-specific and generalizable aspects of reference to people, space, and time. The following notes are not meant to be an analysis of the intricate mechanisms of reference; they only highlight some aspects that are particularly important for our present concerns. In successful reference, a referent is sorted out of a set of possible alternative referents. The set of possible alternatives is defined by the properties of the referential domain, on the one hand, and by various contextual factors, on the other:

(a) The referential domain with its specific properties provides all elements which in principle can be referred to; for example, spatial reference may sort out a component of visual space, and this space is assumed to have a three-dimensional structure with the axes: up/down, front/back, left/right. Not all spatial reference is to this referential domain (for example, deep in my heart is not); but in any case, such a referential domain is presupposed, whatever its nature may be.

(b) In a given situation, the set of possible referents is narrowed
down by what is relevant in the specific context of utterance. The
referential domain for persons may contain thousands of Johns,
but in a given context only a small selection of persons may be at
issue, and this selection may contain only one John; this allows
reference to this person simply by John rather than by John + some
additional discriminatory expression (my uncle John, John, the
Vice-Chancellor, etc.). How this contextual narrowing-down of
"actualized referents" indeed works is hard to describe and need
not concern us here (see for example, Deutsch, 1976; Miller, 1977;
Garrod & Sanford, 1981; Marslen-Wilson, Tyler, Levy, 1982); but it
is clear that all actual reference relies heavily on contextual
restriction.

In an idealized speech situation, the relevant set of possible referents
is identical for speaker and hearer - that is, they share the same referential domain, and the contextual restrictions operate in the same way
for both of them. In real speech situations, this is probably never the
case. In order to be successful in referring, then, the speaker has to
choose his words according to what he assumes to be given for the listener, and, if necessary, to adapt his formulation. This requires a
permanent monitoring of the listener's knowledge by the speaker (cf.
5.2.2), a process which normally involves the eliciting and giving of
feedback (cf. 4.4).

Hence, the choice of an appropriate referring expression depends
on both the ability correctly to estimate the listener's knowledge in
a given situation, and the knowledge of the meaning of words and
syntactic constructions of the given language.

What does this mean from the learner's point of view? Obviously,
he has to learn the meaning of words and structures. However, the situation is different when it comes to ascertaining mutual knowledge. There
is good reason to assume that the way in which referential domains are
structured, and the way in which contextual factors operate, are similar across languages - but they are not identical, and this easily
leads to problems. In particular, differences due to different cultural

background often go unnoticed and thus lead to communicative breakdown, or to misunderstandings. A typical case is found in HDP (1979:162-4), where communication with a Spanish worker almost breaks down because the listeners do not immediately understand the Spanish system of "familia" (where the child gets the second name of both father and mother). In this case, the misunderstanding is recognized and repaired by a long explanation which would have been unnecessary if the Spaniard had been talking to other Spaniards. More generally, referential failure may be avoided by supplying additional knowledge to the listener. This possibility is crucial for an understanding of how reference to people, space, and time is established in learner varieties.

The acquisition problem as regards reference to people, space and time is then to reach a suitable balance between the listener's assumed knowledge, which can be manipulated to some extent, and the means of expressing reference which the learner has at a given moment.

If the learner has just two or three local expressions, or pronouns, etc., the burden on the listener's assumed knowledge is very high; it gradually decreases as the learner's repertoire becomes richer.

7.1.3 <u>Deictic and non-deictic reference</u>. All reference to people, space and time may be either relative to a referent - a person, place, or time - which is assumed to be given, or else without such an "anchoring point". Most obvious candidates in the former case are the person who is speaking, the place where he is speaking, and the time when this is done. They constitute the anchoring point, the "origo" (cf. Bühler, 1934), of deictic reference. All languages exploit this possibility, so that the fundamental mechanisms of deixis need to be learned only once in first language acquisition, where it indeed constitutes a major learning problem. The second-language learner already has them. What is different, however, are the deictic expressions themselves and also the semantic oppositions expressed by them. We will come to this problem in a moment. Reference may also be made relative to other given referents. The two most typical cases are:

(a) Anaphora. A referent introduced in the preceding context (sometimes in the following context) is taken up again with a specific marker, for example a pronoun. In many languages, anaphoric and deictic expressions largely overlap, and Bühler (1934) in his classic treatment considered anaphora to be a special case of deixis. But for language acquisition, deictic and anaphoric use have to be kept apart; thus, in the acquisition of personal pronouns, the former precedes the latter as a rule.

(b) "Fixed origo". The deictic origo has the advantage of always being at hand, but the disadvantage of permanently floating. This flexibility complicates less situationally dependent reference. As an additional possibility, many cultures have chosen a designated time or place as a stable primary reference point. The most obvious cases are the calendar systems, where times are referred to relative to the time of an important historical event, and the system of geographical co-ordinates.

A related procedure underlies so-called intrinsic orientation. Spatial expressions like left, right, front, back relate to the position of the speaker and the direction of his gaze. But a car has an intrinsic left and right, and front and back, which are relative to the normal position of the driver ("frozen origo"). Similarly, expressions like behind, before, etc. may be used either in relation to the real origo, or to such a frozen origo.

Both these types of choice of primary reference points which deviate from the deictic origo may constitute acquisition problems, since cultures and languages show some variance in this respect.

Deictic reference - with its possible variants (a) and (b) - is extremely flexible; it offers rich referential possibilities with comparatively little means, especially since the learner can assume that the underlying mechanisms (but not the individual expressions, of course) are identical or at least very similar across languages. Hence we may assume that it plays a particularly important role in learner varieties.

7.1.4 Links with other research topics. In the preceding sections, we have sketched the kind of acquisition problem that reference to people, space and time constitutes for the learner. Before turning to its more specific aspects, some notes about its relationship to other research topics of the project might be in order.

Firstly, there is obviously a close connection with the thematic structure of utterances, which often reflects the setting of an event in space and time. Some examples are quoted in 5.1.2 and 5.2.1.

Secondly, the acquisition of referential expressions naturally involves numerous semantic processes; thus, the acquisition of modality expressions and their semantics (cf. 6.2.4) is intrinsically linked to the acquisition of temporality and the way in which it is expressed.

Thirdly, referential failure is a major source of misunderstanding and communicative breakdown (cf. chapter 4). As was stated above, differences in cultural background knowledge may often lead to problems for unambiguous reference.

In the following three sections, we will discuss specific problems relating to personal, then spatial, and finally temporal reference. No attempt is made to deal with these domains in a comprehensive and theoretically satisfactory way; rather we focus on some aspects which are particularly relevant from the learner's point of view. Each subsection begins with some notes on how the target language reflects the referential domains in question, since differences in the way in which semantic fields are organized may constitute a major learning problem. Then we will turn to the different kinds of expressions (adverbs, prepositional phrases, tense, etc.) which are used to express reference.

7.2 Reference to people

7.2.1 <u>The referential domain and its reflection in the target languages</u>. Here, the possible referents are persons, and there is little reason to assume the existence of major differences, or of specific acquisition problems due to such differences. The only exception perhaps is the qualification of other people in terms of their personal relation to the speaker. The well-known differences in systems of personal address can often be analysed as depending on differences in power and solidarity (Brown and Gilman, 1960). We will return to this problem in 7.2.3.

7.2.2 <u>Types of expressions</u>. In all the target languages of the project, there are three major types of expressions for reference to people:

personal pronouns, proper names, lexical noun phrases (including titles).

Although they may often be alternatives to refer to the same referent (he - Berthold Schwarz - the man who is supposed to have invented powder), their conditions of use are different, and they constitute different learning problems. Thus, deictic reference by I and you as well as proper names belong to the earliest and most often used NPs of learner varieties, whereas lexical NPs with determiners and modifiers generally occur much later.

7.2.2.1 Personal pronouns. In the sense of the distinction made in 7.1.3, personal pronouns are a typical instance of deictic reference (in the larger sense of the word, including anaphoric use). In principle, they function in much the same way in all the languages involved; but there are numerous differences in detail which may lead to specific acquisition problems. More specifically, the following aspects must be taken into consideration.[1]

Deictic vs anaphoric use. First and second person pronouns usually only function deictically (in the narrower sense of the word), third person pronouns allow both deictic and anaphoric use, with a preference for the latter. In Klein and Rieck (1979) it was shown that in the untutored acquisition of German by Spanish and Italian adults, deictic use in general has a clear preponderance over anaphoric use. This result raises the following questions to be investigated in the project:

- Is this also true for other language combinations?
- Is this true across different text types?(Data in the study mentioned above come only from linguistic interviews.)
- What is responsible for this asymmetry: differences in communicative importance, different frequencies in the input, different discourse functions, or what?

---

[1] For a study of the untutored acquisition of personal pronouns, on which much of the following discussion is based, see Klein and Rieck (1979) and Klein (1981b); for a discussion of pronoun acquisition in the classroom, see Felix and Simmet, 1982.

Speaker vs addressee. This feature of the pronoun system seems to pose
no specific learning problem, except for the choice of appropriate
politeness forms (tu vs vous, du vs Sie, etc.); we will return to this
problem in 7.2.3.

Singular vs plural. All languages under investigation, both target and
source, only distinguish these two specifications of number, and there
seems to be no specific acquisition problem in this respect. On the
other hand, it appears to be the case that in initial learner varieties,
singular forms are clearly predominant and often have plural meaning as
well. In the learner variety of Spanish and Italian adults, a form like
ich is used to refer either to the speaker alone or to the speaker and
some other people, i.e., in place of the target form wir. This observation raises the following three questions:

- Is this also true for other language combinations?
- How is this fact related to the often noted observation that
  acquisition often starts with "unmarked" forms, for example nouns
  which are uninflected and equivalently used for singular and
  plural, whereas this form, morphologically at least, corresponds
  to target language singular?
- What are the causes of this preference for the singular form?

Case marking. Even in languages with limited inflectional case marking,
there often exist case variants for personal pronouns (he-him vs John-
John). In the present context we are less interested in the problem of
acquiring case marking in general (a problem which looks quite different
for the different language combinations) but rather in its possible
complications for learning the appropriate devices for person reference.
It has been found that in learner varieties the nominative form is
often used as an "unmarked" form, covering oblique cases as well. This
raises the following questions:

- What is the "case marking acquisition sequence" for different
  constellations of case systems?
- What are the causes for overgeneralizing specific forms, and why
  just these?

Two more problems are posed by the specific relation between the geni-

tive of personal pronouns and possessive pronouns (mon - de/à moi, le
mien; mein / von mir - mein, etc.), and by special uses of case marking
in some contexts (Who was it? - Me, rather than I):

- How are possessive pronouns acquired in relation to the genitive
  of personal pronouns?
- How do special uses, like the ones mentioned above, affect the
  acquisition of the system?

Obviously, the importance of the latter questions differs very much for
the different language pairs.

Strong vs weak forms. Many languages have developed "strong" and "weak"
variants of personal pronouns, e.g., je-moi, me-à moi in French, je-jij
in Dutch, etc.; sometimes, the weak variant is full omission, such as
the frequently missing personal pronoun in subject position in Spanish
or Italian. The conditions for using either strong or weak forms are
very complex and not identical across languages. There is some evidence
that the existence, and the specific forms, of such an opposition leads
to special learning problems. Adult Italian and Spanish learners of
German often seem to use bei mir as a prominent variant of ich - roughly
in the sense of "as for me" - and the extent to which this construction
is used differs for Italians and Spaniards. This gives rise to the
following questions:

- To what extent is a source language distinction between strong and
  weak forms transported into the learner variety, and how - if at
  all - is it realized?
- How is such a distinction learned, if it is in the target but not
  in the source language?

An answer to these questions is complicated by two problems. First, the
opposition "strong-weak" may interact with other oppositions, e.g.,
with case marking. It is unclear, for example, to what extent the
distinction expressed by je - moi in French is functionally equivalent
to the distinction expressed by me - à moi. And secondly, even languages in which this opposition is not part of the grammatical system
may have related phenomena. Thus, German ich is often reduced to 'ch
in unstressed position, and du is often cliticized when postposed:

haste, willste. It has often been noted that these "merged forms" are perceived as a unit and even combined with other pronouns.

Generic use. Most personal pronouns can be used for specific as well as for generic reference, although the former use is clearly dominant. Generic use is often restricted to special contexts, for example to hypothetical sentences or to generalized orders: If I push this button, the bomb will explode does not specifically mean: "If the present speaker ...", but rather "If anyone ...". Similarly, an order like You should honour your father and mother is addressed to everybody, not to a specific person.

At present, it is unclear whether this use constitutes an acquisition problem. It possibly does in connection with the acquisition of indefinite pronouns in general, such as German man, French on, English one, etc.

Idiosyncrasies. Apart from these general characteristics of pronoun systems, most languages show some idiosyncrasies, which cannot therefore be research problems of the whole project, but which should be included if they are particularly important for some SL-TL combination. German, for example, has an alternative sub-system for third person pronouns: er, sie, es vs der, die, das. The exact conditions of use of these two subsystems are almost unexplored, but at least in spoken language, the second system is extremely frequently used. This is clearly reflected in the initial learner varieties: der, die, das appear to be predominant for a long time. It is difficult, however, to formulate clear research problems here, but it seems clear that where such competing sub-systems do exist, the possible impact on acquisition has to be taken into account. An obvious case is the systems of clitic pronouns in the Spanish-French pair.

7.2.2.2 Proper names. At first glance, proper names do not seem to constitute a serious acquisition problem. Consequently, their proportion among all references to person is very high in the initial learner varieties. On a deeper level of analysis, however, there are indeed some problems with this category:

(a) Different cultures often have different systems of personal names (first name, second name, surname); see, for example, HDP (1979:162-

164) where lack of knowledge of these differences leads to mis-understanding.

(b) The rules which govern the appropriate use of names in addressing someone and referring to someone are highly complicated. Violating these rules often has social consequences: the speaker is considered to be impolite, ridiculous, arrogant, or even aggressive; in any case, he qualifies himself as an outsider.

The second problem is clearly of the greatest importance for communicative and social success. It is closely linked to the appropriate use of address forms of pronouns and of titles, which we examine in 7.2.3.

7.2.2.3 <u>Lexical noun phrases</u>. Lexical NPs offer the most richly struc-tured and flexible possibilities for referring to persons. They often combine deictic and non-deictic reference. Thus, in <u>this</u> <u>man</u>, the first component is deictic (or anaphoric), and the second is non-deictic. This fact, as well as their rich structural diversification make lexical NPs a particularly important acquisition problem.

The problem looks different for the more "lexical" part and the more "determining" part of a lexical NP, the former including nouns and attributes and the latter including determiners, numerals, etc. As has been mentioned in 1.5.3.1, Spaniards and Italians learning German have a certain acquisition order which for lexical NPs is:

1. Simple lexical nouns (<u>Haus</u>, <u>Frau</u>)
2. determiners in the following order:
    numeral + N (<u>zwei</u> <u>Kollege</u>)
    quantifier + N (<u>viel</u> <u>Kollege</u>)
    article + N (<u>der</u> <u>Kollege</u>)
3. adjective + N (both uninflected)
4. combinations of 2 and 3
5. attributes other than adjective (PP, S, etc.).

This order raises some general problems as to the underlying principles at work (cf. 1.5.3.1). In particular, the late appearance of explicitly marked definitely referring NPs (e.g., <u>der</u> <u>Kollege</u>) may be linked with the problems of the listener's assumed knowledge and of word order (cf. 5.2.2 and 7.1.2).

7.2.3 <u>Special problems</u>. The way in which a person is referred to most
often indicates the specific personal or social relation which obtains
between the speaker and that person. This is most obvious when this
person is present in the speech situation and, for example, when he is
addressed or called; but it also holds when he is referred to <u>in</u> <u>absentia</u>
(it clearly makes a difference whether someone is called <u>François</u> or
<u>le Président de la République</u>).

As has already been mentioned, correct application of the appropriate forms is extremely important for communicative and social success,
and incorrect use is strongly stigmatized. This fact, on the one hand,
and the fact that the subtle mechanisms which underlie appropriate use
are rarely made explicit and hence require a lot of analytic labour,
on the other hand, make this problem a particularly rewarding domain
for studying the role of awareness. Immediate social sanctions lead to
higher awareness, and higher awareness is needed to understand the underlying rules.

Among the many aspects which make this problem so complex, at least
the following four should be mentioned:

(a) One has to distinguish whether the person referred to is present
     or absent. A form which is absolutely correct in the latter case
     may be highly offensive in the former.

(b) At least <u>in praesentia</u>, a distinction has to be made as to whether
     a person is addressed or merely mentioned, that is whether he or
     she is treated as a "second" or as a "third" person; in fact, even
     this option may be used to express a specific personal relation
     to the person referred to.

(c) The nature of what has been called here "personal or social rela-
     tions" is far from being clear, and it is most obvious that lan-
     guages differ in this respect.

(d) All types of expressions discussed in 7.2.2 are affected by this
     problem:
     - personal pronouns, e.g., by distinctions like <u>du</u> - <u>Sie</u>, <u>tu</u> - <u>vous</u>,
       etc.;
     - proper names, e.g., first name vs second name;
     - lexical NPs; here, titles and vocative use of other NPs are par-

ticularly relevant cases.

Finally, it should be noted that despite an extensive literature on the problem of "politeness forms" (cf. for example, Friedrich, 1966; Ervin-Tripp, 1969; Svennung, 1958), and related questions, it is by no means clear whether the available descriptions indeed cover the regularities of the specific subgroups which constitute the learning environment of our informants.

7.3 Reference to space

7.3.1 Referential domains and their reflection in target languages and learner varieties. Spatial expressions may denote very different kinds of localities and relations. Consider the following few prepositional phrases with in:

1.   He had ten pence in his purse
2.   He had a hole in his purse
3.   He has a cigar in his mouth
4.   He was born in Spain
5.   ... their reflection in target languages ...
6.   In this paper, we will discuss three questions.

In all of these cases, a relation between two entities is expressed. They differ, however, with respect to the referential domains, that is, to the nature of these entities which range from very concrete (pence in purse) to very abstract (question - or speaker? - in paper). They also differ with respect to the precise nature of this relation: in (1), one entity is fully enclosed in the other; in (3), it is only partly enclosed; and the other cases are more complicated. It seems plausible to assume that some of these uses have a historical or ontogenetic priority, or may be more frequent in everyday communication. But mastering a language beyond a most elementary level requires at least some knowledge of them.

For our present concerns, it will probably suffice to distinguish three types of referential domain, which we will discuss now.

Perceptual space. This concerns objects of our immediate perceptual

experience and the local relations between them, as reflected by perception and possibly, practical operations (moving objects, moving
ourselves, etc.).

It most clearly reflects the anthropological organization of some
aspects of language (Lyons, 1977; Miller & Johnson-Laird, 1976). Human
beings usually move upright on the surface of the earth; they turn
around, look around, move objects up and down, back and forth, etc. A
highly typical feature of perceptual space due to this kind of human
experience is three-dimensionality. Many authors presume an internal
ranking of these dimensions: " ... verticality is physically and psychologically the most salient of the spatial dimensions" (Lyons, 1977:690),
front-back and finally left-right being cognitively derived dimensions.
The poles of these oppositions may again have a different cognitive
status: "Upwards and backwards are negative, in the egocentric perceptual and interactional space based on the notions of visibility and
confrontation" (Lyons, 1977:691).

There are alternative ways of ranking these dimensions, but independently of which version will prove to be most appropriate, such an
internal ranking could be extremely helpful in explaining the order in
which some local expressions are acquired. We will come back to this
point in 7.3.2.

Geographical space. Expressions like in Turkey, behind the French border
still relate to physical space, but they do so in a much more abstract
way; they refer to elements of our geographical knowledge which, of
course, may differ between speakers. Apart from problems due to such
differences in background knowledge, reference to elements of geographical space seems to pose no particular acquisition problem, since
(a) the referents mostly have proper names, and (b) the number and
nature of possible spatial relations are rather restricted here.

Abstract space. As examples (5) and (6) illustrate, we often express
spatial relations between abstract entities of very different kinds.
It is important to distinguish this use from non-spatial uses of prepositions, as in idiomatic expressions (in this respect) or in verb
government (we trust in God), although there are numerous borderline
cases. Spatial reference in abstract space is probably historically

and doubtlessly ontogenetically late, and perhaps its use is less
frequent overall, although this clearly depends on the type of discourse. (In this field manual, it is by far the most important use.)

Within the project, all three uses should be taken into account.
But for two reasons priority should be given to reference to perceptual space:

(a) In foreign workers' everyday communication, it is probably the
     most urgent learning problem: it is much more difficult than
     reference to geographical space, where there are restricted possi-
     bilities and a low probability of misunderstanding these; the
     discourse domains foreign workers are mainly engaged in probably
     require less reference to abstract space.
(b) It is easier to control by experimental techniques.

It should be noted here that this elementary subdivision into three
kinds of space is a gross oversimplification which, apart from the usual
and unavoidable problems of borderline cases, may lead to difficulties
in at least one respect. Perceptual space is often not really
accessible to the perception of the speech partners: it is a space of
possible but not necessarily of actual perception. There may indeed be
a difference between interpreting Give me the book on the table! when
book and table are visually present, and uttering The book was on the
table in a narrative. In the latter case, correct interpretation of the
utterance hinges much more on a precise understanding of the preposition
on itself than in the former case, where it is simultaneously supported
by visual information, and may even be facilitated by pointing gestures.
So, while type of reference and type of spatial relation are fully
identical in both cases, the weight of the preposition for establishing
successful communication is different, and we may wonder whether this
fact is reflected in acquisition. Note finally that if, in the second
case, there were two books, one on and one under the table, there would
still be a difference: although the preposition is no longer redundant,
there would only be two possible spatial relations, and furthermore,
on would normally be stressed.

7.3.2 <u>Types of expressions</u>. Spatial entities and relations are basically expressed by four types of linguistic expressions: simple adverbs,
prepositional phrases (PP), and corresponding inflectional constructions; subordinate clauses; "motion" verbs. All of them can express two
types of relations: positional (or static) and directional (or dynamic).
Following Talmy (1980) and Fillmore (1982), we will call the entity
which is located or moved the <u>figure</u>, and the entity (place) relative
to which it is located or moved, the <u>ground</u> of the spatial relation in
question. Thus, in <u>The book is on the table</u>, <u>the book</u> is the figure,
whereas <u>the table</u> is the ground. In <u>He walked across the meadow</u>, <u>the
meadow</u> is the ground, and <u>he</u> is the figure. For directional relations,
the ground may be either origin or target, or even both. There is some
reason to assume that the target has a certain communicative priority
(cf. Lyons, 1977:695), which is possibly reflected in the acquisition
order of some of these expressions, which we will now briefly discuss.

7.3.2.1 <u>Adverbs</u>. Typical cases of local adverbs are <u>here</u>, <u>there</u>, <u>down-
wards</u>, <u>thence</u>, <u>(to the) left</u>, <u>(to the) right</u> (the latter two being on
the borderline with PPs). Most of them are deictic or may at least be
used deictically. Usually, these adverbs cluster into small sub-systems,
but the way in which this is done and the internal semantic structure
of the sub-systems vary across languages. We can illustrate this with
the following sub-system of German:

hier	hierhin	hierher	von hier (aus)
da	dahin	daher	von da (aus)
dort	dorthin	dorther	von dort (aus)

The morphologically basic <u>hier</u>, <u>da</u>, <u>dort</u> are positional; by suffixes
or additional prepositions, they may be extended to directionals: the
suffixes -<u>hin</u>, -<u>her</u> denote movement to the target, as seen from the
listener's position (-<u>hin</u>) or from the speaker's position (-<u>her</u>).
Movement away from the place denoted by the basic morpheme is expressed
by <u>von ... (aus)</u>. From an acquisitional point of view, it seems plausible to assume that the morphologically simpler forms are learned before
the more complex ones; but this may also depend on whether such differences between positionals and various kinds of directionals are marked

in the source language. We will come back to this question in a moment. But first let us have a look at the semantics of the basic morphemes hier, da, dort.

The best-known way of characterizing the lexical meaning of these components of a sub-system is by a number of specified semantic features. Various proposals have been made in this respect (for a general discussion, cf. Lyons, 1977: 636-724. For numerous examples, cf. the contributions to Weissenborn and Klein, 1982). The most typical features are based on the distance from the origo. Thus, Lyons (1968) uses "proximal" and "remote" to mark the opposition between English here and there; Fillmore (1982) uses [± proximal] for English and [± proximal], [± medial], [± distal] for some other languages. Other systems also take into account the distance from the listener, or from a third person, or factors like whether the place referred to is in the visual field or not, quite independently from how close it is. This approach sometimes runs into problems (for a discussion and some alternative suggestions, cf. Klein, 1981c), but for our present purpose it seems basically appropriate.

Obviously, languages differ in the way in which they subdivide a feature like distance from origo. English probably subdivides it into two distances: here [+ proximal] and there [+ remote]. Spanish is often claimed to have three: aquî [+ proximal], allî [+ medial], allá [+ distal]. German also has three words, but da probably does not denote "medial distance"; it is rather used for every distance, and what it really means depends on what it is opposed to in the given speech situation. Hence it seems plausible to assume a specification as follows: hier [+ proximal], da [± proximal], dort [- proximal]. There are again arguments against this description (for an extensive discussion, cf. v. Stechow, 1982), but at least it covers the elementary facts.

Such clearly structured subsystems offer extremely clear opportunities for disentangling various determining factors in acquisition:

(a) Role of input: all of these words are relatively frequent, but their frequency relative to each other is still different enough to allow testing the role of frequency in the input.

(b) Generalizable factors (cf. 1.5.3), such as the hypotheses:
- that less specified elements are learned first: we should
  expect that German da is learned before dort, and also before
  daher,
- that negatively specified elements are learned later: we should
  expect that dort is learned after hier; or else that von ...
  aus is learned after ...-hin, if Lyons' assumption holds that
  the target is positively specified, and the origin negatively
  specified;
(c) Language-specific factors: the acquisition process should be
  structurally different depending on how similar the sub-systems
  of source and target languages are.

There are also some closely related studies on first language
acquisition of such sub-systems (cf., for example, Clark, 1978b, and
Tanz, 1980). Comparison with the developmental sequences there will
allow us to estimate the relative impact of cognitive factors in
both types of acquisition.

7.3.2.2 Prepositional phrases (PP) and corresponding constructions.
This category includes constructions which consist of an NP (pronoun,
proper name, lexical NP) and a spatial morpheme; this morpheme may be
either a preposition, or a postposition, or else a suffix (as in
Finnish or Turkish). There are some borderline cases, such as preposition + adverb rather than preposition + NP (von dort in German),
or a simple NP without explicit marking of a local relation, which we
will neglect in what follows. We will also neglect the NP-component
since the acquisition problems arising here are by and large the same
as those discussed in 7.2: Reference to People.

There is, however, one point in connection with NP which deserves
mention since it may lead to acquisition problems. In some languages,
such as German, the difference between positional and directional relations is often expressed by the case marking of an NP rather than by
specific prepositions: positional use requires a dative (or genitive),
directional use requires an accusative, for example: auf dem Tisch vs
auf den Tisch (on (to) the table); in der Küche vs in die Küche (in(to)

the kitchen), etc. Since the acquisition of inflectional morphology
in general occurs rather late, this automatically leads to a confla-
tion of directional and positional marking in these cases. This raises
the problem of whether this difference remains unmarked until morphological case marking is learned, or whether the communicative importance
of the distinction is high enough to necessitate the introduction into
learner varieties of other devices for expressing it (such as different
prepositions, rather than same prepositions and different case).

In general, the meaning of local prepositions, postpositions and
suffixes has been extensively studied and described in all the target
languages of the project, and also in most source languages. Moreover,
the basic relations expressed by prepositions like in, on, under, before, behind, when limited to figure-ground relations in perceptual and
geographical space, seem not to be so different in the languages of the
project as to constitute major learning problems. But there are other
problems which may matter for acquisition:

(a) It is unclear how these elementary local relations within
    perceptual space are transferred to abstract space, and whether
    this is done in a similar way across languages.

(b) On a deeper level of analysis, the semantics of local preposi-
    tions is rather unclear even for perceptual space, as may have
    become clear from examples (1) - (3) of 7.3.1. In many cases,
    for example, it is at least unclear how many and which dimensions
    we attribute to the ground and possibly to the figure. Thus it
    seems plausible to assume that in He had no teeth in his mouth, the
    mouth is envisaged as a three-dimensional cavity, whereas in
    He had a cigar in his mouth, the mouth is envisaged as a two-
    dimensional surface. What is unclear, however, is whether these
    ways of "envisaging" figure and ground in different ways are
    language-specific or a kind of anthropological universal: the
    former assumption would point to a specific acquisition problem,
    the latter assumption would suggest that we should expect no such
    problem.

(c) In very many cases, the specific collocation of an NP with differ-
    ent prepositions (or corresponding morphemes) leads to quite
    different interpretations of the whole utterance. Take for example

German: <u>das Fahrrad stand in der Ecke</u> (the bicycle stood in the
corner) vs <u>das Fahrrad stand an der Ecke</u> vs <u>das Fahrrad stand auf</u>
<u>der Ecke</u>. Here, the ground and consequently the relationship of
figure to ground is conceived of in different ways.

(d) Finally, there are numerous idiosyncratic constructions with
local prepositions (and corresponding morphemes) which seem to
escape any systematic treatment but constitute a serious acquisition problem as soon as learner varieties get beyond the most
elementary stage. Take for example Spanish <u>en esta calle</u> (in/on
this street) vs German (<u>die Kinder spielten) auf dieser Straße</u>
(the children played on this street) vs <u>(er lebte) in dieser</u>
<u>Straße</u> (he lived in this street).

These and some related problems make the acquisition of local PPs a
complicated but intriguing research topic. Possibly the best way to
approach it is to start with the third of our central questions (cf.
1.3.1): How are some of these concepts expressed in reduced learner
varieties? A learner has to optimally exploit the limited resources
which he has at his disposal, and the goal of our analysis is to find
out which principles and strategies he is pursuing here. As we saw in
7.1.2, whenever a learner wants to attain some communicative aim, he
has to base his verbal planning on an estimation of the whole contextual situation, including the knowledge of the listener, and on the
repertoire of expressions he has at that stage of his acquisition
process. The more reduced his learner variety is, the more often he
encounters the problem that his repertoire is indeed insufficient to
attain his communicative aims. He then has either to give up his intention, or modify it, or else he has to apply strategies to compensate
for these insufficiencies. At exactly this point, his metalinguistic
capacities may come in and help to solve this problem, thus at the same
time providing a new push to his acquisition process.

In what follows we will briefly consider some examples of how this
is done by Turkish learners. They stem from an experiment which was
run by the Heidelberg pilot group with a group of adolescents who had
lived for about 2-3 years in Germany. In this video-taped experiment,
short silent scenes involving various spatial changes were performed

by the experimenters: the actor moved from one place to another, took objects from one place to another, etc. The learner was then asked to report this sequence of actions to a third person in such a way that this third person could imitate them as accurately as possible. In the following examples, the action was as follows: the actor (sitting at the table) took an ashtray standing in front of him and put it into a bag standing beside his chair. An appropriate target language instruction would have been: <u>Nimm den Aschenbecher und steck ihn in die Tasche</u> (take the ashtray and put it in the bag). Here are some of the learners' solutions:

1. Aschenbecher Tasche
2. Aschenbecher Tasche rein
3. Aschenbecher weg Tasche rein
4. Aschenbecher weg mit dem Tasche
5. Aschenbecher bringt mit dem Tasche
6. Nehmen Sie de Aschenbecher und rein Tasche
7. Aschenbecher legen Sie die Tasche

Let us briefly go through this list. Of all the versions, (1) is most context-dependent. Only the listener's situational knowledge and knowledge of the world tells him that he has to change the position of the ashtray in a certain sense. Both speech partners know: the speaker gives an instruction to the addressee; the ashtray and the bag are locally separated at the time of utterance; the form and size of the ashtray and bag are such that the former can be enclosed in the latter; such a local relation between both makes sense, as this world is. Moreover, word order probably indicates that in this case, the ashtray is the figure and the bag the ground.

In (2), the local adverb <u>rein</u> supplies additional information: it indicates a directional, target-oriented movement resulting in an inclusion of the figure in the ground.

In (3), the movement is split into two components: firstly, dislocating the figure from its preceding position, and secondly, locating it at the new position. The initial position as such is not made explicit.

In (4), the first part is as in (3); but then, the new relation

of figure and ground is not included in the directional <u>rein</u> but indicated by <u>mit</u>; it is rather mysterious how this local use of <u>mit</u>
(with) could be derived from the target language use; but there are
other occurrences which demonstrate that this overgeneralization indeed exists in learner varieties of Turks.

In (5), the movement is expressed by a verb form <u>bringen</u> (bring).
As used here, it maintains some but not all features which it has in
the target language; it focuses on the target and on the causative
aspect of the action but neglects the deictic component: <u>bringen</u> in
the target language includes movement to the speaker or to somebody
whose perspective is taken.

In (6), the movement is again split into two components, but in
a more elaborate way than in (3): the first component - dislocating
the ashtray - is indicated by a verb form <u>nehmen</u> (take), which exactly
corresponds to its target variety use; the final state in this case
is expressed with the same words as in (1) and (2), but for completely
unclear reasons, their order is reversed.

In (7), only the movement is expressed, but all explicit indication of the initial and final spatial relation is omitted. Hence, it
is rather similar to (1) with respect to the expressed spatial relations, although it is much more elaborate in other respects (as, for
example, the existence of the definite article illustrates).

Examples of this sort may be interpreted in the light of two
general principles which often underly learner variety use:

<u>The principle of redundancy avoidance</u>. Learners construe their utterances
as economically as possible:

- information which can be derived from situational context or can
  be assumed to be available for some other reason is not made
  explicit;
- implications and presuppositions are used whenever possible;
- the intended meaning is expressed by a minimal number of lexemes.
  If, for example, the verb already includes specification of a
  direction, then this information is not repeated with an appropriate preposition, even where the target language would require

this. Here are some additional examples: dann er gehe Stuhl (then
he goes chair); jeden Tag kommt Türkischer Volkshaus (every day
comes Turkish community centre); kommt Deutschland (comes Germany).
If, however, the verb is not realized, then the local relation is
expressed by a preposition and, in the following example, case
marking: Jacke auf die Tür (jacket on the door); or by local adverbs: und dann wieder zurück zu Tür (and then back again to door).
Shortly after, the same speaker rephrased his instruction in the
following form: und dann wieder gehs (and then again go). That is,
he alternatively used the verb or the local adverb to express the
intended directional relation.

The principle of semantic generalization. Initially, the learner's
lexicon is sparse. To fill the gaps, he takes related lexical items
and neglects some of their semantic features. He may be fully aware
of the fact that the item in question is not fully appropriate (for
examples, cf. chapter 6); but it may also be that he does not yet have
the full target language meaning. An instance of such a semantic generalization is bringen in (5) above. The same technique also applies
to prepositions: Jacke auf die Tür (intended: Häng die Jacke an die
Tür). It occasionally happens that the neglected feature is exactly
the one which would be crucial in the given situation. This occurs,
for example, when exactly the wrong member is chosen from an opposition: Mütze aufsteigen (hat get up) (intended: abnehmen, take off)
vor dem Aschenbecher (in front of the ashtray) (intended: hinter,
behind). Clearly, vor and hinter share numerous semantic features;
but still, no element of this opposition can be generalized without
leading to communicative problems.

A final and quite different strategy which the learners may use
here are gestures - a strategy which is particularly appropriate if
the spatial relations concern perceptual space. For example, when
asked to verbalize the action "to put a hat on your head", a learner
first says Kopftuch then hesitates and points to his head with his hand.
When asked to try again, he finally says Mütze trage Kopf.

These examples, though disputable and still unsystematic, may
illustrate the way in which a careful analysis of the use of learner

varieties may lead to deeper insights into the process of how spatial relations are expressed. Let us now briefly turn to the two remaining classes.

7.3.2.3 <u>Subordinate clauses</u>. In the target languages, spatial relations may also be expressed by two types of subordinate clauses:

(a)   Relative clauses, such as: <u>the house in which he was born</u>. This case may be considered as a simple variant of PP, in which (!) the NP is simply expressed by a relative pronoun. If there is a specific acquisition problem, it probably has to do with relative clauses as such but not with their specific spatial aspects.

(b)   Indirect questions, such as: <u>I don't know where to go</u>. These cases indeed play a role in learner varieties, although the difference between main clause and subordinate clause may be left unmarked. But again, this is much more a problem of question structure and question words as such rather than a specific problem of reference to space.

Consequently, this type of spatial expression should play only a minor role within this research topic.

7.3.2.4 <u>Motion and position verbs</u>. Here, this expression is meant to include directional verbs (verbs of "locomotion"), which express a change in the position of the agent or an object (<u>to go</u>, <u>to bring</u>, etc.), as well as positional verbs, which describe a spatial state (<u>to lie</u>, <u>to locate</u>, etc.). The latter verbs usually require an additional spatial expression which relates the figure to the ground; they are less interesting in the present context except that they often enter into systematic oppositions with "real" motion verbs, for example German <u>stellen</u> vs <u>stehen</u> (to place vs to stand), <u>legen</u> vs <u>liegen</u> (to lay vs to lie), etc.

Directional verbs, on the other hand, often form an interesting and semantically well structured subclass. They differ with respect to: the direction of movement (<u>to rise</u>, <u>to fall</u>); the type of movement (<u>to run</u>, <u>to walk</u>, <u>to stroll</u>); the instrument of movement (<u>to walk</u>, <u>to drive</u>, <u>to ride</u>, <u>to sail</u>); the object of movement (<u>to come</u>, <u>to throw</u>);

origin and target of movement (to go, to come). As has been shown in
a previous study (HDP, 1978: chapter 4), the most important of them in
the acquisition of German are the deictic verbs kommen (to come) and
gehen (to go), where the former is target-oriented and the latter is
origin-oriented. Target and origin are identified with the position of
the speaker at time of utterance (the origo), or correspond to a perspective which he is taking. It was shown that kommen is strongly
overgeneralized in the initial learner varieties - a fact which
could possibly be explained by the assumption that the target is
positively and the origin is negatively marked (cf. Lyons, 1977: 695).
Similar acquisition orders have been observed in child language (Clark,
1978b). This suggests that universal rather than language-specific factors
determine the acquisition process here.

7.4 Reference to time

7.4.1 The referential domain and its reflection in the target languages.
All the languages of the project, both source and target, allow the
expression of three characteristics of events (or actions, states, etc.,
briefly "events"): temporal reference, aspect, manner of action:

(a) Temporal reference (or "temporality" in the narrower sense) refers
     to the location of events in relation to a designated reference
     time. This designated reference time has to be given - either in
     the situational context, or in the general knowledge of the speech
     partners. In the most straightforward case, it is implicitly de-
     fined by the (unmarked) time of utterance; but there may be all
     kinds of complications, such as important events in the cultural
     background which may function as reference times (the calendar
     system), fictitious reference times, chains of reference times,
     etc. Temporal relations include those expressed by before, immedi-
     ately before, after, being contained in, simultaneous, since, and
     others.

(b) Aspect refers to the various perspectives the speaker may take
     with regard to an event, such as viewing it as "perfective" vs
     "imperfective", "progressive" vs "non-progressive". The role of

this category and the precise meaning of its various specifications varies across the project languages. Thus, English clearly
has a systematic aspect opposition (sleeps vs is sleeping), which
functions orthogonally to temporal reference; French has some
rudiments of it (passé simple vs imparfait vs passé composé);
in German or Dutch, it is quite unclear whether there is any
grammaticalized aspect marking; in any case, it is not independent of tense marking. In all languages, of course, there are
various lexical means to express perfectivity and non-perfec-
tivity, but clearly, the acquisition problem is then different
for the various languages.

(c) "Manner of action" refers to quasi-objective time characteristics of an event: durativity, transformativity, iteration of
sub-events, etc. It is mostly expressed by the lexical content
of the verb (e.g., "stative" vs "non-stative" verbs), by adverbials, and sometimes by derivational affixes; thus, German has
a rather rich though not really systematic repertoire of pre-
fixes (cf. blühen - aufblühen - erblühen - verblühen; to blossom
- to wither, etc.).

Acquiring the appropriate means of expressing manner of action and
(although to a lesser extent) aspect are mainly problems of lexical
development. They will be included here only to the extent to which
they are interwoven with the acquisition of temporal reference.

Turning now to temporal reference, it appears that the underlying
conception of time, its rooting in deictic origo or calendar reference
time, and the underlying temporal relations as such do not essentially
differ for the project languages (although differences of this kind
cannot be excluded in principle and might then constitute an interesting cultural background problem). The acquisition problems arise with
the way in which temporal relations are expressed.

7.4.2 Types of expressions. Temporal reference requires linguistic
devices for reference times and for temporal relations. In all languages of the project, there are three such devices:

(a) tense systems (expressed by affixes, auxiliaries, vowel

alternation);

(b) time adverbials (adverbs; prepositional phrases and corresponding constructions, including simple NPs; subordinate clauses);

(c) discourse principles (such as "unless marked otherwise, order of mention corresponds to order of events").

In what follows, (a) and (b) will be discussed only briefly; (c) will be considered in more detail, since it plays a particularly important role in learner varieties.

7.4.2.1 <u>Tense systems</u>. The tense systems of source and target languages differ considerably, both in the form and meaning of the tenses which they include. This makes them a particularly suitable sub-topic for the study of language-specific factors and their role for acquisition. In what follows, we will briefly point firstly to three aspects which seem particularly fruitful in this respect, and secondly to three difficulties in contrasting tense systems.

(a) Basically, tense marking has three forms, two synthetic and one analytic. These are affixes and vowel alternation, on the one hand, and periphrastic constructions, on the other. This offers an opportunity for testing and formulating input-oriented general principles, such as Slobin's (1973) operating principle A: "Pay attention to the end of words", and similar ones.

(b) The weight which different target languages attribute to tense varies considerably. Thus, the tense of lexical verbs in spoken German is more or less reduced to present and perfect (the latter possibly being more of an aspect), whereas English and French, for example, tend to a much more systematic marking of tenses. A comparative study of learners of different TLs with the same SL could answer the question whether acquisition is driven more by the specific communicative needs of the speaker, or by the "codified" communicative needs reflected in the grammatical system of a language: for example the need to mark an event as being in the future, which is codified in French but not in German.

(c) Similarly, the role of tense in the source languages is quite different. The most interesting contrast in this respect is

Turkish and Arabic, with target language Dutch (though similar
considerations hold for all other combinations as well). Turkish
has a rather rich tense (and aspect) system, Arabic has a limited
tense system, where an inflected verb has (primarily) aspect-
marking. Dutch has almost no grammatical aspect and a "medium
weight" tense system. If the learner's source language bias indeed plays a crucial role, then we should clearly expect differences in the acquisition of Dutch by Turkish vs Arabic speakers,
either in speed or even in structure.

In these respects, an investigation of the development of tense
marking would essentially contribute to disentangling the relative
impact on acquisition of various determining factors. There are, however,
some problems in doing so, which deserve mention.

Firstly, inflection seems to be acquired very late in general;
hence, it might be that the learner varieties to be studied in the
project are not differentiated enough for a systematic study of tense
marking even at the end of the longitudinal study.

Secondly, the information about tense usage in descriptive grammars
is often not very reliable. This even holds for intensively studied
languages like English or French, as soon as the description goes beyond literary use and touches on everyday language. But it is exactly
this latter language form to which the learner is exposed. Hence, it
is indispensable to include a study of the specific tense usage of this
everyday language form.

Thirdly, there is good reason to assume that tense usage depends on,
or is linked to, specific discourse types, or rather different functions
connected to these discourse types (reportative vs narrative, etc.).
Thus, reference to past in "vivid narrative" is often established by
present tense rather than by past tense (preterite or perfect). Hence,
different discourse types have to be kept apart in the study of tense
(cf. Weinrich, 1964).

In early learner varieties, tense usually plays a minor role; its
functions are partially taken over by adverbials, to which we will now
briefly turn.

7.4.2.2 <u>Adverbials</u>. The nature of the acquisition problem here is
quite similar to that of local adverbials which have been discussed
in the preceding section. We will therefore not discuss this further,
especially since the temporal relations are less differentiated than
the spatial relations, but simply point out two aspects in which both
domains differ. (Obviously, there are many other differences, but from
an acquisitional point of view these two deserve special mention.)

(a)   The transition from no-tense-marking to tense-marking is often
      characterized by the specific use of some adverbs, in German for
      example <u>schon</u> (already) and <u>fertig</u> (finished). Similar phenomena
      have been noted in first language acquisition and in pidgins. A
      more careful investigation of the distribution, semantics and
      language-specific variation of these forms would shed some light
      on the "constructive role" of the learner in building up his
      learner varieties.

(b)   Subordinate clauses play a much more important role for tempor-
      ality than they do for locality. Now, the acquisition of subordi-
      nate clauses occurs in general at rather a late stage, and it is
      unclear whether the learner varieties attained by the learners of
      our project are sufficiently rich in this respect to allow the
      inclusion of this subdomain of grammar in our investigation. But
      there are at least two aspects in which a study of early sub-
      ordinate clauses (and related structures) would be particularly
      rewarding:

      - The opposition main clause vs subordinate (temporal) clause
        is often used to express the opposition between foregrounded
        vs backgrounded knowledge (together with an aspect or even tense
        distinction between the verb forms). This links them to questions
        discussed in 5.2 (cf. also, de Lemos & Bybee, 1981).
      - In early stages of acquisition, it is often impossible to dis-
        tinguish temporal and conditional subordinate clauses. This may
        lead to serious misunderstandings and hence is important to the
        questions discussed in chapter 4.

The justification for including temporal subordinate clauses is, then,
not so much their role within the system of temporal reference as such,

but their possible relevance to other research topics.

For a very long time, learner varieties are marked by an almost complete lack of inflectional morphology and by a very limited range of adverbial constructions. But still, learners at these stages may handle the expression of temporality in a very effective way by the optimal application of certain discourse rules, to which we will now turn in more detail.

7.4.2.3 <u>Discourse principles</u>. What is meant by "discourse principles" is best illustrated by a well-known example. In each of the following co-ordinate sentences,

(1) Kate married and she became pregnant

and

(2) Kate became pregnant and she married,

the same two events are reported, one in each clause, but we interpret the temporal order of both events differently in (1) and (2). There seems to be a general discourse rule which says that, if two events are reported, and their temporal relation is not specifically marked, then the event reported first is <u>before</u> the event reported after; that is, the linear order of clauses corresponds in the unmarked case to the temporal order of what is reported. Stated in this way, the rule is clearly false. In:

(3) They played a wonderful string quartet. Peter played the violin, John played the cello, Mary played the viola d'amore, and Henry the bass

we do not assume that the musicians played one after the other. We simply know that they played, more or less, at the same time; that is, our knowledge of the world (of string quartets in this case) tells us that the time relations between the events reported in the linearly ordered clauses is simultaneous. This is roughly what is meant by "discourse principles" in the present context. Obviously, there are also some discourse principles of a more general sort which may be important to temporality, such as the Gricean maxims. For example, it is these

conversational maxims that make an answer like "Very often" to the
question "Have you seen my glasses?" somewhat inappropriate, whereas it would be perfect after a question like "Have you ever eaten
a frog?" In this chapter, we will not deal, however, with maxims of
this sort.

The examples given in (1) - (3) clearly demonstrate the important
role of discourse rules in the sense just explained for temporal reference. But nobody has ever made a serious attempt to work them out.
It seems, however, that in German at least, the following rules hold:

(4) Let α and β be expressions denoting events a and b, respectively[1]:

   1. If ⌜α,β⌝ are co-ordinated to ⌜α and $\bar{\beta}$⌝ or as ⌜α,β⌝, then the
      time relation a <u>after</u> b must be marked, if world knowledge
      admits a <u>after</u> b, a <u>before</u> b, and a <u>simultaneous</u> b.

   2. If ⌜α⌝, ⌜β⌝ are co-ordinated as ⌜α and $\bar{\beta}$⌝ or as ⌜α,β⌝, then
      the time relations a <u>contained in</u> b as well as b <u>contained in</u>
      a must be marked, if world knowledge admits a <u>before</u> b, a
      <u>after</u> b and a <u>contained in</u> b.

   3. If ⌜α⌝ , ⌜β⌝ are non-co-ordinatively linked (e.g., in adjacent
      sentences), then the time relations a <u>after</u> b must be marked,
      if world knowledge permits a <u>before</u> b, a <u>after</u> b, a <u>simulta-
      neous</u> b, and a <u>contained in</u> b.

These rules are very tentative, and we will not try to justify them
here. But they clearly illustrate the principle.

We will now see how principles of this sort are used to solve the
specific communicative problems a learner may be faced with. The following examples and analyses are taken from Klein, 1981a(cf. also HDP,
1979: chapter 2). The learner in this case is a Spanish worker who has
no tense marking and an extremely restricted lexicon. More specifically,
his only expressions for time intervals and time relations are single
words like <u>Stunde</u> (hour), <u>Jahr</u> (year), <u>heute</u> (today), as well as some

---

[1] The signs ⌜   ⌝ are used to quote concatenations of object-language
expressions and meta-language expressions.

numbers which he uses to refer to years. So, when faced with the problem of communicating a complex event with a rich temporal structure,
such as telling a narrative, he is essentially dependent on discourse
principles. Indeed, a careful inspection of his utterances shows that
he uses discourse rules most systematically and economically. His
strategy may be roughly described as follows:

(5) Introduce a time interval a as a first reference time by an expression α, let β, γ, δ ... follow in such a way that not b
after g, not g after d, ... That is, take the time of event a as
a reference time for event b, that of b as a reference time
for g, etc., where the relation is <u>before</u> or <u>simultaneous</u>; if
this is impossible, introduce a new basic reference time.

The best way to explain the functioning of this strategy is probably
to consider how it works in his texts. The first example is the beginning of one of his most marvellous stories:

(6) In erste Jahr ich komme in Urlaub, in Madrid, eine Frau
In first year I   come on vacation, in Madrid, (there was) a woman

naja (wie) du groß, (wie) ich, nee (wie) du. Ich komme,
well (as) you tall, (as) I , no (as) you. I   come

ja, hier (deutet auf eine Stelle) Frau, Kollege nicht verstehen,
yes, here (pointing to a spot) woman , colleague not understand

Frau nicht verstehen; y meine Frau sage: "Name P..., esa
woman not understand; y my   wife say: "Name P..., esa

mujer es alemana o francesa!" Ich sage: "guten Tag", buenas
mujer es alemana o francesa!" I   say: "good day", buenas

tardes; y (zu) Kollege spreche Frau: "wieviel Uhr Zug Paris?"
tardes; y (to) colleague speak woman: "what   time train Paris?"

Kollege spreche: "no te comprendo", nicht verstehen, no te comprendo
colleague speak: "no te comprendo", not understand, no te comprendo

nicht verstehen. Ich ...
not   understand. I ...

What he does here is to introduce one temporal interval "last year, when I was on vacation in Madrid", and within this interval, a second, more specific one is introduced by the rheme of the first utterance: "there was a woman", or "I met a woman" or "I saw a woman". And this interval is then the starting point of the following chain of events; at no point is the relation after or simultaneous violated; hence, the whole story can run through without it being necessary to introduce any explicit new reference time.

The second example is much more ambitious in this respect. He is comparing the school system at different times in Spain:

(7) ("Und wo sind Sie zur Schule gegangen?") - ja, (als ich) klein
     ("And where did you go to school?)   - well, (when I) little

     (war) - nicht viel Schule. Heute - hundert Prozent besser
     (was) - not much school.   Today - hundred percent better

     Spanien. Mein Sohn, zehn Jahre - immer Schule, alle Schule.
     Spain . My   son, ten years - always school, all school.

     Ich vielleicht zehn Jahre - fort, arbeite, verstehn? (...)
     I   perhaps   ten years - away, work, understand?

     Heute - vier Schule neu, mein Dorf. Ich klein Kind - eine
     Today - four school new, my village. I little child - one

     Schule vielleicht hundert Kinder. Heute vielleicht ein Chef o
     school perhaps one hundred children. Today perhaps one boss o

     maestro ("Lehrer") - vielleicht zwanzig Kinder o fünfundzwanzig
     maestro ("teacher") - perhaps twenty children o twenty-five

     Kinder; ich Kind - vielleicht hundert Kinder alle Tag.
     children. I child - perhaps one hundred children all day.

Here, he first introduces a reference time "when I was a child" and says how the situation was then. In the second pattern he switches to another time, "today", contrasts the situation now to the former one and illustrates this with the example of his son. He then switches back again to the past, and this reference time has to be re-introduced; he does this with Ich vielleicht zehn Jahre - when I was about ten years old; and this constant back and forth goes on until the end of his long explanation.

These two examples may suffice to illustrate how he overcomes the problems of expressing temporality in the absence of tense markers and most adverbials and are remarkable examples of the organisation of information in discourse (cf. chapter 5). He just makes the most systematic use of a discourse strategy based on discourse rules; these rules play a role in any expression of temporality but they are less apparent in fully-fledged language use, as compared to the overt tense expressions.

7.5 Summary

In the preceding sections we have outlined numerous but by no means all aspects of reference to people, space and time which constitute specific acquisition problems. Special emphasis has been given to the internal communicative functioning of a learner variety at a given point in time, since an appropriate understanding of the acquisition process, its internal systematicity and the forces which drive it seems hardly possible without understanding how the given intermediate systems are used to satisfy (or not to satisfy) the communicative needs of their users.

7.6 Data collection

In principle, all types of data which we are planning to collect can successfully be used to investigate reference to people, space and time. In practice, their suitability depends on the particular aspects of the problem to be analyzed.

Generally speaking, for each of the three sub-topics we should have data for comprehension and production, and from more and less controlled situations, i.e., data which are as close as possible to authentic, unrecorded interaction vs data which are closer to laboratory situations. A cross-classification would lead to four types of data, but in practice, the possibility of studying comprehension in fully uncontrolled situations is rather limited, and we will neglect it in what follows. So, for each of the three sub-topics described in this chapter, we should have the following three types of data:

(a) Complex verbal actions which are what we termed "authentic" in

2.5.1, or which, although controlled, can be supposed to reflect pertinent aspects of authentic interaction (we will term these "complex verbal action").

(b) More strongly controlled data focussing on production ("semi-controlled production").

(c) More strongly controlled data focussing on comprehension ("semi-controlled comprehension").

In what follows, we will indicate some possibilities of (a) - (c) for each of the three sub-topics. Needless to say, this does not preclude other possibilities, nor does it preclude that those suggested here for one sub-topic could not be successfully used for another one as well.

Reference to people

(a) Complex verbal action. The first source are selections from play scenes: this type of simulation regularly involves reference to numerous persons and also permanent deictic shift. As the play scene is video-recorded it will be possible also to ascertain, at least partially, the role of para-linguistic devices in establishing and maintaining reference to persons.

A secondary source are narratives within (audio-recorded) interviews, which offer less interesting deictic reference (in the narrower sense) but possibly more anaphoric reference.

(b) Semi-controlled production. Film watching, and some of the experiments outlined in 8.3.4 (e.g., verbalizations of picture-sequences) involve the informant having to focus on changing actors, to whom reference must be made, or on different actions of the same actor(s), for whom reference must be maintained.

(c) Semi-controlled comprehension. A productive technique will be ad hoc oral translation from selected, orally presented texts in the target language.

Reference to space

(a) Complex verbal action. Room descriptions, apartment descriptions, description of complex objects (e.g., machines, bikes, etc.), route

directions. Depending on the specific situation, they could either be
video- or audio-taped (for more details on this, cf. 5.3).

(b) Semi-controlled production. The most productive technique here is
likely to be stage directions, such as those described in 7.3.2.2.
A small scene involving all sorts of spatial rearrangements is
acted for the informant, who then is asked to instruct a third
person to replicate the actions. This schema can easily be modi-
fied in various ways, e.g., by asking the informant to do something and to describe it simultaneously.

(c) Semi-controlled comprehension. There are two major possibilities
here: ad hoc translations, which will be particulary important
for reference to more abstract space, and a variant of the technique described under (b): instructions are given in the target
language, and the informant is asked to perform them.

Reference to time

(a) Complex verbal action. Here again, narratives can be used, but they
usually only include reference to past time. Reference to the
present (and often to the past) can easily be obtained by asking
for the informants' living conditions or their situation at work.
Reference to future time is more difficult to obtain. One possibility is asking for future plans (short-term: "What will you do
next weekend?" or long-term: "Will you go back to your country?")
or future events (the results of next week's football matches, etc.).

(b) Semi-controlled production. The techniques used to elicit reference
to persons should be equally suitable here. A further technique
which can be prepared in such a way that it elicits reference to
all times is the retelling in the TL of stories given in the SL.

(c) Semi-controlled comprehension. Ad hoc translations, as before, or
telling a (temporally richly structured) story or event in the TL
with the following conversation about this story or event in the
SL.

8. Data Collection and Preparation of Data for Analysis

8.1 Introduction

This project is conceived as an empirical study. Its outcome will largely depend on whether the five teams involved will be able to obtain the appropriate amount of good, reliable and comparable data.

In this chapter, we will discuss how the necessary data will be elicited, recorded and prepared for further analysis. There is no sharp borderline between the various elicitation techniques that we intend to apply: it will be convenient, however, to discuss them in relation to the three main methods of data recording - audio-recording, video-recording and field notes - as these correspond to a large extent to the three main types of activity envisaged: the audio "session" (cf. 8.3), the video "session" (cf. 8.4), and observation (cf. 8.5). Practical considerations, such as the periodicity of "sessions", and their overall structure, will be discussed in 8.2. In 8.7, we will give general guidelines for the transcription of data, and, in 8.8, a description of some optional data collection techniques.

Before turning to these points in detail, a few general remarks are in order, which hold equally for all methods of collecting data from informants used in this project.

(a) We are dealing with four types of informants (cf. 2.3): the native speaker group, from whom data will be collected twice during the field work phase of the project; the initial learner group, from whom data will be collected three times; the long residence group, from whom data will be collected six times; and the main sample, the longitudinal group, from whom data will be collected (at least) thirty times.

This programme immediately raises two practical problems: the first is simply organizational: each national team will have to adhere to a relatively strict time schedule in order to fit in all the data-collection sessions (cf. 8.2); the second one is much more fundamental: the longitudinal informants (especially) must feel that it is worth their while to be observed and recorded systematically over a period of thirty months.

This chapter deals with data collection, and not data giving; i.e., we approach the problem here essentially from the point of view of the researcher. Motivation of informants will be discussed in detail in chapter 9. We will simply outline here the type of rapport to be created with the informants which, we think, represents what we can do to minimize the danger of informants "dropping out":

- the researcher is an observer, but not a neutral observer; he is interested, both professionally and personally, in the phenomenon of working in a foreign country, and of using a foreign language;
- the researcher should be seen to be interested. If the informant should need help, help should be forthcoming, be it in terms of availability outside scheduled meetings, or in terms of solving concrete problems. If the informant proposes an activitiy or gives an invitation, this should be accepted if at all possible: the researcher may also feel that it is useful, or agreeable, to invite informants to dinner, or propose excursions, etc.;
- the informant should see the point of the regular meetings, and should be briefed, as far as possible, as to the reasons for having the next meeting, and what kind of activity in relation to these reasons the researcher proposes. It should also be made clear to informants that it is they that have the expert knowledge.

The researcher is thus an observer, and should become a confidant, and an enabler. We have already mentioned in 2.3 that regular contact with informants, and the type of attitude outlined here (which, we hope, will ensure regular contact), will produce a strong control effect. We have taken measures to "control" the control effect, but we feel that it is the price we have to pay to undertake this kind of longitudinal study at all.

(b) As was stated in 2.5, SSLA is language acquisition in communication

- mainly in everyday interaction with the social environment, and
to a lesser extent by one-way communication (TV, radio, newspapers).
This communication, therefore, must ideally be our primary data
source. That is, the data should be representative of this communication and the various factors involved in it. This does not mean,
however, that it would be sufficient to record selections from
everyday interaction, even where this is possible, since not all
relevant factors are immediately manifest in this "recorded performance". For example, it usually gives no immediate evidence about
what the informant felt, his attitudes, what he as speaker intended
to say with a particular word or construction, what he as listener
understood from the total input, what the differences in background
knowledge were. In other words, recording "authentic communication"
- communication which is most typical for the learner's everyday
interaction with his social environment - is fundamental, but it
has to be completed by other kinds of data.

(c) Turning now to "authentic communication", we are simply faced with
the problem that, as a rule, it cannot be recorded. Foreign workers
interact with their co-workers, with their neighbours, with shop-
owners, with people in authority. Academic researchers do not belong to their everyday social environment. Informants rarely stand
in front of a microphone, and even more rarely a video-camera, and
the verbal tasks they have to solve in their daily communication
are usually not to outline their moral norms to people more or less
alien to them, or to play little scenes from their lives. There is
no ideal way to overcome this "observer's paradox" (Labov). We have
to apply various methods, each of which will correctly represent
some aspects of authentic communication and will distort others,
to an extent unknown to us. Therefore, for all topics to be studied
in the project, a combination of various data types will be necessary.

(d) Collecting data for a specific purpose always embodies two risks,
namely having not enough and having too much data. The first point
is obvious. It has to be kept in mind, however, that "not enough"
has to be seen in relation to a specific topic; that is, having a

large amount of recorded conversation does not mean that we would
have enough data for background knowledge. The other point - having
too much data - is much less obvious, but no less important for the
practical success of a project with a limited time span, limited
working capacities and clearly defined aims that have to be
attained within that time and with those capacities.

   To illustrate what this means in practice for this project
it may suffice to mention two points. The main group of informants
is observed over thirty months; suppose this would result in 100
hours of video-taped interaction per SL-TL pair (20 per informant).
Looking once through these data would take 12.5 days - under the
unrealistic assumption that somebody is able to watch eight hours
of video-recorded interaction per day during almost a fortnight.
Now, the analysis of only one aspect (e.g., feedback eliciting and
giving) requires at least five repetitions if the analysis is not
to be completely superficial; it also involves playing back and
slow motion. As we have allowed ourselves about eighteen months
for data analysis (cf. 2.3), we will have to adopt a restrictive
attitude in general, and in particular, try to calculate and to
select severely the data needed for further analysis as soon as
they come in. That is, if it is not possible to restrict recording
of data in a way which would be appropriate to the size of the
project, this restriction would be made before the analysis phase;
the data preparation protocol given in the annexe to this chapter
will be extremely important in this respect.

(e) Since the project is planned as a comparative study, the data must
be comparable across the five groups. This concerns the amount of
data (at least the minimal amount collected in each group), the
elicitation techniques, the way in which they are stored (and pre-
selected for analysis), and finally the transcription systems.
The two last points are less problematic; but it may be that
differences in local situations will lead to differences concerning the two first points. It may be, for example, that specific
techniques are difficult to use with some informant groups while
being very fruitful for others. How problems of this sort are to

be solved cannot be planned in advance. But they may result in co-ordinated changes in the data collection schedule.

Recapitulating the main points of this general outline, we have seen that the data collection techniques and the methods of observation used in the project should have the following qualities:

(a)   they should be agreeable, and meaningful, to the informants;

(b) & (c) they should be valid: i.e., the data and observations they yield should reflect in as unbiased a way as possible the phenomena under investigation;

(d)   they should be productive: i.e., the amount of relevant data obtained should be as high as possible whilst involving as little time, effort and equipment as possible;

(e)   they should be reliable: i.e., yield comparable data irrespective of who the individuals (investigator and informant) involved are.

To these, we must add another quality: the data-collection techniques should be ethical (cf. 9.4).

These qualities are of course partially contradictory: it is therefore necessary to employ a combination of different methods and techniques which will reconcile them as far as possible.

8.2 Practical organization of data collection

In this section we will try to define, from a practical point of view, the common core of data collection which will be undertaken by all the teams involved in the project. This does not, of course, prevent any team carrying out additional work with the techniques described in 8.3 to 8.5, or from using other techniques (cf. 8.8). Indeed, the situation in some countries may contribute to making such extra work highly interesting, giving valuable results.

8.2.1 Longitudinal group (LG), long residence group (LRG) and initial learner group (ILG).

It is planned to interview not only the LG, but also the LRG and the IRG at the outset of the project. Those teams working with a LG and a LRG are, of course, dealing with informants with different

biographical characteristics. For those teams working with a LG and an
ILG, on the other hand, an initial effort will have to be made to find
a large number of informants with similar biographical characteristics.
We will discuss this latter case here (although the practical implications for the first months of the project are the same in either case).

There will be time (at least two months, and preferably more) before the actual start of data collection for teams to become acquainted
with the field, and to prospect for informants. For the teams working
with a LG and an ILG, it may prove helpful to cast the net wide at the
beginning: that is, efforts should be made to interview once any
potential informant. In this way, the teams will have a minimal empirical base (contacts and one interview) for selecting those informants
to whom the longitudinal study will be proposed, and those to whom
three interviews over a period of two and a half years will be proposed.
Criteria for selection will include objective elements - linguistic and
biographical - and also subjective elements: does a given informant
seem interested enough to accept being systematically observed over a
long period?

The practical result of this, for all countries, is that the first
month (ideally), or the first two months (more practically) will be
marked by an extremely large number of interviews to be carried out
(cf. 8.6). The TL researcher may count on an average of one interview
per day, for example. However, this period of intense activity will
result in the accomplishment of the first short encounter for all types
of informant. We return in detail to the first encounters in 9.3:
Motivation of Informants.

8.2.2 "Authentic" data collection and "project-specific" data collection. We described "authentic interaction" in 2.5.1 as interactions representative of informants' everyday life. Collection of data from
"authentic interactions" is therefore to a certain extent dependent on
the individual circumstances, and willingness, of the informant. For
accompanying observation, for example (cf. 8.5.5), we cannot force ourselves on an informant; we are dependent on him proposing that we
accompany, or on him accepting our offer of accompanying. This type of

observation will, however, be of immense value to the project, and, if
successful, will strengthen the rapport between researcher and informant.
All efforts should therefore be made so that this activity not only happens,
but happens regularly.

One type of observation which is not directly dependent on informants,
and which is recommended for all researchers on the project is participant
observation. Here, the researcher spends some time in the field - preferably working - in order to gain personal experience, not of a given informant's
daily life and linguistic interactions, but of the type of situation this
type of foreign worker often encounters (cf. 8.5.4).

We are hoping to achieve a balance between the amount of data collected from authentic interactions and project-specific interactions. This
means that at least every second month, data should be obtained from accompanying observation (or neutral observation, cf. 8.8.1, or, failing
these, from a simulated interaction with a TL-speaker other than researchers, cf. 2.5.2). For participant observation, we envisage that all researchers on the project will do at least one week during the data-
collection period, and preferably more, to the extent that time constraints allow.

By "project-specific" data collection, we mean the actual encounters
we will propose to the informants. It is worth recalling (cf. 2.5.1)
that the term project-specific encounter is used to refer to encounters
of a type that informants would not have were they not participating in
this project: the distinction project-specific vs authentic does not
therefore imply that interactions with researchers are not authentic.
As we said in 8.1, there will be two encounters with the TL-speakers,
three encounters with the ILG, six encounters with the LRG and thirty
encounters with the LG during the data-collection period.

For this last group, we therefore plan to meet each informant once
a month. This frequency has been decided on for theoretical and practical
reasons. We want to obtain data often enough to be able to trace informants'
acquisition. From this point of view, one month is perhaps the longest
possible period we can allow ourselves between encounters. However, as
we have said, great efforts will be made to see informants outside the
planned encounters, and especially in accompanying observation. Thus

we expect to see informants more than once a month, and will obtain additional data from these extra meetings in the form of field notes and recordings (cf. 8.5). Furthermore, we will be asking informants to record themselves about four times per year (cf. 8.2.3).

On the other hand, the project-specific encounters are perhaps those where the pedagogic potential of the project is greatest, and we wish to avoid a situation where informants would look forward to frequent, informal "language tutorials". From this point of view, one month is perhaps the smallest possible period we can allow ourselves between planned encounters.

Practically speaking, reducing the work load - i.e., having encounters less than once a month - would be easy: it would, however, be unrealistic to expect to be able to fit into the data-collection period more encounters than those envisaged (cf. 8.6). As the schedule stands, there are "critical periods" once every nine months, approximately, where the TL linguist will be doing one interview per working day.

The project-specific encounters are of two types: a shorter, audio-recorded encounter of about an hour and a longer, video-recorded encounter of about two hours. For the LGs, each three-month cycle of the data-collection phase of the project will contain two shorter encounters and one longer one. The data collected for each informant during such a period will therefore consist (very broadly speaking) of two hours' audio-recording, two hours' video-recording and (sometimes) forty minutes' self-recording by the informant, plus data from observation.

The ILGs will be interviewed three times during the data collection phase (audio-recording, about one and a half hours). Data obtained from the LRGs will represent the equivalent of two three-month cycles of the longitudinal study. The group of TL-speakers will be interviewed once, will participate in one film-watching session (cf. 8.2.3), and their everyday interaction with informants will be observed.

8.2.3 Project-specific encounters

8.2.3.1 Pretexts and reasons. As we said in 8.1, the researcher's attitude is one of professional and personal interest, and of willingness to help. This is the overall reason why he is working on the project.

In the longitudinal study, researchers will have to convince informants that it is important that they meet on a month to month basis. The informants should therefore feel that the next meeting is taking place _for a reason_, and be briefed about it. This reason would then serve at the meeting as a pretext for engaging in conversation.

It would be unrealistic to attempt to imagine precisely what reasons will be motivating for a given group of researchers/informants. However, a possible way of establishing regular contacts in the early months will be outlined in the sample schedule of 8.6.2. Here, the reasons evoked could be: mutual information about the project and about the informant; film-watching; self-recording.

Overall, the reasons given in the sample schedule of 8.6 are purely indicative. However, the principle should be clear. We cannot expect informants simply to turn up every month and tell us what has happened to them (the more so as ideally, no month should go by without seeing the informant ouside the regular encounters). Thus no encounter should end with the researcher saying "See you next month", but rather "Next month we must talk about so and so", or "Next month, if you wish, we can do so and so".

Two pretexts for meeting will, however, be used throughout the period of data-collection: self-recording (about ten times) and film-watching (about three times). As both require some organization, they will be briefly discussed here. Finally, some other possible pretexts will be mentioned.

Self-recording. Self-recording with an audio-tape can serve two purposes:

(a) it can be used by the informant as a "diary" to recall events and impressions, his movements during a week, etc.;

(b) it can be used to collect samples of the informant's use of the TL in interactions when researchers are absent, and when their influence on events is therefore minimal.

It should be possible to persuade all informants to accomplish (a) during the data-collection period, more especially if they record

information in their SL to start off with. This information may then
serve to initiate conversation in the following regular encounter. One
type of event which will prove very fruitful in the video encounters
incorporating play acting, is any interaction the informant has had in
the TL and which he found difficult or unsuccessful. We can then let
him elaborate on it by asking who was present, what were the goals of the
participants, what was the interlocutor's status, what went wrong, etc.
This would constitute a natural prelude to the grounding phase preceding play acting: the interaction would, of course, be the subject
matter for the scene (cf. 8.4.2).

If it proves possible to accomplish (b), which is more likely after
the first year of data collection, we may obtain relatively authentic
data, perhaps from interactional events to which researchers would have
no, or only limited, access (cf. Becker and Perdue, 1982). However,
there are obvious practical problems in recording interactions with TL-
speakers. Concealed recording is not to be recommended, as it can cause
harm both to the informant and to the project in terms of public confidence. It is also unethical. Asking people's consent to be recorded may
(depending on their country, their status or the situation) result in
refusal. This type of recorded interaction may therefore be difficult
to obtain, and hence cannot constitute an essential part of the data
we wish to analyze.

Film watching. We plan to invite informants of the LG to watch short
film sequences about three times during the data-collection period: at
the beginning, towards the middle, and at the end. The same sequences
will be shown to informants at the beginning and at the end for comparative purposes. These sequences will also be shown to the NSG and
to the LRG.

The informant is shown carefully selected film sequences of typical
communication patterns in the target culture and language. The informant
is then asked to recall or reconstruct what he was shown, and is asked
to interpret the beliefs, intentions, actions, linguistic behaviour and
social relations of the interactants in the film. This technique is
employed to explore how the informant's perception and understanding is
dependent on his background assumptions (cf. 4.3.2).

   The criterion of selection for the film should therefore be "interaction and speech typical of target culture, preferably involving things
which are fairly culture specific".

   When a film has been found which may be suitable for the project,
the next task is to choose two short sequences from it. One should be
such that the interpretation of the actions is to a relatively small
extent dependent on the understanding of what is said. The other should
be such that the interpretation is to a large extent dependent on the
ability to understand what the interactants on the screen say.

   The film-watching session with an informant can be divided into
three steps:

(a) First show the film sequence to the informant to comment on what
    he has seen. Follow up the informant's spontaneous interpretations
    (e.g., "They're having an argument" or "This is bad manners")
    with questions like "How can you tell (e.g., that they're having
    an argument)?" and so on.

(b) You now ask questions prompting the informant more systematically
    for interpretations of the setting, the events and episodes, the
    persons and their roles, relations and socio-economic status, their
    attitudes and emotions, and language and markers of speech: "What
    do you think they're up to now?"; "Would you say that his way of
    conduct/language is correct/appropriate?"; "Where (in Sweden...
    in what part of the town...) do you think the people in the film
    live?"; "What job do you think he has?"; "What is the atmosphere
    like in this scene... How did she take what he said?"; "What sort
    of mood is he in, do you think?"; "Why do you think she is saying
    that?"; "How do target language speakers generally say that?";
    "When and where can you see and hear things like this?", etc.

   It is also possible to ask informants to take the point of
view of characters in the film by asking questions like: "What
would you feel like if you were the one who entered that room?";
"Let's say you are the mother in this family waiting for your
husband to come home after work...". You can then test the informant's knowledge of different speech styles and conventionalized
role expectations in the target culture by following up the last

utterance with "...How would you greet him?". As we will see, there are many parallels between these questions and the techniques used in role-play (cf. 8.8.3).

(c) The film watching session should then lead into general conversation on differences between the source and target cultures. In this way, the film constitutes a pretext for the rest of the session.

Other pretexts. These two groups of pretexts are obviously only suggestions. What motivates their mention here is firstly, that they give an indication of the type of rapport we wish to build up with informants (cf. 9.3) and secondly, that the type of activities listed may indeed serve to make the monthly encounters agreeable for informants and researchers, as well as providing relevant data. Use of these pretexts would lead to the monthly encounters being seen not only as an opportunity to talk, but as an opportunity to do things together while talking.

A first group of activities could be termed "do it yourself". If an informant is doing work on his flat, offer to help. Explain, or have explained, how to change the tyre on a car or bicycle. Show how you prepare your food, learn how informants prepare their food. Other activities which may be possible with some informants are: beauty, make-up, hairdressing; sewing and knitting; care of plants, gardening.

The other group of activities is games. Be taught how to play the card games, or dominoes, etc. of the source countries. Explain some target country games and play them.

These types of activity will elicit speech which is relevant for all four major topics of investigation. The success of giving and receiving the instructions involved (i.e., understanding or not) can be checked against the manipulations to be performed. The situations in which these activities will take place is moreover "co-operative" in the sense of 4.3.2. The themes of the activities are relatively precise and involve the linguistic organization of possibly complex information (one could imagine, for example, learning about the game of chess towards the end of the data-collection period); this is directly relevant for the thematic structure of utterances. Such activities systematically involve reference to space (cf. 7.6). Finally, as many of them involve a relatively specialized vocabulary, which will very probably not be known in the TL, they should elicit a wealth of compensatory strategies (the "detour devices" of 6.3).

8.2.3.2 <u>Long and short encounters</u>. The informant and researchers will therefore meet once per month, for a reason. The reason, as in the examples given in 8.2.3.1, serves as a pretext for the conversation. Other activities, such as play acting and small <u>ad hoc</u> experiments, will be built into the conversation in ways outlined in 8.3 and 8.4.

The short encounters will consist basically of conversation, and the experiments incorporated into them can be loosely defined as activities which interrupt the natural flow of conversation, for a reason. As we have said, these encounters will last approximately one hour, and will be audio-recorded (or video-recorded, if circumstances permit this).

The long encounters will be video-recorded (with the exception of some passages, cf. 8.4.4), and will, in much the same way as the short encounters, start with a conversation. Here, the pretext for the conversation will often be the informant's self-recording, assuming this is possible. These encounters will be prolonged either by play acting, or by experiments which require video-recording (apartment descriptions, spatial relationships, cf. 8.4).

A three month cycle would therefore have the following form:

Month minus 1. Brief informant for next meeting. Prepare any
                materials necessitated by the briefing, and the
                type of informal experiments envisaged.
Month 1 (a)   Short encounter: 1 hour's conversation starting from
                the pretext and incorporating, if possible, the planned
                informal experiments.
        (b)   Listen to recording, select passages for transcription
                in relation to the topics (data preparation protocol).
        (c)   as month minus 1.
Month 2 (a)   as month 1
        (b)   as month 1

(c)   Brief informant on what aspects of the next month it
        would be interesting to (self-) record. Prepare experi-
        ments, if any, to be video-recorded.

Month 3 (a)   Long encounter. One hour's conversation, taking the
        informant's recording as a pretext. Let the conversation
        take its course and then <u>go back</u> to any interesting
        episode the informant has mentioned in order to do play
        acting. Or: explain and carry out the prepared experi-
        ments.

(b)   as month 1

(c)   as month minus 1.

This schedule would be repeated five times, minimally, and twenty
times, maximally, for a given researcher. In one of the "minimal"
cycles, arrangements would be made for participant observation. Accompanying observation would ideally happen systematically.

8.3 Short encounters

8.3.1 <u>Conversation</u>. As we said in 8.2.3.2, the short encounters will
consist basically of conversation, i.e., a type of verbal interaction
which is as close as possible under the given circumstances to everyday conversations the informant would have with his social environment,
and is loosely and cautiously guided by the interviewers (cf. 8.3.2.2).
The informant should be made to feel not too disturbed by the fact that
he is being recorded and is talking to people from a different social
environment. He should feel free to display his full competence, both
in respect to verbal skills and to subject matter. Whenever possible,
the conversation should follow its own internal dynamics. However, careful planning will be needed from the interviewer, who has not only to
initiate the conversation, but to reactivate it if it begins to tail
off, and to introduce those topics that should be talked about in order
to get particular information.

The function of these conversations is to provide us with actual
manifestations of informants' communicative competence in the TL, to
obtain information about their background and present life in the host

country, and to give interviewers the opportunity of obtaining more
precise linguistic data by means of ad hoc experiments.

To fulfill the first function, the interview should include
different types of verbal interaction, in particular:

(a) dialogues, and especially question-answer sequences;

(b) narratives, both about personal events from the informant's life,
     and fictitious events;

(c) descriptions which lead the informant to handle complex amounts
     of information;

(d) argumentative sequences, which would provoke the expression of
     complex relations (cause, condition, intention, etc.).

The topics suggested for discussion (cf. 8.3.3) are chosen with a
view to provoking to a greater or lesser extent, these types of interaction.

8.3.2 Implementation

8.3.2.1 External parameters: place, time, participants. The setting
should be chosen to help the informants feel relaxed and self-confident.
This probably does not correspond to the majority of their everyday
interactions in the TL, but is rather a situation where there is a minimal amount of external constraint (stress, time, etc., cf. chapter 4)
on their opportunity to display their full communicative skills in the
TL. Thus, at least the first interviews should be made in an environment which is familiar, and where they feel they have equal status.

A particularly good place for conversations with adult informants
is the informant's home where his social role is at least partially
defined: he is the host. In later stages, it is also possible to choose
more neutral places, but again, care has to be taken that the informant
is not made to feel too uncomfortable.

It may, however, not be appropriate to hold meetings with young
people in their homes (a) because there are normally too many people
present (parents, brothers and sisters), and (b) because they often cannot express their opinions freely in the presence of their parents. The
pilot studies showed that young people are ready to come to the university.

In order to make them familiar with the place it is useful to arrange, first, an informal meeting with a larger group during which potential informants can become acquainted with the rooms, the technical equipment, etc.

For the right time, two factors are important. Firstly, most foreign workers are under a considerable work load, and immediately after a day's work at the conveyer belt or in a cement factory (or queuing in the unemployment office), they may not be enthusiastic about holding a long conversation. Secondly, neither the informant nor the interviewer should be under time pressure. There are two reasons for this: it distorts the natural dynamics of a conversation and may cause an abrupt stop at interesting points, and at least in some cultures, it would be extremely impolite to stop an ongoing conversation for external reasons.

Both reasons do not allow us to fix the duration of an interview in advance. The pilot studies have shown that one hour is a good average time. Each interview should consist of three phases: a warming-up phase (pre-interview) with small-talk about everyday events, the main interview in which the interviewer introduces the topics he is interested in, starting with the pretext, and a final period of relaxation and leave taking (post-interview).

Normally speaking, a native speaker of both SL and TL will be present. The TL speaker should act as the main interviewer and the SL speaker should monitor the recording. Having more than two interviewers is unwise since the informant may feel dominated. Certain constraints must be observed with informants from some cultures: for Turks, interviews with female informants should be made by female interviewers or, if the husband is present, by a female and a male researcher. Similarly, it is preferable to have at least one male interviewer in the case of male informants from some countries, e.g. Morocco.

In principle, the interview will be held in the target language. The pilot interviews suggest, however, that it is absolutely impossible to stick systematically to this language as long as a SL speaker is present. Even if asked several times to communicate in the TL, the learner will immediately switch to his mother language when meeting the first difficulty and appeal to the SL interviewer for translation. This does not mean, however, that the presence of a SL interviewer is unnecessary:

(a) He should be present in the warming up phase to make the informant feel more at ease.

(b) He has to be present in part of the main interview if the level of TL competence of the learner is low. If the informant only knows twenty words and three constructions, it is simply impossible to hold a one hour conversation. But even here, the learner should, if possible, be left alone with the TL interviewer for a short time because otherwise it is difficult to get any idea of his competence.

(c) In later stages of acquisition it seems useful to have the interviewer knowing the source language nearby (not in the same room) so that he can be called (e.g., in the case of a communication breakdown), or to have him participate in part of the interview (e.g., if one wants to ask what the learner meant with a specific utterance, and for self-confrontation in general).

8.3.2.2 <u>Guiding the conversation</u>. The interview should be as close as possible to everyday conversation, but at the same time, it should provide the required information. This requires very cautious and careful guiding of the conversation by the interviewers. The following points are particularly important:

(a) The informant must have the feeling that there is enough time.

(b) Initiatives on the informant's side should not only be tolerated, but encouraged; the interviewer should not interrupt him too often and give him enough feedback.

(c) The interviewer should introduce a thematic frame, that is, he must not just ask a question but briefly explain what it is about and, if necessary, give an example (without suggesting an answer); then he should leave the floor to the informant.

(d) The interviewer should show that he is really listening and trying to understand what the informant wants to communicate.

(e) The transition to a new topic the interviewer wants to bring up should be organic and the interviewer should have clearly in mind what this topic is.

(f) The interviewer should speak clearly and distinctly (without ex-
     aggerating, of course).
(g) He should include into the conversation other people who may be
     present, but should prevent these people from dominating the con-
     versation.
(h) He should use the informant's SL only if it is unavoidable, and
     should prevent longer passages in this language.
(i) He should show involvement (actually, he should be involved) and
     express his own attitudes and opinions in a non-agressive manner.

All this requires considerable effort on the part of the interviewers.
It also requires preparation. In particular, a list of topics to be
touched upon at the appropriate occasion has to be worked out beforehand and memorized. We turn to these topics now.

8.3.3 Topics to be discussed. As we said in 8.2.3.2, the first part of
the long encounters (the video "session") will be similar to the short
encounters (the audio "session"). The following indicative list of
topics to be discussed therefore holds for both types of encounter.
Activities and topics which are more specific to the long encounters
will be described in 8.4.

The early encounters. For all types of L2 informant (LG, ILG, LRG) the
early interviews should consist of an exchange of the same type of information between researchers and informants.

  From the researchers' side, it is important to inform (potential)
informants of what the main characteristics of the project are, in order
to motivate them to play a role in the project, and to explain to them
what this role might be. It is also important to obtain general information about the informant's social and linguistic background, present
situation, etc. Both types of information are set out in detail in
chapter 9.

Suggested topics to be discussed. The main topic of conversation in a
given interview will be the "pretext" for the interview (cf. 8.2.3) and
will be worked out by individual teams on a month to month basis.

However, some of the linguistic topics of investigation require that certain topics of conversation be touched upon regularly, and we will briefly mention them here.

Work, home, social relations. As we are following the development of learners' vocabulary in these three areas (cf. 6.2.1), it will be important to return to them at regular intervals. When they are not the pretext for an interview, they should be evoked in the pre- or post-interview.

The urban environment. It is to be expected that many of the informants will come from rural backgrounds. The theme of the urban environment, and the difficulties that such informants may have in adapting to it, should prove to be interesting, the more so as experience of this environment will in all likelihood be shared by researchers and informants. Furthermore, two of our major research topics concern reference to space and reference to time, both of which should be systematically provoked in a conversation about getting around town (the time it takes to get from x to y, the best way of getting from x to y, etc.). Route directions may thus be naturally introduced into the conversation.

The telephone. Although it is unlikely that all informants will have a telephone, virtually all informants will have at some period to use the telephone (which is in any case part and parcel of the urban environment). Conversation about use of the telephone will in itself be instructive, and may in addition provide a pretext for acting out a scene in which the face to face integration of contextual and uttered information is not possible.

Abstract ideas. Well-tried topics (sex, freedom, violence, death ....) should be introduced into the conversation if at all possible, although it must be remembered that some of these topics will be taboo for some informants. Talk about these topics is a plausible means of solving the "observer's paradox" (Labov), as well as providing subject matter which involves argumentation (cf. 8.3.1).

The project. We are briefing informants on what our role in the project is. It would seem advisable to return from time to time (every year, say) explicitly to the subject of the project in order to have informants' opinions on how it is developing, and in order to ensure their continued co-operation.

Self recording, film watching. These two pretexts for interviews were discussed in 8.2.3.1. Conversation about informants' own recordings, or about a film sequence that both researchers and informants have watched, should prove fruitful in ascertaining informants' attitudes and emotions as regards the TL and its speakers, and give rise to argumentative discussions.

8.3.4 Experiments

8.3.4.1 General remarks. As we said in 8.3.1 the conversations will also serve to gather data by more experimental techniques. Inserting these techniques into a conversation may well interrupt the natural flow of the conversation; care and preparation is therefore required both in introducing such techniques and in steering the conversation back to a more spontaneous course after the task is done.

The type of informant we are working with on this project precludes the use of standardized testing or formal laboratory situations. "Experimental techniques" means, in the context of the project, semi-formal procedures designed to provoke a specific type of linguistic activity in our informants in order to obtain from them additional data in relation to a given topic of investigation. In this way we hope to neutralize some of the many psychological, social and situational parameters that govern an informant's use (or non-use) of TL-material.

Given this very broad description, there is no hard and fast distinction between some of the "experiments" described below, and some of the "topics" described in 8.3.3 ("the urban environment" was mentioned in 8.3.3, and "route directions" appear below, for example). This is a practical consequence of our wish to incorporate different types of activity into an encounter which has some meaning for the informant, and which can develop in as organic a way as possible.

It follows that we cannot predict exactly what (types of) experiments a given informant in a given situation will be prepared to participate in. Although it is highly interesting for us that an informant gives route directions (cf. 8.3.4.2), if he finds the activity pointless it is unproductive for us to insist. However, the experiments described below have been successfully tried out during the pilot year, and attempts will be made to replicate them in all groups and for all informants during the project.

Normally speaking, we will be dealing with one informant per encounter, and the description of the experiments assume that the encounter will take place between this informant, a SL-interviewer and a TL-interviewer. However, the pilot study showed that young people - and especially those who are acquainted with each other outside the project - seem to be more motivated when performing in small groups some of the activities described below. This makes it difficult to isolate and analyse the language behaviour of the individual subject (unless ways are found of preventing the temporarily inactive part of the group from participating nevertheless). However, the extra preparation that this requires, and possible transcription difficulties, are a price worth paying for maintaining high motivation.

8.3.4.2 Some suggested experiments.

(a) Repetition and ad hoc translation. These two extremely simple devices can be worked into the conversation very naturally indeed: the interviewer, not understanding an informant's utterance, asks for a repetition or a SL-translation. (Both repetition and translation can of course be used much more systematically, and are so used in self-confrontation, cf. 8.4.4).

Asking for a translation allows the interviewer to get a closer idea of what the informant intended to say by some word or expression, information which, as we said in 8.1, is vital to all the topics of investigation. What should be particularly kept in mind here is however that in chapter 6: Processes in the Developing Vocabulary, we hypothesized that the learner would use TL lexical items systematically to express a meaning different from that of

the TL: translation is an important means for testing such a hypothesis.

In the French pilot study, it was found that asking for a repetition provoked either a repetition or - very frequently - a reformulation. The reformulation was frequently revealing as to what
the informant had originally intended to say. Both repetitions and
reformulations also gave indications as to the degree of the informant's linguistic awareness; this last point is taken up again
in 8.4.4.

(b) Flat descriptions and route directions. These two types of experiment were described in 5.3. It is worth repeating here that we are
using "apartment" as a mnemonic for the type of experiment first tried
by Linde and Labov (1975), and plan to ask for descriptions of
other locales, such as the work-place.

Depending on the type of informant, it may be possible to
extend these experiments to descriptions of more "abstract" space,
such as the moves of chess, or to carry them out on the telephone,
as this eliminates the contextual information provided by face-to-
face interaction. Route directions may be extended to other settings
than the studio. A possibility successfully accomplished in the
Swedish pilot study was to drive informants to places they had to
go to in town, and record their authentic route directions.

(c) Verbalization of pictures or picture sequences. Here, the informant
is shown a picture, or a sequence of pictures, and asked to comment,
describe the scene or the story, etc. This experiment is in many
ways a less onerous version of film watching (cf. 8.2.3), and can
elicit similar types of data - in particular the effect of the informant's background assumptions on interpretation. In the case
of picture-sequences, the informant's organization of the information contained in the sequence can give relevant data for the
thematic structure of utterances (cf. chapter 5, and Dietrich,
1982).

Another possible use of pictures is to show the informant a
mail-order catalogue and to ask him to give the TL-name of selected
objects. The pictures can be chosen so that the data elicited is
relevant for the more concrete aspects of some of the lexical

domains of chapter 6, home and work, for example.

(d) <u>Parlour games</u>. Depending on the willingness and interest of the
informant, selected games can be introduced, both as a way of
eliciting data, and as a way of varying the tempo of the encounter.

Two possible games for eliciting yes/no questions from the
informant are "twenty questions" and "Botticelli". In the first,
the interviewer thinks of an entity that is either animal, vege-
table or mineral, and gives the relevant category. The informant
then asks up to twenty questions in order to find the entity,
questions to which the interviewer replies either "yes" or "no".
In "Botticelli" the interviewer thinks of a well-known person and
gives that person's initials. The game then proceeds in the same
way as "twenty questions".

These examples are purely indicative, and, as with many parlour games, linguistically limited. Persons and objects will have
to be chosen carefully, moreover, in relation to the cultural background of the informant. However, the essence of these games is
reference to person, place and (present or past) time, and questions, and they would serve as a phase of relaxation in the encounter.

(e) <u>Comprehension</u>. The four activities mentioned here can be used to
test the informant's comprehension more directly. Thus he could be
asked to repeat, or to translate into SL, utterances of the interviewer ("How <u>does</u> one say that in SL?"), or to reconstruct with
pencil and paper a verbal description of a map, or a picture, given
by the interviewer. In the two parlour games mentioned, the informant, having chosen an object or a person, will have to understand
the interviewers' questions in order to be able to answer "yes" or
"no". "Wrong" answers - "no" for "yes" and vice versa - are easily
identified at the end of a turn and can then be discussed.

(f) <u>Self-confrontation</u>. As this technique will be used in a systematic
way in the long encounters, we will discuss it in the following
section. We mention it here simply to remark that <u>ad hoc</u> self-
confrontation is relatively easy to carry out and should be used
when necessary as a means for verifying what the informant

understood, or intended to say.

8.3.4.3 <u>Conclusion</u>. Obviously, the successful accomplishment of experiments such as those described here depends above all on the willingness of the informant. Much will therefore depend on the relationship between informant and interviewer, and on the persuasiveness of the latter in introducing them. It is therefore difficult to give precise indications on how often or under what circumstances these experiments will occur. The rule can only be to have thoroughly prepared the experiments in order to be ready to introduce them at an appropriate moment.

8.4 <u>Long encounters</u>.

8.4.1 <u>Introduction</u>. A long encounter (about 2 hours) with informants will take place every three months, and will make use of video techniques. The form it will take will be essentially that of the short encounter, completed by play acting, video-recorded experiments or self-confrontation. As these extra activities are of an experimental nature, it may perhaps not prove desirable to incorporate other experiments into the interview phase of the encounter.

As we have already described the short encounter in 8.3, we will merely describe the additional activities of the long encounter in this section.

8.4.2 <u>Play acting</u>. The main purpose of play acting is to get the informant to simulate, briefly, some interaction in the TL in which he was a participant. This activity may present some problems for certain types of informant, and will have to be carefully prepared. As with all data collection techniques the informant must be made to <u>see the point</u> of the activity. Here, we will limit ourselves to one possible pretext, which has proved to be efficient when used by the Swedish and English teams. Other teams may wish to use other pretexts.

The <u>pretext</u> for play acting can be one of the situations in the previous month which the informant has logged in his recorded "diary" or even recorded directly (cf. 8.2.3.1) and which posed some communication difficulty in the TL. This recording will constitute the main topic of the interview, thus allowing the interviewer to choose the situation the informant will be persuaded to play. However, once this situation is chosen, the interview should be allowed to continue in a natural way, thus giving about an hour's recorded conversation which is comparable to the recorded data of the other months. At the end of the interview, the interviewer should then go back to the situation, and suggest to the informant that an efficient way of understanding what was unsatisfactory, or difficult, would be to simulate the situation. This will also mean that the informant will be better prepared if the same type of situation should occur again. In order to do this, we need to know who the participants were, their respective status, their respective goals in the interaction.

Grounding. The "grounding" phase of the play scene consists in getting the informant to re-construct as precisely as possible the physical context of the situation: the place, the participants, and their respective positions, the furniture, movements that happened during the situation, etc. The effect desired is that the informant remembers as vividly as possible what the setting was, and furthermore, instructs the interviewer on what furniture to move, where to place himself, whether to stand or sit, what attitude to adopt, etc. In this sense, the grounding phase can be seen as a more natural variant of stage directions (cf. 8.4.3).

Role designation. The grounding phase culminates with role designation, where the interviewer explicitly tells the informant that the participants are now in their roles at the time and place of the event in question. The here and now of the scene to be simulated is thus symbolically marked off from the here and now of the recording studio.

Play scene. The scene then takes place. It is not expected that this will be particularly long - say three to five minutes. It will consist of an uninterrupted improvisation, on the basis of the information established in the preceding discussion, with the informant playing himself, and the interviewer(s) the other participant(s). As was mentioned in 2.5.2, a TL native speaker who has everyday contacts with the informant may be persuaded to come to the studio and simulate such contacts.

Speaker perspective analysis. After the play scene, the interview explicitly brings the participants back to the here and now of the studio.
Discussion of the play scene then takes place: how the informant felt
in his role, what was good or bad, like or unlike the original situation,
etc. This type of analysis should concentrate on how things could have
been done/said otherwise in order that the interaction be more successful, that the informant get his point across better, etc. Once the
analysis is finished to the participants' satisfaction, the encounter
develops into leave-taking, arrangements for next time, etc.

The advantages and disadvantages of this method of data-collection
are similar to those of the "stronger" optional technique of role play
by action interview, and will be discussed together with this latter
technique in 8.8.3.

8.4.3 Other video-recorded experiments

Apartment descriptions. As we said in 5.3, we propose to record (variations
of) apartment descriptions in both the audio and the video "sessions". We
therefore obtain the same activity, accomplished respectively in absentia and in praesentia, and bearing directly on many topics of investigation in chapters 5, 6 and 7.

Stage directions. Here, the TL-interviewer leaves the room, and in his
absence, the SL-interviewer performs a short, silent sketch to the informant, usually involving body movement, or manipulation of objects.

The TL-interviewer then comes back into the room, and the informant instructs him to perform the same actions as the SL-interviewer
has just performed. It goes without saying that this activity should
be prepared by the SL-interviewer independently, i.e., without the TL-
interviewer's prior knowledge.

Examples of possible sketches are given in chapters 5 (the "egg
hiding" sketch) and 7 (the "ashtray" sketch). In the Heidelberg pilot
study, such scenes were imagined with the specific intention of eliciting spatial prepositions - auf, hinter, zwischen, etc. The data resulting had a three-fold interest: use of prepositions, strategies used by

informants to express spatial relationships when such prepositions were not known, and the thematic structuring of utterances.

8.4.4 Self-confrontation

8.4.4.1 Introduction. In self-confrontation, the informant is confronted with an audio- or video-recording of some interaction in which he himself took part, e.g., a conversation or play acting. In the latter case, self-confrontation should not be confused with the speaker perspective analysis of play acting. The speaker perspective analysis takes place immediatly after the play scene, and is designed to obtain extra information about the informant's feelings during it, his attitudes to the other protagonists, how closely the scene corresponded to the real situation it was based on, etc. Self-confrontation is concerned, however, with getting the informant's reactions to the detail of the communicative interaction - was there a misunderstanding here? was something said inappropriately? etc. - and needs at least some preparation on the part of the researcher.

Other-confrontation, as its name suggests, involves confronting the informant with an audio- or video-recording of somebody else, either another informant, or members of the target community. Thus film watching (cf. 8.2.3.1) is a special case of other-confrontation. The idea here is again to obtain the informant's understanding of, and judgement on, various aspects of the interaction: what is going on? what type of people are involved? why did the woman say that? etc.

The techniques involved in both activities are very similar; here, we will concentrate on self-confrontation. Self-confrontation is broadly speaking a metalinguistic activity. This fact provokes three general remarks:

(a) informants will be asked to pay attention to utterances as objects, some of whose aspects they will comment on. This, together with the tension provoked by hearing/seeing recordings of oneself, will contribute to make informants' production different in some aspects from their production in other elicitation techniques (although their production in other techniques is again not necessarily comparable);

(b) given (a), the technique is certain to increase informants' awareness of the TL in general; furthermore, they may (justifiably) try
to benefit from its pedagogic potential. Thus the technique should
be used sparingly, and this will mean that the unease informants
will feel at hearing/seeing themselves may not diminish over time;

(c) the researcher should maximally adapt to the informant's way of
talking about language, and language-related topics, whether the
conversation is held in the SL or the TL. (As far as the TL is
concerned, some indication of this may be obtained from the type
of metalinguistic vocabulary the informant uses, cf. 6.2.3.)

8.4.4.2 <u>Aims of self-confrontation</u>. Self-confrontation is the most
direct technique we have at our disposal for ascertaining the informant's
comprehension of the TL. "Comprehension" is taken here in the broad
sense of understanding the propositional content of utterances, their
illocutionary and perlocutionary effects, differences in background
assumptions leading to misunderstandings, etc. It is also a privileged
means of obtaining informants' attitudes to the TL, their perception
of sociolinguistic norms, of difficulties they find with the TL, etc.

Viewed in this way, it is a technique that is complementary to
play acting, where we attempt to ascertain the emotional and attitudinal
factors underlying successful or unsuccessful interaction with native
TL <u>speakers</u>. Here, we are trying to obtain specific information (to confirm or invalidate a hypothesis, or simply to clear up a doubt) on
specific <u>linguistic</u> (or interactional) phenomena. Self-confrontation is
therefore an elicitation technique which has to be prepared.

Going into more detail on these general aims, we can distinguish
three types of information that can be obtained from self-confrontation:

(a) <u>Ensuring mutual understanding</u>. Whatever the level of analysis, we
wish to be sure that we have understood what the informant meant.
For example, in tracing the semantic processes at work in the informant's developing lexicon, we will need supplementary data to
complete those obtained from the informant's spontaneous output. A
possible way of achieving this is to ask the informant to paraphrase
(in the SL or the TL) the relevant part of his output, to give

"another word meaning the same thing" or "meaning the opposite",
etc. On a more global level, we will need to ask him why, for
example, he answered a question in the way he did, what he was
talking about in a stretch of narrative, etc.

There is another side to the picture. It may turn out that
the informant did not understand some aspect of the investigator's
speech, and this caused him to answer in a surprising way, or
change the subject, etc. It will be of great importance to obtain
supplementary data on the way the informant processes the input:
whether he "switches off" if speech he hears is too fast, right
down to the important words in an utterance (cf. 4.3) that he identifies (correctly or incorrectly) as important for comprehension.
In other words we are also seeking to understand what the informant thought the interlocutor meant.

(b) Informants' attitude to language. Some work (summed up in Meisel,
1981) has been done on the relationship of the informant to the
TL-object, and has resulted in distinctions such as "form-orien-
tated learner" vs "risk-taker", "monitor over- vs under-user",
etc. This work indicates the possibility that at least some of
the communication strategies a learner uses depend on his attitude to the TL-object, and that use of these different strategies
provokes differences in the output.

A stronger hypothesis (cf. the Neuchâtel project mentioned in
2.1) is that an informant's linguistic awareness partly determines
the speed and structure of the acquisition process.

We will need to ascertain the informants' attitudes to
language both for these reasons, and in order to be able to speak
to them about language (and we will spend some considerable time
over the project speaking to them about language). We will be
looking for what aspects of the TL (or languages in general) are
salient for the informants: do they notice, and talk about spontaneously, the enunciative properties of an utterance, its appropriateness, its meaning, its form? Here, confrontation ties in
closely with the acquisition of metalanguage (cf. 6.2.3). It is
all the more important that we roughly understand early on the
nature of an informants' linguistic awareness, as confrontation

especially (but, to a lesser extent, most of the elicitation
techniques at our disposal) has distinct pedagogical potential:
if the informant has to adapt to our way of speaking about
language (rather than we to his) then we will be seriously increasing the already present control effect.

(c) <u>Self-confrontation will also give us text</u>. The audio-recordings
of confrontation are obtained in a situation where, generally
speaking, the informant is somewhat tense, and where his attention is centred on the language-object. He may therefore pay
greater attention, when he speaks, to the form of his utterances.

It is interesting to see if this is indeed the case for two
reasons: firstly, it may give us indications of how he is acquiring the TL. For example, do certain forms obtained in this situation appear before they appear in more spontaneous data?;
secondly, it may happen (more so, perhaps, towards the end of the
study) that an informant shows an ability to style-shift. Does he,
for example, achieve more TL-like pronunciation and intonation in
this situation than in those where his speech is more spontaneous?

8.4.4.3 <u>Frequency of self-confrontation</u>. We said above that confrontation is a technique which will certainly increase informants' awareness of the TL in general, and that it is a technique that needs to be
prepared.

We thus have two sets of contradictory aims:

(a) We need to use confrontation frequently enough to obtain the information we want, and infrequently enough to affect as little as
possible the informants' awareness. This problem can only be solved
empirically: as a rough guideline, systematic confrontation should
not be used more than once every four months (<u>ad hoc</u> use of self-
confrontation must be left to the initiative of the individual
researcher).

(b) We need sufficient time to prepare the relevant questions, and we
need to confront the informant as soon as possible after the inter-
view/play scene, etc. with which he is to be confronted, i.e.,
whilst his memory is still relatively fresh. Again, this problem
can only be solved empirically: a possible solution would be to

ask the informant to hand in a self-recorded tape one week before
the encounter, or to use a recording from an accompanying observation which happened shortly before an encounter.

In any event we want to avoid the informants' guessing at "what
they must have meant" when they said something: with some of the subjects in the French pilot study the time-lag between interview and
confrontation was too long, and some answers were indeed preceded by
j'ai dû vouloir dire.....

8.4.4.4 Procedure. It is only possible here to suggest general guidelines for the procedure to be followed, as the questions to be asked
will vary considerably.

Generally speaking, therefore, it is a good idea not to play iso-
lated utterances to the informant, but rather to give a fairly broad
context to what is for us the interesting utterance/exchange. It is
then possible to play the passage to the informant a first time, without interruption. For self-confrontation, people often do not like
hearing the sound of their own voice, or seeing themselves on video,
and this first run-through at least allows them some time to accustom
themselves. (It can be useful to make a "joke" out of the audio-video-
tape: for certain informants in the Swedish pilot study, self-confrontation came to be known as the "film-star session", and this considerably lessened the unease of these informants.)

The passage can then be played through a second time, with the
informant commenting on anything of note: this second run-through serves
both for the informant to hear the passage again without the intervention of the researcher (which gives him that much more time to accustom
himself) and for the researcher to observe and note what the informant
himself becomes aware of. Our expectations on this last point should
not, however, be too high: the most frequent reaction to this phase in
the French pilot study with both Spanish and Arabic speakers was self-
deprecatory comments - je parle mal - which are to be expected given
the situation the informant finds himself in, both in the project and
in his daily life.

The passage can then be played through a third time with the researcher asking the questions he has prepared.

   If, however, the researcher can ask any of his questions <u>naturally</u>
during the second run-through, by following up an informant's comment,
for example, this chance should be seized: the more confrontation
approximates to conversation, the less the informant will consider
himself to be in the position of a pupil.

   This last point is important, both from a sociolinguistic point
of view and from the point of view of the almost inevitable pedagogical
effect of this technique. The informant will almost certainly ask metalinguistic questions - "how do you say that in the TL?" etc. - and these
questions <u>should be answered</u>. On the other hand, <u>great care</u> must be
taken by the researcher not to turn the confrontation session into a
listening comprehension exercise or into a grammar lesson, two dangers
which became apparent during the pilot year.

   A last general point for the procedure concerns the danger of translated enunciation (Trévise, 1979) in self-confrontation: we are more
interested in what the informant said or understood <u>on the tape</u> than we
are in what he now thinks he said/understood. Care must therefore be
taken to make questions referentially as unambiguous as possible. For
example, addressing the informant as <u>you</u> can be understood as the in-
formant-on-the-tape, or the informant-in-confrontation, thus "what <u>are</u>
you trying to say <u>here</u>" is a less effective question than "what <u>did</u> you
try to say <u>there</u>".

   The informant is of course reporting on his speech/understanding:
when this reported speech is marked explicitly, as in the <u>j'ai dû voul-</u>
<u>oir dire...</u> case, we have a clear indication that the informant is
guessing. However, it may sometimes be difficult to decide whether the
informant is reporting faithfully or whether he is in fact learning.
Imagine the following situation:

Acting a scene in the police station:

Facilitator/policeman: "Where is your residence permit?"
Informant: "I do ... I not have it".

Self-confrontation:

Investigator: "What are you trying to say here?"
Informant: "Ah! I lost it".

Did the informant really mean "I lost it" in the role-play? or did the specific question provoke him to find a more adequate answer?

A general question to be borne in mind when writing up the protocol of self-confrontation is therefore: given the informants' double situation, on the tape and in confrontation, what does a given answer tell us?

8.4.4.5 <u>Protocol</u>. As in the case of the procedure, it is only possible to give general guidelines for the protocol (cf. the relevant parts of the annexe to this chapter), since the main task here will be to mark the informant's responses to the researcher's specific questions.

However, one should look systematically for the following phenomena:

(a) the informant's own comments or questions on the TL (whether these comments be given in the SL or the TL), and the way he expresses them;

(b) indirect speech: by this we mean not only passages where the informant indicates specifically that he was presumably trying to say x, but also passages where the informant quotes the speech of others "you/he/were/was saying x". This latter case is likely to occur in confrontation more than in the linguistic interview, in play acting (where the informant is quoting himself) or in specific experiments, and can serve as an indication of his sociolinguistic awareness: does the informant try to speak like the people he is quoting?

Both aspects of (b) can be illustrated from the French pilot study or similar work in France on the expression of negation in the French of Spanish learners. One informant, whose use of <u>-pas</u> was systematic, nevertheless produced some instances of the "interference" form, <u>no + V</u>, when quoting her own speech in past situations where she had been in contact with French authority. Other informants, whose use of <u>-pas</u> was also systematic, nevertheless produced some instances of the hypercorrect <u>ne + V + pas</u> in indirect speech where utterances of social superiors (teachers, foremen, the investigator, etc.) were being reported, or repeated;

(c) (as in other types of elicitation) hesitations, self-corrections, and exaggerations. By this last term, we mean places where it seems (to the researcher) that the informant is being unduly careful in his pronunciation, his marking of verb-endings, etc., and particularly where this seems to have an effect on intonation (long pauses between words, assigning an intonation contour to each word, etc.). This type of phenomenon may occur frequently in answers to the researcher's specific questions, and may give us some idea of the difficulties he is having at a specific time.

8.5 Observation

8.5.1 <u>Motivation</u>. None of the techniques outlined so far allows us to observe the foreign worker's real everyday interaction - that is, those forms of communication in which he indeed acquires and applies his second language. This means, amongst other things, that we have no control over the real input; for example, the possible influence of "foreigner talk" simply cannot be taken into account. One method of gaining access to what we are calling "authentic" interactions is observation. In this project, observation has three major functions:

(a) It should give the researcher an impression of the informant's real way of living: the scope of his possible activities, experiences and social contacts.

(b) It should increase the researcher's awareness of the informant's communicative habits, and the communicative and other problems he is faced with from day to day; this will help the researcher to get a better understanding of the informant's communicative behaviour and the reasons for his communicative failures and successes.

(c) It will provide information about the informant's communicative abilities, communicative needs and actual communicative contacts in certain everyday situations. This last point also includes information about the real communicative behaviour of the informant's social environment, for example the varieties of the TL that he hears. Observation should also assess the informant's

need for TL literacy: in the observational domains listed below,
what sort of TL material does he have to read? what forms must he
fill in using the TL? etc. How does this compare qualitatively
and quantitatively with his use of the written SL?

8.5.2 <u>Observational domains</u>. The learner's communicative contacts with
his social environment fall into several more or less distinct fields,
such as contacts at work, in leisure time, etc. These fields constitute
the frame for the possible domains of observation. Five domains seem to
be particularly important for the purposes of the project:

(a) Work place interaction.
(b) Leisure time interaction.
(c) Practical everyday interaction (shopping).
(d) Interaction with authorities.
(e) Consultation (medical, legal, etc.).

All these fields should be covered.

8.5.3 <u>Types of observation</u>. We may distinguish three types of observation:

(a) Participant observation, defined as observation in which the re-
     searcher becomes a member of the informants' social environment,
     participates in a part of their everyday interaction and at the
     same time observes this interaction. The people who are observed
     are not fully informed about the researcher's status as an obser-
     ver. Ideally they are not informed at all.
(b) Accompanying observation, defined as observation where the re-
     searcher is present (he accompanies the informant), but takes no
     active part in the interaction.
(c) Neutral observation, where the researcher is not present (or not
     visibly present).

In the following sections the first two types of observation will be discussed in detail. With the exception of the informant's self-recording,
neutral observation in the project is optional.

8.5.4 Participant observation

8.5.4.1 Role of the observer. The role of the researcher as a participant should be chosen such that it gives access to all situations which are thought to be relevant, but does not change the field too much. It should also give him enough time for his observations. How this is handled in detail depends very much on the specific local conditions. In any event, successfully accomplishing participant observation requires some previous familiarity with the domains of observation.

8.5.4.2 Observation scheme. For both practical and ethical reasons, the interaction cannot be recorded, except by the classical means of human memory. What is remembered has subsequently to be transformed into field notes, and these must be selective. In order to control what is observed and to order one's impressions, observation should be guided by some observational scheme which should minimize the risk of the researcher's becoming overwhelmed by a flood of impressions or of proceeding unsystematically. The scheme should be ready before the first day of observation but checked and possibly adapted to special characteristics of the field after some experience has been obtained.

It should include an exact description of what one's attention has to focus upon within a certain stretch of time, and it should contain a survey of various factors which characterize the observational domain, such as:

(a) The wider frame into which the observational domain is embedded, for example: large factory with 400 workers, three divisions, in which this and that is produced, etc.; unemployment office in working class area, etc.

(b) Characteristics of the observational domain itself, for example: hall of such and such a size, eight large machines, permanent high noise level, workers' position largely stable, but occasionally changing, etc.

(c) Participants, with more specific features such as: classification according to age, sex, composition in terms of foreigners and non-foreigners; grouping of participants according to job requirements or personal relations (in leisure time), etc.; general activities

in the field; social structures of the field, such as professional
hierarchies, social status, particular roles.

The precise nature of these factors, of course, varies with the specific
field.

8.5.4.3 _Forms of observation_. For observation to be effective, attention has to be focussed on: specific persons; specific recurring types
of events, for example, greetings, complaints, etc.; specific recurring
features of situations, for example the way in which a verbal interaction
is initiated or ended.

What has to be observed and registered is somewhat variable. In
general, the following points are important:

(a) Context, that is the preceding and following situation.
(b) Structure, that is spatio-temporal characteristics like duration,
     persons involved, objects involved, etc.
(c) Features of interactive processes in the narrower sense, that is,
     purposes of interaction, distribution of verbal and non-verbal ac-
     tions, speech-act types, topics, initiation, turn-taking, endings,
     symmetry or asymmetry of communication, specific code and code
     switches, and others.

Observation should focus on recurrent events or situations; this does not
mean that unique, unexpected events should be neglected - they might even
be particularly revealing - but obviously they cannot be systematically
looked for.

All observations are recorded in the form of "field notes". They
should be written up as soon as possible after being made. In addition,
each observer should keep a "linguistic diary" in order to document observations that do not fit the observational scheme of the field notes.
It may also include more subjective impressions of the observer which -
apart from their personal use - might be helpful in evaluating his interpretation of what he thinks he has observed.

8.5.4.4 _Disadvantages and frequency of participant observation_. Participant observation involves the following _problems_:

(a) The researcher has almost no control over the variables involved.

He just has to wait and to observe, and it may be that those aspects of communication he is particularly interested in simply do not occur.

(b) The written data are a result of subjective interpretation and the reliability of these data therefore suffers.

(c) In many fields the presence of the observer presupposes the permission of the institution concerned. Unfortunately, in Germany, most of the institutions are not willing to co-operate, and in England, the level of unemployment has made it virtually impossible for a firm to agree to taking on a researcher even for a limited period of time.

With these problems in mind, our ambitions for participant observation are modest. The researchers on the project will endeavour to work for a period of <u>one week</u> during the data-collection period in some relevant institution. If this proves impossible, other measures will have to be envisaged: one practical possibility proposed by the English team is to propose to firms that they allow researchers onto the shop floor specifically as <u>investigators</u>. This solution would obviously change the field to a certain extent, but would be better than no observation at all. One final point is that it would be wise for all researchers to have done participant observation early in the data-collection period (and preferably in the period before regular project-specific encounters start), as this experience will serve in choosing the relevant questions to ask informants, relevant situations to simulate in the studio, etc.

8.5.5 Accompanying observation

8.5.5.1 <u>Purpose</u>. Here, the researcher accompanies a foreign worker to authorities, to a lawyer, a physician etc. He thus has the possibility of observing a large variety of situations which he would not have access to by participant observation, whether through lack of time or lack of official permission. This kind of observation is the only one which is in direct relation to the informants of the project (in participant observation the presence of an informant in the observed field is unlikely) and the results of accompanying observation can be easily integrated into other already existing data about the informant. The observer is looking for a better understanding of the informants' problems and for in-

sights into situations in which foreign workers, with their specific cultural and linguistic backgrounds, are confronted with the official institutions of the country of immigration and their representatives (the
"gate keepers" of chapter 4). The researcher's understanding of the situation will be all the more profound if he is informed by the foreign worker about the entire background and the circumstances which led to the
situation in question. This type of background knowledge is more difficult to obtain in participant or neutral observation.

8.5.5.2 <u>Role of observer</u>. There are many opportunities for helping the
informant in a difficult official matter. The informants often ask for
support and complying with this request gives the researcher one of the
rare opportunities of concretely helping them (cf. 8.1). The paradox is
however that the researcher should participate as little as possible in
the interaction between the informant and the official in order not to
distort unduly the "authentic" situation. Thus the researcher is playing
two contradictory roles: while wishing himself to remain external to the
interaction, he is endowed with the role of an agent both by the immigrant and by the official, and is expected to manage the interaction.

8.5.5.3 <u>Data documentation</u>. One can either make field notes and/or
(given the agreement of the participants) audio-recordings. All efforts
will be made to use the latter technique, as recordings of this type,
completed by self-confrontation, are the most effective means of verifying an informant's understanding of "authentic" interaction.

8.5.5.4 <u>Disadvantages</u>. The great disadvantage of accompanying observation is, of course, the researcher's double role. Careful briefing of
the informant will be necessary before accompanying observation takes
place, in order to resolve, if only partially, this contradiction. Nevertheless, accompanying observation is important to give the researcher
deeper insight into social and communicative problems and to sharpen his
awareness of attitudes and motivations. It is also the activity which
best represents the researcher's general motivation for working on the
project: that of an interested and concerned person who is prepared to
offer concrete help. With this in mind, every effort will be made to use

accompanying observation as systematically as possible.

8.6 Summary: individual techniques and sample schedule

8.6.1 Individual techniques. For our main investigation - the longitudinal group - we have discussed a number of elicitation techniques, combined into audio- and video-recorded "sessions", whose backbone is conversation (cf. 8.3.1). These data are completed by data from observation (cf. 8.5).

These techniques all distort, in some way, the linguistic interaction that adult immigrants have with their social environment. Each technique is designed to capture one or more aspects of what we suppose this interaction to be.

Taking our criteria for choosing the techniques(cf. 8.1):

(a) We have tried to organize data-collection in a way which will prove agreeable and meaningful to informants. Efforts will be made to help the informant - particularly in accompanying observation - and the reasons for each encounter will be explained;

(b) each technique is productive, and valid, for some aspects of linguistic communication, while being less so for others;

(c) the techniques are not all simple, and this may affect their reliability. However, the project starts with a training week which is being organized precisely in order to achieve maximal familiarity with the techniques for all researchers, and this should considerably augment each technique's reliability.

Participant observation will give researchers a clear idea, not of the language an individual informant is exposed to, but of the type of target linguistic environment in which our informants live. Accompanying observation will give researchers some idea of the type of interaction an individual informant has, although the internal structure of the interaction will be changed by their presence. More details on the "authentic" internal structure of these interactions may be obtained from play acting and the speaker perspective analysis following play acting.

Conversations will give us the main body of data, and will be prepared in such a way that they naturally elicit different types of speech - question-answer sequences, narratives, argumentation, phatics, etc. -

as well as essential biographical information, including the informant's account of his communicative needs and wishes, and attitudes towards the society he lives in.

This combination will, we feel, give us some understanding of the role of two of the three determining factors in each informant's acquisition (cf. 1.3.3), namely propensity factors and exposure to language. From this point of view, the successful accomplishment of the two main tasks we have chosen as pretexts for encounters (cf. 8.2) - film watching and informants' self-recording - would result in particularly valuable data.

The set of elicitation techniques is completed by tasks of a more experimental nature (cf. 8.3 & 8.4) whose purpose is to elicit specific aspects of informants' communicative competence - the expression of spatial relationships, for example - and to allow us a deeper insight into the third set of determining factors in acquisition which we mentioned in 1.3.3, namely cognitive/perceptual factors: self-confrontation is the privileged technique from this latter point of view.

8.6.2 Sample schedule. The practical organization of the considerations of 8.6.1 on a month to month basis is a problem which will face all teams. Obviously, it is impossible to predict how this will be achieved, given the very different local circumstances in each country.

We give below a sample schedule for the first year of data-collection. This schedule is fictitious, and we would be surprised if it corresponded to the year of any group of informants/researchers. It does serve, however, three purposes:

(a) It gives an idea of the amount of work a researcher on the project may expect to be faced with.

(b) It gives an idea of the organization and preparation which the data-collection period will entail.

(c) It attempts to set out - in very broad terms - the type of data we may anticipate from each type of encounter and thus, implicitly, the amount of selection of data for analysis which will have to be accomplished each month.

Sample schedule for first year's data collection

Month: Pre-project (leave time for all teams between training week
        and start of data collection)

Project-specific interaction: None

Type of encounter:

Reason for encounter:

Type of data anticipated:

Brief for next time:

Authentic interaction :

General observation of field, including 1 week's participant observation
for 1 researcher. Establish preliminary contacts with organizations,
networks, etc., and, towards the end, potential informants: arrange
meetings with potential informants.

Month: 1

<u>Project-specific interaction</u>:

<u>Type of encounter</u>: Introductory encounters. About 12 per SL =
about <u>24</u>!

<u>Reason for encounter</u>: Introductions. Preliminary explanation of the
project.

<u>Type of data anticipated</u>: Some biographical data from informants: age,
length of stay, region or origin, etc. Evaluation of informants' initial attitudes to the project → sort out candidates for the LGs and for the ILGs.
England, Germany and Sweden: establish <u>LRGs</u>.

<u>Brief for next time</u>: LG: Mutual information: more about the project,
more about the informants.

<u>Authentic interaction</u>:

None.

Month: 2

Project-specific interaction:

Type of encounter: LG: 6 short encounters per SL.

Reason for encounter: Mutual information (these informants should have
a clear idea of their role in the project at the end of
this month: financial arrangements finalized).

Type of data anticipated: In SL, biographical data, narratives (past
time); if appropriate, TL vocabulary on work, home;
difficulties with target language, speakers (and esp.
authorities). I.e. a linguistic interview with no "experimental" interruptions.

Brief for next time: (Pick up on e.g. TL speakers) "Come and
watch a short film with typical aspects of target life,
and we can talk about it."

Authentic interaction:

Accompanying observation starts.

Month: 3

Project-specific interaction:

Type of encounter: 6 short encounters per SL.

Reason for encounter: Film watching.

Type of data anticipated: With as much TL as possible: attitudes to
        target speakers; comprehension of film; background as-
        sumptions; reference to people, places and movements on
        film; question-answer sequences.
        SL probably necessary: give cassette players to LG: com-
        prehension of manipulations of cassette; first informal
        confrontation with own voice. I.e. an interview leading
        off from film watching, and ending up with a detailed
        brief.

Brief for next time: LG: "Log" (in SL, but with TL words if you can)
        two or three situations where you felt TL communication
        did not go as well as it might have.

Authentic interaction:

Accompanying observation continues.

Month: 4

Project-specific interaction:

Type of encounter: 6 long (i.e. videoed) encounters per SL.

Reason for encounter: Self-recording.

Type of data anticipated: Conversation: informal self confrontation,
argumentation, narrative past time, reported speech.
Grounding: instructions, spatial relations.
Play scene: dialogue (perhaps rudimentary at this stage).
Speaker perspective analysis: attitudes and emotions;
(comprehension data on interviewer's utterances during
play scene).

Brief for next time: LG: $\begin{Bmatrix} \text{Can I play back to you} \\ \text{Come and listen to} \end{Bmatrix}$ short extracts from

some of the recordings $\begin{Bmatrix} \text{you have made up to now.} \\ \text{we will make when I accompany you} \\ \text{to see X.} \end{Bmatrix}$

Authentic interaction:

Accompanying observation continues.

Month: 5

Project-specific interaction:

Type of encounters: 6 short encounters per SL.

Reason for encounter: Self confrontation.

Type of data anticipated: Self-confrontation: paraphrases, self-correc-
                tions; judgements (deprecatory comments on own performance
                compared to TL-speakers: comments and judgements on TL):
                this general part of the conversation takes place in the
                SL, in order to obtain some idea of informants' linguistic
                awareness when speaking in the SL.
                Other theme for the conversation (in TL): work and social
                relations. I.e. an interview with a self-confrontation
                "session" embedded in it.

Brief for next time: LG: (Pick up on "work" and "social relations"):
                "I would like to have your opinions on the economic/social
                climate of the country".

Authentic interaction:

1 week working in field for 1 researcher. Accompanying observation continues.

Month: 6

Project-specific interaction:

Type of encounter: 6 short encounters per SL.

Reason for encounter: General discussion on the (economic) state of the
country.

Type of data anticipated: Work and social relations vocabulary; attitudes
and opinions; reference to past, present and future
time; argumentative sequences; transport (route directions,
getting from home to work); narratives; comparisons source
and target countries. I.e. an interview with no explicit
"experimental" interruptions.

Brief for next time: LG: Self-recording: see month 3.

Authentic interaction:

Accompanying observation continues.

Month: 7

Project-specific interaction:

Type of encounter: 6 long encounters per SL.

Reason for encounter: Self-recording.

Type of data anticipated: Play-scene etc., see month 4.
                    If play scene is not particularly productive, or if there
                    is in any case time to do both, simulation of route
                    directions: e.g. the informant is in front of his house,
                    someone asks the way to the street where his work-place
                    is, how would he give directions?

Brief for next time: LG: Log movements around town during one week.

Authentic interaction:

Accompanying observation continues.

Month: 8

Project-specific interaction:

Type of encounters: 6 short encounters per SL.

Reason for encounter: Informant's movements.

Type of data anticipated: Route directions, getting about town in absentia (i.e. in front of a microphone with no reliance
on gestures). I.e. an interview with route directions
embedded in it.

Brief for next time: LG: Leisure activities. What are your leisure time
activities/where do you go on holiday/have you got any
holiday photos/how about going to a football match/
whatever is appropriate.

Authentic interaction:

Accompanying observation continues.

Month 9:

Project-specific interaction:

Type of encounter: 6 short encounters per SL.

Reason for encounter: Leisure activities.

Type of data anticipated: Narrative of past event (e.g. football match); reference to future time (e.g. next holidays); reference to place; informant's holiday photos → picture descriptions, reference to persons. Attempt to introduce target leisure activities: e.g. parlour games → question/answer sequences; seaside post-cards → picture descriptions etc.; reference to home, social relations. I.e. an interview with experiments embedded.

Brief for next time: LG: "Log" or record communication in TL which was interesting or difficult; hand in recording a few days before next meeting.

Authentic interaction:

Accompanying observation continues.

Month: 10

Project-specific interaction:

Type of encounter: 6 long encounters per SL.

Reason for encounter: Self-recording.

Type of data anticipated: Self-confrontation: cassette of months 9/10
and/or video recording of month 7: corrections, paraphrases,
judgements. "Stage directions"experiment: spatial relations,
thematic structure of utterances or: videoed route directions if not possible in month 7 (cf. month 7). I.e. more
experimentally orientated video session with interview-like
discussion on content of self-recording.

Brief for next time: LG: Post office (backed up if possible by previous
accompanying observation); LRG: see you next month; we
would like you to simulate an interaction (with a TL speaker you know).

Authentic interaction:

Accompanying observation continues.

Month: 11

Project-specific interaction:

Type of encounter: 6 short encounters (LG) per SL / 6 long encounters
         (LRG) per SL.

Reason for encounter: LG: Post office; LRG: how are things? Play acting
         (with a non-researcher).

Type of data anticipated: LRG: Conversation; dialogue; attitudes and
         emotions. LG: form-filling; telephone calls (phatics;
         reference to person, place, time in absentia). I.e. an in-
         terview with embedded experiments.

Brief for next time: LG: Taking stock of the project so far.

Authentic interaction:

England/Germany/Sweden. As little as possible ("critical period" for
project-specific encounters).

Month: 12

Project-specific interaction:

Type of encounter: 6 short encounters per SL.

Reason for encounter: Taking stock of project.

Type of data anticipated: Reference to past, present and future time;
            attitudes, opinions; argumentative sequences. I.e. an in-
            terview with little or no experimental interruptions.

Brief for next time: Self-recording: see month 9.

Authentic interactions:

Accompanying observation continues.

Month: 13

Project-specific interaction:

Type of encounter: 6 long encounters per SL.

Reason for encounter: Self-recording.

Type of data anticipated: Conversation followed by play scene, see month 4.

Brief for next time: Brief LG.

Authentic interaction:

Accompanying observation continues.

8.7 Transcription of Data

Introduction. In what follows, we give the conventions adopted for
initial transcription of data. This transcription is "all-purpose", that
is, it serves as a general base which can if needed be made more detailed
for specific purposes of analysis (for example, for some questions discussed in chapters 4 and 5, the transcription of intonation given here
will have to be refined for the relevant selection of data). For this reason - and in order that subsequent computer storage can be facilitated[1] -
efforts have been made to keep the conventions described here relatively
simple.

The majority of teams engaged in the project have developed during
the pilot year - or even earlier - differing methods of transcription.
Although ideally it would be desirable to have a standardized alphabet
for a comparative project such as this, it was felt that the advantages
of each team's keeping its own alphabet were more important for the following reasons: each alphabet has evolved in order to deal with phonetic
phenomena which seem specific to the type of learner variety studied;
each team knows its system well, and any time which can be saved in the
time-consuming activity of transcription is precious; all teams involved
have familiarized themselves with reading each other's transcriptions;
use has been made in establishing each alphabet of characters on the
different TL typewriters - ö, ç, å, etc.

Although the alphabet used by each team will be to a certain extent
idiosyncratic, the presentation of the text, and the conventions for
transcribing non-segmental phenomena, have been standardized. In what
follows, we give the transcription conventions common to all teams. (As
a rule, ordinary orthography will be used to transcribe interviewers'
utterances.)

---

[1] It is planned that transcribed data will be stored on a computer.
For practical reasons of availability and programming, this possibility
will not materialize until some time after the data collection period
has begun. Thus, all transcriptions will be initially hand- or type-
written, and will not contain programming conventions.

8.7.1 <u>General presentation of the transcription</u>. Transcripts are writ-
ten/typed on double paged, lined sheets. The left page is used for the
text, and the right page for making comments on vocal features not usually found in a lexicon, comments on the speaker's attitudes and emotions,
information about visually observable features, and for close phonetic
transcription.

There is no one language that is common to all researchers in the
project: English is the one that most closely approximates. Whilst there
will be no English glosses of the text of the transcription, efforts will
be made to note comments on the text - the right-hand page - in English
in all transcriptions. The text should, however, be triple-spaced, allowing room for an English gloss if particular circumstances make this necessary.

The text should be headed with information concerning the type of
activity - e.g., audio-conversations, video-preposition experiment - the
pseudonym of the informant and information on where in the study the
transcription comes - e.g., longitudinal group, audio-conversation 11 -
the name of the interviewers and their initials; the date of the recording;
the cassette reference.

Participants' (pseudo)initials will be used in the left-hand margin
of the left-hand page to indicate who is speaking. In general (but see
Fig. 1) each new speaker will be assigned a new line. The text should be
numbered every fifth line. For video recordings, each interval of 30 secs
on the tape will be marked in the transcription.

8.7.2 <u>Inter-utterance, and left/right page correspondences</u>. Overlapping
utterances are signalled by the following conventions:

[at the beginning of two or more consecutive lines indicates a re-
         lationship of simultaneity between the utterances on those lines.
         This sign therefore marks a block of simultaneous speech.

⌐ or ⌐,⌐ indicates the end of simultaneous speech. The beginning of simul-
         taneous speech is indicated by the vertical positioning of ut-
         terrances on consecutive lines within a block of simultaneous
         speech.

     indicates an interruption of one speaker by another.

< >   indicates correspondences between the left- and right-hand pages,

accompanied by a subscript (see Fig. 1) if there are two or more correspondences on the same line. The terminology used between the angled brackets on the right hand page is listed immediately below.

8.7.3 Notations in < >

Deviances from the speaker's "normal speaking style". The terms below are used relatively to the intuitive notion of an informant's "normal speaking style". This notion cannot be "measured" by the transcriber, whose job is to assess intuitively for each informant when he is speaking at his "normal" speed, with a "normal" pitch range and "normal" intensity, using "normal" stress, etc. Deviations from this norm will be marked.

The most important phenomena to be noted here are: softer, louder, faster, slower (lengthening every word/syllable), and emphatically (with special stress on every word/syllable).

Sentence stress. Sentence stress used in the speaker's "normal speaking style" and which does not deviate from TL (or TL variety) use will not be marked. A word which wrongly receives sentence stress, or which is given emphatic/contrastive stress by the speaker, is enclosed in < >, with the corresponding right-page notations: < wrong stress > , < emphatic stress >. The term < emphatically > (see above) is therefore reserved for sequences longer than one word.

Non-articulated sounds. Angular brackets will also be used to indicate coughs, laughs, yawns, etc.

Other features. Angular brackets will also be used to give on the right-hand page the transcriber's impression of the informant's attitudes and emotions as indicated e.g., by his tone of voice - ironically, angrily, enthusiastically, hesitantly, etc. - as well as to describe relevant visually observable features - gestures, etc. - of the interaction. Background information relevant to understanding the text may be indicated in angular brackets:

tü 4: ich sprache mit sie + hier + < folks > /
    (I   spoke with she + here +   folk
	< Türkisches
	  Volkshaus >

ich habe gesagt ...
    I   have   said)
	(Turkish communi-
	  ty centre)

The overall presentation of the transcript will therefore have the following form (aaa, bbb represent sequences of articulated sounds):

See Figure 1, page 233

8.7.4 Conventional notation used within the text

Intonation. Without special training, intonation is extremely difficult to describe and analyse. In view of this fact, we will limit ourselves to an approximate description of this phenomenon, namely: "rise" - marked ↑ - and "fall" - marked ↓.

With the exception of questions (see below), "normal" intonation will not be marked. Use of ↑ - and use of ↓ - will therefore depend on the transcriber's evaluation of the rise or fall being contrastive, unusual in relation to the speaker's normal speaking style, or otherwise "interesting".

Questions. If the transcriber feels that a sequence is unambiguously a question, he may enclose the sequence in ? ?. Use of question marks does not therefore preclude the possibility of marking "non-normal" intonation in:

? what did you do ↑ ?

Sense-units (or T-units). If the transcriber feels that he can unambiguously isolate a sense-unit he may enclose the sequence in

@ @

Non-TL words and sequences (excluding loan words) are enclosed in asterisks: * *

Figure 1

1.6.82 1st Audio-conversation with Jamal (J); also present, Jamal's friend Fawzi (F).
Interviewers: Daniel Véronique (DV); Daniel Faïta (DF). Cassette reference: LGA.J1

```
1      DV: aaaaaa <      > aaa                        <coughs>

2      J : bbbbbb

3      F :  ┌aaa
           │
4      DV: └bb ┌bbbb

5 005  F : <₁aaaa <₂aaaa₂> aaaaaaaaaaa ₁>             <₁slower > <₂emphatic stress >

6      DF: ┌bbbbbbbbb
           │
7      DV: └    aaaaaa

8      J :  ┌<bbbb~~~        bbbb>                    <in reply to DF's utterance, line 6>
           │
9      DV: └     <aaaa>                               <faster>

10 010 F :  <bbbb>                                    <hesitantly>
```

Line 1: DV speaks, and coughs within his utterance; L.2: J speaks; L.3-4: F and DV start speaking simul- taneously, DV finishes his utterance, F waits before finishing his utterance (see also lines 8, 9); L.6-7: DF speaks, DV speaks in the middle of his utterance, both finish together (this is not an interruption, as both speakers finish what they are saying - see lines 8 - 9); L.8-9: J speaks, his utterance bearing on DF's previous utterance, DV interrupts J, J then continues to speak about DV's previous utterance (in the latter part of L.8, although J is technically a new speaker, the presentation adopted saves one line's space: this saving would not have been possible in lines 3 - 5); L.10: F speaks.

Word stress is normally not marked; the cases where it is correspond to places where the speaker wrongly assigns stress within a word, as in:

de'viant [də'vijənt]

Unfilled pauses are indicated in the text by +. The length of the pause is normally assessed intuitively by "speaker subjective time units" (Schegloff, personal communication), which can be obtained by counting "one one thousand, two one thousand, etc." in the rhythm of the speaker's normal speaking style. One + corresponds to one speaker subjective time unit. If, however, the transcriber wishes to specify the length of a pause objectively, he may indicate this length in seconds between two +, e.g.:

aaa + 5s + aaa

It is sometimes difficult to establish for silences between utterances of two speakers whether speaker 1 or speaker 2 is "responsible" for the silence (is speaker 1 pausing before going on to say something else, and "interrupted" by speaker 2, or is speaker 2 pausing before replying to speaker 1?). When the transcriber has no intuitions about this, he can end one utterance by a +, and start the following utterance by a +, as in the following example taken from a Swedish informant's tape:

```
1   de    e    som    fogelns    mjölk +
    (it   is   like the bord's    milk)

2   + va   sa   du   + 0.8s
    (what said  you)

1   + fogelns   mjölk   ++   fågelns   mjölk   +++
    (the bord's milk          the bird's milk)
```

In the last line of this example, there is therefore a pause of 0.8 seconds before the first two words, a two-unit pause between the second and third words, and a three-unit pause at the end of the utterance.

Absence of pauses between utterances of different speakers are of course indicated by absence of +.

Filled pauses and unarticulated backchannel signals. These are transcribed as closely as is feasible: "ah", "mm","euh", and differentiated using the < > convention. Backchannel signals, but not filled pauses, are indicated on the right-hand page by < backchannel >.

Self-interruption is indicated by a slash / in the text. Self-interruption may also be followed by pause, as in the following example:

I didn't thou/+ think about it

Liaison. A circumflex may be used to indicate liaison between two words: aaa^bbb. Non-liaison where liaison is obligatory (or "normal") will be marked by a full stop: aaa.bbb.

Inaudible stretches of speech are indicated between parentheses: ( ). In cases where the transcriber has some idea, but is not sure, of what was said, he can add this between parentheses, as in:

he said that (habibur) would come.

Otherwise, some estimation of the length of the inaudible stretch can be given by using an X for the number of perceived syllables:

he said that (XXX) would come.

8.7.5 Summary

There follows a recapitulative list of the conventions used by all five teams in the project.

1. Left-hand/right-hand page correspondence is indicated by   < >ᵢ   < >ᵢ

2. Simultaneous speech blocks are indicated in the left-hand margin by

3. End of simultaneous speech is indicated by

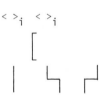

4. Speaker shift without pauses or interruption is indicated by   change of line

5. Speaker shift by interruption is indicated by

6. Unfilled pauses are indicated by   +   ++   +++

7. Intonation rise is indicated by   word ↑

8. Intonation fall is indicated by   word ↓

9. Self-interruption is indicated by   /

10. Clear questions are indicated by   ? sequence ?

11. Clear sense units are indicated by   @   sequence   @

12. Non TL words and sequences are indicated by   * word *

13. Non-normal liaison is indicated by   word‾word

14. Lack of normal liaison is indicated by   word.word

15. Inaudible stretches are indicated by   (XXX)

16. Incorrect word stress is indicated by   syl'lable

8.8 Optional data-collection techniques

In this paragraph we give three data-collection techniques which were tried out during the pilot year, but whose successful accomplishment depends to a great extent on either the type of informant, or on a very high willingness to co-operate on the part of the informant or people he encounters.

While we feel that these techniques are extremely interesting, we feel it unwise to include them in the central core of data-collection techniques since it is difficult to guarantee that they can be successfully carried out.

8.8.1 Neutral observation

Purpose. In this type of observation the researcher is not present when the interaction takes place, either not present at all, or else watching the situation without being visible. Thus situations can be covered without distortions caused by the direct presence of the researcher, or his being involved, as is the case with participant observation and accompanying observation. Nevertheless, the persons in the field have necessarily to be informed about their being observed and consciousness of this fact may cause distortions again.

Data documentation. The following ways of documentation are possible:

(a) The researcher observes under cover: in this case, field notes can be taken and/or audio-recordings can be made (provided, of course, the persons concerned give prior agreement).

(b) The researcher is not present at all: here, audio-recordings
have to be made by the person working in the office/institu-
tion. This person has to get permission from the informant
to record. Furthermore, he has to supply the researcher with
background data on the situation, the informant, his request,
etc. In an optimum case the documentation of the interaction
can be almost complete.

Disadvantages. This data-collection method requires a high degree of
co-operation on the part of the institution involved. This is usually difficult to obtain. In the pilot year it was only possible to persuade a
few personal acquaintances to help, and even these agreed without enthu-
siasm, so that the real amount of data was in fact small in comparison
to the effort involved.

This means that one cannot rely on this method, but can use it as
an additional source for data-collection under especially favourable
circumstances, which are seldom met.

8.8.2 The diary method. The diary method draws on the informant's own
voluntary and to some extent informed co-operation. It has certain advantages and can be very fruitfully used in combination with other methods.
However, it is only possible to use it with informants who are literate
(Finnish informants, for example) and these informants are a minority case
in the project overall.

Procedures for diary writing. In principle, the procedure is simple
and only consists of requesting an informant to write in his SL, about
TL interactions. However, there are certain instructions that have to be
given in order to guarantee that the diary entries are of value to the research project.

(a) The diary method is a complementary research device, and is particularly suitable as a pretext for conversation or play acting in project-specific encounters. This means that an informant has to be
briefed on the use that will be made of the diary in the following
encounter.

(b) Information of interest in the diary largely coincides with what
the researcher is trying to obtain in participant observation
(cf. 8.5.4). The informant should note:

- the place of the communicative event;
- activities taking place: what sort of interaction it was, when it happened, what other activities were going on at the same time;
- interaction partners: sex, nationality, age, status or functions in the place of interaction, roles in the interaction itself;
- why and how the interaction came about, the aims of the encounter, whether, and if so how, these were attained;
- observations on the initial and final phases of the interaction;
- interactional difficulties and communicative co-operation: whether, and if so how, the informant was aided in comprehending and in expressing himself in the target language, and what was found to be especially difficult;
- what the themes of the interaction were;
- the emotions and attitudes of the speech partners.

8.8.3 Role play by action interview

8.8.3.1 Introduction. The term "role play" can be associated with a wide range of activities; e.g. the things that take place on the stage in a theatre, or the simulation of some past or future event where one aims at as detailed and objective an account of the event as possible. Furthermore, the term "role play" is encountered in various pedagogical contexts. Thus, role play is sometimes used for training people to be skilled participants in future interactions, or in an ordinary class-room situation to help students to memorize the items to be learned. The role play elaborated by the Göteborg team represents yet another kind, whose main objective is to get the informant to act out a certain experienced, expected, or imagined event, as well as to talk about it. A possible name for this type of role play would then be action interview. Its main point is not simulation, but rather to stimulate the informant to be more emotionally involved while at the same time activating his memory. Thus, it offers a tool for exploring motivational and other explanatory factors behind the interaction and course of events being enacted. Besides this, target language material of a different kind than in an interview will be elicited.

The action interview will thus produce data on how the informant's own reported and enacted needs, desires and attitudes influence his language use and acquisition. It will also provide information on the informant's general conception of communicative events.

8.8.3.2 <u>The structure and techniques of role play as action interview</u>. The action phase proper is preceded by a <u>warm up</u>. The warm up consists of a conversation in which the researcher tries to see whether there are any suitable topics brought up by the informant which could be developed into role play and action illustration. The role play or action phase is thus a logical extension of the conversation. The event which is enacted can be either something that the informant has experienced or something that he expects to happen, or imagines. In the context of our project we will be more interested in the informant's own experience of communicative difficulties. Suitable pretexts for role play therefore include diary notes or self-recordings by the informant.

The warm up is followed by <u>grounding</u> (or anchoring), a phase where the situational circumstances of the event to be enacted are made vivid by the informant. A good thing to say when you are on the edge of transforming the event that has been talked about into illustration by role play is "Let us take a look at what happened". It is the researcher's job to make the informant feel in charge and to help him (re)create the event. It is often useful if two members of the research team work together during a role play session. It is important, however, that one and only one person should bear the chief responsibility as "facilitator", while the other provides assistance and support as "co-facilitator".

The grounding phase culminates with the <u>role designation</u> procedure. This is the threshold to the role play proper and consists in the facilitator explicitly giving the informant his role at the time and place of the event in question ("O.K., now you are X at time t"). The here and now of the role play proper is thus symbolically marked off from the surrounding here and now. To the extent that the informant indicates that other persons are to take part in the event, the facilitator can introduce these persons into the play by asking whether the co-facilitator or some other person available could impersonate the needed counterpart(s) and subsequently giving them roles in the same way as for the informant.

It should be noted however that other people present (such as friends
that the informant has brought with him) should only interact with the
informant through the role play. No asides should be allowed during this
phase.

The informant thus builds up a symbolic space. The symbolic value
of the stage props will be strongest if the informant is encouraged to
introduce the symbols or props himself. In building up such a symbolic
space the informant puts himself under strong pressure to fill this space
with something, and he fills it with verbal as well as non-verbal behaviour. As speech events in the target language are the point of our role
plays, we have here a good way of stimulating them: an informant who is
reluctant to use the target language during an interview will often use
the target language in recreating a speech exchange during role play.

Thus, the more grounding the informant can accomplish himself, the
better. Generally, do not rush, but let the informant take his time, and
adjust to the informant's mood and perspective in building up this symbolic space during the warm up and grounding phases. Listen to what the
informant wishes to tell you, so that the role play can develop as an
extension of the informant's words and thoughts, and not as a thing
which is forced upon him from outside. During the grounding phase, as
during the other phases, try to reduce the informant's possible anxiety
by asking him questions he can answer. It is useful to ask questions
about the spatial setting of the interaction to be played: "What was behind the desk?", etc. Tell the informant to take his time, and help him
to relax.

Switching and doubling. As an alternative to choosing a person for
a minor role during the action phase of the interview the facilitator
can chose to designate the role to a stage prop or dummy, e.g. a chair.
In this case the informant must also play the role of the counterpart
in order to carry out the interaction properly. The facilitator can help
the informant with this task by asking him to take a stand behind the
dummy (chair) and to say what the counterpart is supposedly to say. He
then reverses back again to his own role. The technique of reversing
roles is known as role switching. Role switching can also be used to
allow the informant to correct and edit moves and utterances made by the
person playing the counterpart. The facilitator should be active and

help the informant make the actions and utterances of the other conform
to the informant's conception of how the event happened. The facilitator can do this by intervening and asking questions like "Did he say that?"
or "Is this the way he did it?", or, in order to reduce the risk of the
informant's feeling interrogated, the facilitator can simply say "Possible?" If the answer is negative, the facilitator goes on: "O.K., could
you step over and say what he really said?". In cases where the role play
concerns an event experienced by the informant, the switch technique ef-
fectively calls up the informant's memory and makes him more emotionally
involved. It also increases his awareness and memory of what was said
and communicated.

Another technique which can be used within the play is <u>doubling</u>.
When doubling, a person other than the informant - preferably the co-
facilitator - stands behind the back of one of the role players, touches
his shoulders and makes a remark that he thinks would suit the impersonated character or that could plausibly be made by the impersonated
character. (The credibility of the thoughts and attitudes communicated
through doubling should be checked with the informant to a certain extent.)

<u>Exploratory side sequences</u>. Interventions by the facilitator, like
"Did he say that?", initiate side sequences to the role play proper. The
obvious risk with such digressions is that they create discontinuity in
the role play. (If you do not manage to accomplish the return to the role
play, the role play should then be transformed to a narrative.) On the
other hand, these side sequences are necessary to remedy cases where the
informant has lost control of the course of events, e.g. when a role play
develops in a direction which is not in accordance with the experience or
(in case of a future interaction) expectations of the informant.

The problem, then, is to return to the role play proper in a way
which allows continuity in spite of the digression. A solution to this
problem is to go back to the sequence which occurred immediately before
the digression. The facilitator can do this by instructing the role playing interactants to resume their positions previous to the digression
and to say their last utterances again (or, in cases where the side sequence was aimed at changing a previous action or utterance, to go back
in the course of events and act or say something in the new way required).

Care should always be taken, however, to follow the informant's own directions. If he does not wish to return, a return should not be attempted.

An important advantage with digressions is that they allow the facilitator/researcher to explore the motivational and other explanatory factors behind the informant's behaviour. The facilitator can ask questions like "How do you feel now that you're entering the housing office?", "Did you find his course of action correct?", "Why do you consider this the appropriate thing to say?" etc. We shall briefly mention in this respect the problem of backward-pointing and forward-pointing dimensions in discourse analysis. In most cases students of discourse are forced to do their analysis of, for example, a conversation <u>post hoc</u>. During a role play the researcher/facilitator finds himself, so to speak, <u>in medias res</u> and he can profit from this by asking the informant questions about his purposes, expectations and other dimensions pointing forward in discourse. Thus, exploratory side sequences during role play allow us to view discourse from the forward pointing perspective to a greater extent than is normally the case.

So far we have talked about the exploratory sequences as "side sequences" or "digressions", thus making the role play proper stand out as the most important component. However, as the purpose of role play is to explore the motivational and other explanatory factors behind the informant's language use and acquisition, we may to some extent conceive of the exploratory sequences as crucial components of the technique described here. The role play proper is then an activity which embeds and enhances these exploratory sequences. In short, the kind of questions asked in an exploratory sequence might be hard for the informant to answer in an interview, whereas they can often be much more naturally dealt with by the informant in the context of role play.

<u>Cooling down and deroling</u>. After the action phase or role play has ended it is extremely important to go through a <u>cooling down</u> phase. An obligatory procedure in this phase is <u>deroling</u>. The facilitator explicitly tells the informant and the other role players to be themselves again in the here and now of the studio or whatever the location of the role play is. The message is therefore: "O.K., now you are no longer X at place p and time t, but X in the here and now of the studio." As a rule it is

best to start the cooling down phase with deroling. It is useful to let
the cooling down phase consist of talking about the content of the role
play, how the informant and other participants felt in their roles, what
was good or bad, how things could have been done otherwise, etc. Thus,
cooling down is to a great extent a phase of analysis for the informant,
giving us information about his awareness and understanding. It is very
important also for other participants in the role play, e.g. the facilitator and co-facilitator, to share their own experiences with the informant so that he feels that he is in a sympathetic environment.

Choice of language during role play. It is important that the informant is as free as possible to express his thoughts and feelings during the warm up, grounding and cooling down phases. As a rule, therefore,
the source language could be used during these phases. This goes also for
the side sequences or digressions made during the role play proper. However, in interviews some informants have reported that when they use the
target language in interactions, the target language plays a part in
their thinking. This suggests that the target language sometimes could
be used in the exploratory side sequences during the role play. The role
play proper should take place in the target language.

8.8.3.3 Some problems and solutions. Firstly, we should emphasize the
danger of raising more than necessary the informant's awareness of what
goes on in communication. In this respect, role switching and doubling
are techniques which must be handled with care. We suggest that role
switching should be employed only to clarify what the other said, not
what he felt. As regards doubling, we suggest that it should concern the
feelings and beliefs of the informant only. In this way the awareness
raising effect of role play will be limited to motivational factors and
not so much to the linguistic output per se. Increased awareness of motivational factors is a price we will probably have to pay in view of the
utility of using role play for exploring such factors and the fact that
we know very little about them.

Secondly, there is a potential ambiguity of reference to be coped
with (cf. 8.4.4.4, the translated enunciation of self-confrontation).
It could be unclear whether a certain linguistic expression - e.g. "I" -
is used by the informant to refer to the informant in the role play, or

to the informant in the real event on which the role play is based, or
to the informant in the here and now of the studio. To the extent that
such an ambiguity of reference actually arises during role play a method
of repair or clarification is called for. Such a method is provided precisely by the type of exploratory intervening sequence discussed above.
In order to clarify this type of ambiguity, the facilitator can intervene with questions like "Sorry - are you talking about what you are
feeling right now in this role or are you talking about what you feel
outside of the play?" In general, this type of data should prove very
valuable as indicators of informants' acquisition of reference to people,
place and time.

It is therefore important explicitly to designate roles initially
and to derole after the role play in order to delimit the here and now
of the role proper from the here and now of the studio. It is the facilitator's job to see that the informant is not confused in this respect. At the same time we can expect the role players themselves spontaneously to use disambiguating cues and the researcher should be sensitive to such cues or markers, e.g. uses of past vs present tense or
of deictic terms such as "here" and "now" vs "there" and "then".

8.8.3.4 <u>Final remarks</u>. In general, action interview by role play is a
strong technique, and the informant might get more emotionally involved
in the play than you wish him to be. It is therefore important that the
facilitator keeps the possibility of observing, thinking, and intervening or regulating the course of events, by keeping at some distance and
not stepping into a role himself. The facilitator should interfere as
little as possible and leave the job of building up the situation to the
informant. As the term indicates, the facilitator's task should be to
facilitate - not dictate - the informant's task in this process.

It is furthermore important that the informant is not forced to do
or say anything he does not want to. Confidence and trust are essential
ingredients in the kind of long term relationships that this project
aims for. The informants themselves should always have the last say.

Annexe: Data preparation protocol

Data preparation protocol

This protocol is used immediately after an encounter takes place in order to organize data for subsequent transcription and analysis, and to note other relevant aspects of the interaction.

1. Coding

Protocol number ———— corresponding to cassette number ————
                                    Is cassette numbered?

Group: (longitudinal, long residence, etc.
                            and source language)

Informant's pseudonym:

Type of encounter: (e.g., second video "session")

Date:

Place:

Time:

Project researchers present:

Pretext for meeting: (cf. 8.2.3)

Objective of meeting: (e.g., social security claim, accompany
                            to social security office)

Successful/unsuccessful: (see also 8 below)

2. Description of setting

Other people present:

Extent of their participation:

Effect on recorded quality of informant's speech:
(For audio-recordings) sketch of setting (placing of participants, position relative to microphone, etc.)

Hospitality: (sweets, drinks, etc. offered to whom
                            by whom?)

3. Informant's (other participants') attitude to recorder:

4. Short summary of the main episodes of the encounter
   (This summary should be a brief chronological account of the encounter, giving the reader a general idea of its structure, and allowing
   him to locate the approximate place on the audio-cassette - and the
   precise place on the video cassette - of the activities, etc., described in 5 and the passages for transcription selected in 7.)

5. Features of the encounter
   Atmosphere during the encounter:
   Development of the conversation: (strongly guided by researcher,
                                    informant's initiatives, etc.)
   Noteworthy reactions to specific subjects of conversation/activities:
                                    (interest, suspicion, etc.)
   External interruptions:

   Specific activities: (experiments, self-confrontation,
                                    etc.,with descriptions)
   Languages used:
   Non-verbal communication: (eye contact, noteworthy gestures,
                                    etc.)

6. "Noteworthy" words, expressions, etc.
   (Here, the researcher should note phenomena which on a first impression seem "new" or "interesting", for subsequent comparison with
   other recordings.)

7. Passages selected for subsequent transcription
   (Here, some indication should be given of the place of the passage -
   see 5 above - and in respect to what area(s) of investigation:
   e.g.: "The holiday narrative", episode IV in 5.

   Thematic structure of utterances   use of anaphor, placing of
   Reference to persons, place, time   time/place adverbials, tensed
                                        verbs)

8. Suggestions for next time
   (e.g., biographical information lacking, specific elicitation tasks,
   what was unsuccessful in the encounter and possible remedies ...)

9. Quest for Informants

9.1 General problems and criteria for selection

9.1.1 Informant selection in relation to previous studies. In 2.3, a summary was given of the type and number of informants from whom data will be collected during the project. For convenience it is repeated here:

1. Main, longitudinal, group (LG): 40 adult immigrant workers, 8 per target language, 4 per source-target-language pair. They will be regularly observed over 30 months.
2. Initial learner group (ILG): 36 adult immigrant workers with similar biographical characteristics to those in the main sample. 12 per target language (Dutch, French, Swedish), 6 per source-target-language pair. Data will be collected from them three times during the longitudinal study.
3. Long residence group (LRG): 36 adult immigrant workers with at least five years' residence in the target community. 12 per target language (English, German, Swedish), 6 per source-target-language pair. Data will be collected from them six times during the longitudinal study.
4. Native speaker group (NSG): 20 adult members of the target community, 4 per target language. They should belong to the social environment of the other informants. Data will be collected in two encounters during the longitudinal study, and their interactions with SL-speakers will be observed.

We will briefly recall the function of each minor group:

- Initial learner group. These informants will give us some idea of the "control effect" (cf. 2.3) on the acquisition process of informants in the LG caused by the researchers' continued contact with them, and by the effect on their motivation that this contact may have;
- Long residence group. These informants will provide a more general picture of the communicative difficulties that may persist even after

several years' residence in the target country, and of possible links
between language and social disadvantage for this type of population;
- Native speaker group. These informants will allow us to control for
the actual varieties of the TL that informants of the LG are exposed
to. We will also ask these native speakers for their opinions of their
linguistic communication with non-native TL-speakers.

Overall, the number of informants in each group for whom data will
be analysed is felt to be maximal. It was stated in chapter 8 that the
encounters planned at certain periods during data collection average
about one per day, and require preparation beforehand and selection of
data for transcription and analysis immediately afterwards (cf. chapter
8, Annexe). Furthermore, the transcription and detailed analysis of data
required to test hypotheses about informants' acquisition is very time-
consuming: for transcription alone, the pilot studies showed that fifteen
minutes were necessary to give a fairly detailed transcription of one
minute of a video-taped interaction. Even with this limited number of informants, and with a relatively strict selection of data for transcription
and analysis, the task is large. Practical reasons therefore preclude the
study of larger samples of informants.

There are, however, other reasons for limiting the number of informants, and for being circumspect in the criteria used to select them.
To obtain valid results from a more superficial analysis of the language
acquisition of a statistically significant number of informants in the
time available, it would be necessary to have established with some confidence what the relevant variables are on which informants could be
selected. As one of the aims of the project is precisely to obtain a
clearer idea than we have at present of what role the groups of cognitive,
propensity and exposure factors described in 1.3 may play in the acquisition process, and which factors within each group are important, it follows
that it is difficult (for us at least) to state a priori what the relevant parameters for SSLA may be on which to select statistically significant groups of informants. It also follows that the groups of informants
who will be studied cannot be termed statistically representative. At the
present time, more case studies are needed.

Few attempts have been made so far in studies on SSLA to link informants' linguistic performances with the factors which may determine them.

We will briefly discuss three well-known studies - those of the Heidelberger Forschungsprojekt "Pidgin-Deutsch" (HDP), Zweitspracherwerb Italienischer und Spanischer Arbeiter (ZISA), and Schumann (1978) - as they give an idea of what progress has been made in this respect, and have in part determined the criteria adopted in this project for selection of informants in the LG (and, therefore, in the ILG). As this chapter is about this project's quest for informants, discussion of these three studies will suffice to describe the problem as we see it.

The HPD study attempts to relate certain measurable factors - "bias" factors such as linguistic origin, age, previous schooling, professional qualification, sex; and "environmental" factors such as contacts with Germans at work or at leisure, abode, duration of stay - with their adult Spanish and Italian informants' linguistic performance, measured by a syntactic index. The results indicated that length of stay in the target community played no significant role after the first two years (this fact contributed to our choice of thirty months as the length of the longitudinal study). After this period, the higher an informant came on the syntactic index, the more likely he was to have been aged 22 years or less at immigration, to have contacts with Germans at work and during leisure time, and to have attended school and have a formal professional qualification. HPD chose not to consider motivation as a factor as they considered it hard to define precisely, and questioned the possible measurement criteria. The determining factors they found to be relevant thus belong under what we have called cognitive and exposure factors.

Schumann conducted a longitudinal study of the acquisition of English by Alberto, a 33 year old Costa Rican, whose linguistic development had fossilized by the end of the study (i.e. after 14 months in the United States) and whose speech showed features of pidginization. (This case study formed part of a larger study, directed by Cazden, on the untutored acquisition of English by six native speakers of Spanish: two children, two adolescents, and two adults. Cf. Cazden, Cancino, Rosansky and Schumann, 1975).

These linguistic phenomena were explained in the following way: a language has three functions - the communicative, the integrative and the expressive. Pidginization is related to the restriction of language use to the communicative function[1], this restriction being the result of the learner's social and/or psychological distance from the target language, itself determined by social factors such as the size and cohesion of the SL community, its relation of dominance, non-dominance or subordination to the TL community, and these communities' attitudes towards each other; and psychological factors such as resolution or not of culture and language shock, stress, integrative vs instrumental motivation, ego permeability.

His argument would lead us to expect, therefore, that for example a Turkish worker in Germany, in a large, cohesive and dominated group, who has not overcome initial language and culture shock, and is under stress, and whose motivation for learning German is instrumental, will restrict himself in his use of German to its communicative function. His German will therefore fossilize at a low level, and be characterized by features of pidginization.

The factors which play a determining role in Schumann's argument belong essentially to what we have termed propensity and exposure.

Meisel, Clahsen and Pienemann (1981. Cf. also Meisel, 1982), reporting on ZISA's results, point to two weaknesses in both these approaches:

- social and psychological factors are relevant, but they are interdependent;
- these factors are used to explain the rate of acquisition, or the stage in acquisition that a learner attains, but not the variation observable between learners who can by certain criteria be deemed to be at the same stage of acquisition: "It is quite a remarkable fact that even those researchers who underline the importance of sociopsychological factors seem to view second language acquisition as a linear process. According to this position, social distance, attitudes, etc. only determine the degree to which the second language is acquired." (p.119).

They argue against this "uniformity hypothesis" and for an approach

---

[1] Defined as the transmission of referential, denotative, information. Roughly speaking, Givón's "pragmatic mode" (cf. 5.2) is used in situations where linguistic interaction serves strictly a communicative function.

whereby certain properties of learner varieties are not interpreted developmentally. In this alternative socio-psychological approach "one may be able to explain some features as being the result of strategies which are not shared by all speakers" (p. 131).

The "simplification strategies" Meisel (1982) observes in ZISA's informants' use of German are of two types - restrictive and non-restrictive - both of which result in structural simplification (and pidginized forms) but which serve different functions for the learner and correspond to different types of motivation. Both types of strategy can be used at all stages of acquisition: social/psychological factors should therefore be used to explain why a person might be of the type that uses certain strategies rather than others.

Both individual variation of the type described by Meisel, and "exceptions" to "overall" tendencies have to be accounted for. Von Stutterheim (1982) points out that about a quarter of the Turkish workers she studied were relatively successful in acquiring German:

"Workers who were interested and willing to make some effort in language learning usually had a relatively high level of social/political and linguistic awareness. They were conscious of the important role of language as a condition to express and carry out their personal needs. Their approach towards language is definitely 'communicative'[1] ... They regard the foreign language as an instrument to formulate their interests as Turks ... as a way to preserve their particularity as an ethnic minority." (p.3).

Such speakers are counter-examples to the pidginization hypothesis.

To sum up, the studies discussed suggest partially different cognitive, propensity and exposure factors as determining the acquisition process.

Others may turn out to play an important determining role in acquisition: for example, in the preceding quotation, v. Stutterheim mentions "awareness" as a possible factor not taken into account in the three other studies discussed. In the French pilot study (cf. Dubois et

---

[1] In the sense that Schumann uses this word.

al, 1981; Trévise, 1981; Mittner and Kahn, 1982; Véronique and Faïta, 1982),
an attempt was made to characterize some aspects of the linguistic awareness of informants, and some correspondence was found between informants'
linguistic background and social experience, and the different manifestations of this awareness. The study was, however, cross-sectional, and no
firm conclusions could be drawn as to the possible role of linguistic
awareness in the acquisition process. It is intended to investigate further
this possible factor in this project.

Thus, in our opinion, the position seems to be for SSLA that more
case studies are needed, which build on previous work, and which attempt to
define further the relevant factors which may determine the acquisition
process, and to characterize more precisely their relative role in this
process.

9.1.2 Criteria for informant selection. Given the considerations of
9.1.1, our criteria for selecting informants should be seen as an attempt
to build on the results of previous work, in that we have adopted some of
the explanatory factors put forward. These criteria cannot, however, be
seen as controlling for all the factors which may be significant for the
acquisition process (this is particularly true for propensity factors),
but rather as safeguards against too much obvious dispersion in the background and present situation of informants.

In what follows, the criteria discussed are valid for all SL informants, unless there are indications to the contrary.

(a) Cognitive/perceptual/motor factors. It was stated in 1.3.3 that
these factors were partially biologically given, and partially formed
by previous linguistic experience.

Obviously, informants should have no apparent impediment to
production and perception of speech, on the motor or pathological
level. The word "apparent" is used here as it is clearly impossible to test for this.

One of the major concerns of the project is to attempt to
characterize language-specific vs generalizable phenomena in the
acquisition process; that is, to examine the extent to which the
informant's SL determines the acquisition process. It is therefore
necessary to ensure that the TL is indeed the second (rather than

the third) language that informants are acquiring, and furthermore
to ensure that for each SL-TL group, the SL background of informants is as similar as possible. In other words, informants who speak
the same source dialect should be selected wherever possible.

The importance of studying the acquisition process from as
near as possible to its outset was stressed in chapter 1. It follows
that informants in the LGs (and in the ILGs) should have extremely
limited knowledge of the TL at the start of data collection, and,
preferably, have recently arrived in the target country.

Some recent research (Krashen, 1975; Rosansky, 1973, 1975)
has suggested that, in contradistinction to child acquisition,
adults acquiring a second language are helped by "instruction"
("instruction" refers here either to being taught the language,
or consciously structuring for oneself the input of the second language environment, this latter activity being facilitated by one's
formal education). Schumann sees age not as the critical factor,
but as an indication of the social and psychological development
of adults, which creates distance between them and the TL. In brief,
the older one is at first contact with the TL, the more psychologically and socially distant one is from the TL, and the less likely
one is to acquire it successfully. If "instruction" plays a role,
it is via one's distance from the TL, which determines one's in-
clination to benefit from "instruction".

Klein and Dittmar (1979), reporting an HPD's work, are also
careful not to state that age alone is a critical factor (despite
its high correlation with proficiency), and suggest that "both
cognitive or neurological factors and the different accessibility
[at different ages] to social contacts are responsible for this
result" (p.205).

Whatever the precise relationship between age, "instruction"
and previous formal education may be, it should be recalled that
HPD found that age upon arrival, educational level and formal professional qualifications correlated significantly with TL proficiency as measured by the syntactic index.

With these considerations in mind, informants of the LG and
the ILG will be chosen who are between 18-30 years old at the start

of the data-collection period. Klein and Dittmar state that "The
ten speakers with the highest syntactical index were 20 years on
the average when they immigrated, and the seven speakers who arrived when they were 40 years or older all belong to [the weakest]
group" (p.204). In the French pilot study, the three speakers (out
of eight) who were forty years or older on arrival form a homogeneous
sub-group both from the point of view of the (pidginized) forms they
used, and of the type of variability in their production. The five
other informants were all under thirty years old on arrival.

As opinions in some previous work vary (see above) as to the
precise effect of previous and current education in SSLA, it has
been decided to select informants who are not receiving regular
tuition in the TL, and who have had limited formal education in the
SL. This latter choice means that they are likely to be, broadly
speaking, working class.

As a final point, it is proposed that in the light of the
studies on sexual differentiation in speech and its role in linguistic
evolution (for an account of these studies, see Labov, 1972a: chapters 8 and 9), no sub-group of informants should be exclusively male
or exclusively female.

No formal tests are planned to measure informants' literacy
in the SL, or command of the TL; firstly because such tests would
have to be elaborated specifically for the type of informant we are
selecting, and secondly because it is not clear how these tests
would be accepted by informants at the appropriate time of administration, i.e. before data collection starts. Rather, such information
will be sought informally in the SL and TL during the preliminary
contacts and at the first interview, by asking the type of question
outlined in 9.1.3 below.

(b) Exposure. The choice of informants for the LG and the ILG with extremely limited knowledge of the TL entails finding informants who
have had hitherto little or no exposure to the TL. We will therefore be looking for informants who have either recently arrived in
the target country, or who, despite having lived there, have had
little or no opportunity for linguistic contacts in the TL, and
whose situation is such that they will have such contacts during

the data-collection period.

The LRGs, on the other hand, should have lived in the target country for at least five years, and be in a situation where their exposure to the TL is undergoing a change.

For the first two groups, informants should be living/working in an environment which is favourable to TL acquisition. The term "favourable" is difficult to define, and will have to be assessed intuitively on the basis of the first encounters. Broadly speaking, informants should have some daily contact with the TL in more than one of the observational domains listed in chapter 8, and repeated here: work place, leisure time, authorities and/or consultation, practical everyday interaction. Two extremes should be avoided: informants with much less contact with the TL than this intuitive mean - for example, a Moroccan wife who looks after the house and does the majority of her shopping in Moroccan shops - should not be selected; informants with significantly more contact with the TL than this intuitive mean should not be selected: that is, for example, informants who are married to a TL-speaker, or informants who have children receiving full-time education in the TL, or (as we said above) informants receiving regular tuition in the TL.

(c)   Propensity. The only "propensity" factor taken into account will be (the researcher's assessment of) informants' motivation to participate in the project and their willingness to co-operate with the proposed data-collection techniques.

Information will be collected on informants' expressed attitudes to the target language and culture, their communicative needs, and their expected length of stay in the target country. This information will, however, not serve to select informants, but rather to see if and how attitudes and expectations change during the course of data collection. Even on the (dubious) assumption that valid tests could be found to measure informants' attitudes, motivations and needs, it seems not feasible to administer such tests to such a population before data collection starts.

9.1.3 Conclusion

The longitudinal and initial learner groups. Here, the "ideal" infor-

mant will speak his/her SL, have extremely limited knowledge of the TL
and of no other language, will have had little formal education in the
SL and will not be receiving tuition in the TL. She/he will not be married to a TL speaker or have children attending school in the target
country, will be between the ages of 18 and 30 and entering an environment which is propitious to the acquisition of the TL.

It will prove difficult in some countries to find ideal informants.
Finns receive compulsory schooling until the age of 16; Finns, Punjabis
and informants from the Maghreb will in all likelihood have had some exposure to Swedish, English and French respectively, etc. However, the
criteria discussed will only be waived in cases of force majeure, the
overall priority being to find adult monolinguals with very little TL
knowledge and with a good prognosis for acquisition.

The long residence group. Here, the "ideal informant" will be between 23 and 35 at the start of data collection, will have been resident
in the target country for at least five years, and will be in a position
where changing personal circumstances make it seem plausible that a pre-
viously stable variety of the TL will undergo further change.

The native speaker group. Here, we wish to find informants who have
daily spoken contact with informants of the LGs, and whose speech is representative of what these latter informants hear. Members of the NSGs
will be matched as far as possible with the age, occupation and educational
level of the relevant members of the LGs.

Selection procedure. It was stated in chapter 8 that in the countries
dealing with LGs and ILGs, the net will be cast wide. The overall stragegy
will be to attempt to find at the outset of the project groups of about
15 informants for each SL-TL pair, with whom, minimally, an initial contact in the SL will take place, followed by a recorded conversation during
which some use of the TL will be made, if possible. On the basis of these
two (or more) encounters, informants will be asked whether they are prepared to participate in the LG or the ILG.

This means that during these encounters, the questions relevant to
the criteria discussed above will be asked, concerning:

(a) Information about the informant's social background: age; precise
     linguistic origin (dialect area); education (in particular reading
     and writing skills); professional status (occupation before emi-

grating); family status; time and circumstances of immigration,
etc.

(b)   Information about the circumstances of his life in the target
country, such as kind of job; abode; kind and intensity of contacts at work place, in leisure time, with authorities; whether
he (or she) regularly reads source- or target-language newspapers,
watches TV, etc.

(c)   Attitudes towards the host society and its language, including
evaluations of different communicative habits and other differences related to cultural background.

The first two types of information can be gained by either asking directly or, preferably, by making these issues thematic and talking about
them. The last kind of information may require a newspaper article or a
film sequence (cf. 8.2.3: Film Watching).

These questions will also serve in the initial encounters with potential informants for the LRGs.

The information gathered is organized under detailed headings in
the questionnaire given in the annexe to this chapter.

9.2   Finding and contacting informants

As the most important SL informants to find, contact and (cf. 9.3)
motivate are those of the LG, the following remarks are directed above
all towards the quest for such informants, unless stated otherwise.

The situation as regards potential informants in the different
countries is very different. Here, it is only possible to give, as an indication, the very different experiences of the Swedish and German pilot
teams in their quest for Finnish and Turkish informants, and to draw from
this account some very general guidelines. Their experiences also illustrate how practical considerations may interfere with the criteria for
informant selection described in 9.1.

9.2.1 The Swedish pilot study. The Swedish team started by building up a
contact network of organizations and made efforts to give the project maximal publicity, by printing an information leaflet, and contacting Swedish
and Finnish newspapers and radio stations in the Göteborg area.

The organizations were of several types; Swedish authorities (tax, immigration, housing); Swedish employers (Volvo, SKF, Hasselblad, etc.); small businesses (barber's shop, garage) and trade unions (the Lands Organisationen); Swedish educational institutions and churches. Foreign organizations contacted included the Finnish consulate and several Finnish immigrant groups.

As well as providing leads for personal contacts with informants (cf. below), these organizations provided statistics on the present state of immigration in Sweden and its likely development, material such as video-tapes, films, etc., and promises of concrete help. This last aspect is particularly useful in the quest for informants for the project itself:
- at the Swedish Ministry of Immigration, the official responsible for the sending of all official information to immigrants has agreed for the Swedish team to have use of his services at the start of the data-collection period; the Finnish Vice-Consul in Göteborg is arranging for personal introductions to Finnish workers;
- the Lands Organisationen's Göteborg branch held an official meeting on the project, which resulted in a decision to co-operate during the data-collection period of the project. This decision is important, as it may open up leads to hospitals, small businesses, etc., as well as to factories. The Swedish team were present at this meeting and were introduced to representatives of Göteborg's main immigrant groups, with whom contacts are being actively maintained.

Participant observation. During this initial contact period, the Swedish team also took part in, and recorded, group leisure activities such as billiards and drinking, and worked for short periods at Hasselblad and SKF.

Personal contacts. Several methods of primary contact were tried in Sweden: those directly arising out of contacts with organizations - contacts on the shop floor of factories, presentation to groups - as well as more direct means such as telephoning, sending literature to potential informants, and random contacts on the street and in trams. Friendship networks were also explored. These contacts resulted in the team obtaining a sufficient number of informants for pilot study data collections.

The implications for the project itself of the Swedish team's pilot work are as follows: there is access to a large number of adult Finnish workers through the organizations mentioned above. All of these workers are more than minimally literate, as schooling is compulsory in Finland. Many of them will also have had some prior contact with Swedish because of the important role Swedish plays in Finnish society. The vast majority of recently arrived workers go into large factories, where the environment does not stimulate language acquisition. Other, more favourable working environments are usually reserved for workers who have spent some time in Sweden and who can communicate in Swedish. The choice for the LG and the ILG is therefore between newly-arrived immigrants in a working environment which is not ideal for language acquisition, and workers whose knowledge of Swedish is considerably less than minimal, but whose working environment is conducive to communication in Swedish. Unless the trade union contacts established during the pilot year do provide information on, and leads to, newly-arrived workers employed in hospitals, small businesses, etc., the informants available who most closely correspond to the criteria described in 9.1 would therefore appear to be the newly-arrived factory workers.

9.2.2 <u>The German pilot study</u>. The German team started by contacting the relevant German authorities. However, political events in Turkey, and the general mistrust on the part of Turkish immigrants of German authorities made official lines of approach both difficult and unfruitful. For example, the aliens' office (<u>Ausländerbehörde</u>) furnished a list of over 20 addresses of Turks in the Heidelberg area who had lived in Germany for less than 3 years. One of these addresses proved to be correct.

 Rather than concentrate on these areas, the German team decided therefore that it would be more fruitful to try through less official channels, such as small business, the <u>Türkische Volkshaus</u> and the German-Turkish project group in Mannheim, the Weinheim project group, social workers and individual teachers of training courses, the most important of which is the MBSE (<u>Maßnahme zur Berufsvorbereitung und sozialen Eingliederung</u>). This line of approach was successful in providing the facilities for observation and personal contacts described below.

 <u>Observation</u>. Participant observation was possible in Heidelberg in a chemist's shop with a high proportion of Turkish customers, in a Turkish food shop also used frequently by Germans, and in a hospital with a pro-

portion of Turkish patients.

Personal contacts. The German team's contacts resulted above all from the "friend of a friend" approach, starting principally with contacts made at the MBSE, whereby researchers were introduced to a potential informant by a Vertrauensperson (person of trust), the introduction typically taking place in the informant's home. This approach also resulted in finding a sufficient number of informants for pilot study data collection.

The implications for finding informants for the LG of the pilot work undertaken in Heidelberg are difficult to assess, as legislation on immigration was changed at the end of 1981 in some Länder, including Baden-Württemberg where Heidelberg is situated. Hitherto, the situation had been as follows: in general, two types of potential Turkish informants still immigrated:

1.   recent political refugees, who are few and far between, reluctant to co-operate and extremely suspicious of tape-recorders;
2a. adult family members being re-united with a spouse who had worked in Germany for three years. A large majority of these are wives, who live typically in a home environment which is not conducive to the acquisition of German, and for whom our data-collection techniques are difficult to accept;
2b. young adults (aged 17-20) being re-united with a parent who had worked in Germany for three years. These young people were both easy to find (through the MBSE) and willing to co-operate fully with all data-collection techniques.

(1) and (2a) pose problems for data-collection that are difficult to resolve. As an illustrative example, the first Turkish adult woman to be interviewed in the pilot study had been in Germany for one month at the time of the interview. She is the most "Europeanized" of the Turkish women, with a city background (Istanbul), European clothes, sons with German friends and at least one German woman in her circle of acquaintances. Yet she had been out of her flat only twice since arriving, did not know the names of the streets in her area and remained extremely distrustful of tape-recorders even after the third visit. It would appear therefore unlikely that a newly arrived adult Turkish wife will be persuaded to be video-recorded: the invasion of privacy that video-techniques would cause in the home is out of the question,

and home is where such informants spend virtually all their time.

For (2b) however, there was access to over 700 informants in the Heidelberg-Mannheim area who could be divided by age into three sub-groups: (a) about 17; (b) about 18; (c) about 19. (These ages are approximate, as these young people give an "official" age to the administration which is often less than their real age.) Sub-group (b) would have been following a course, one day per week, at trade school (Berufsschule), sub-group (c) would have taken this course and would be looking for employment, sub-group (a) would have this course ahead of them.

The change in legislation means, however, that the age for being re-united with one's family has been reduced to 14 years for children, and that only those spouses may immigrate who were married in Turkey more than three years ago. These spouses may not work for the first five years of their residence.

For 1982, the choice of Turkish informants for the LG seems there-fore to be limited either to sub-group (b) or sub-group (c) of the young adults, or to informants with similar biographical characteristics who have not attended the Berufsschule, if they can be found. These latter are more likely to be young women than young men and it is hoped that their exposure to German will have been limited.

Preliminary enquiries by the Dutch team, and other independent stu-dies, show that the situation in Holland is similar to that before the change of legislation in Germany. A similar approach by both the German and the Dutch teams in 1982 is therefore likely to produce the best re-sults, and to ensure that both Turkish populations in the project are com-parable.

9.2.3 Summary. The quest for informants by the Swedish and German pilot teams suffices to illustrate the very different problems that all teams will encounter in the first months of the project. It also indicates the three main tasks each research team is undertaking or will undertake: (a) contacts with organizations, (b) participant observation, and (c) personal contacts, either directly or through a network. A fourth task (d) should be added to these three: personal research on the SL communities.

(a) Organizations. Organizations may provide, as in the Swedish case, information on the political conditions for immigration and the

working and living conditions of immigrants, as well as direct contacts with informants. There follows an indicative list of questions
that the Swedish team put to representatives of the different types
of organization:

Political and social authorities responsible for immigrants:
rate and manner of arrival; places of residence; living conditions
(standard of houses and sizes of rooms, residential density, services in vicinity); problems immigrants frequently face finding a
place to live, aid offered by public interpreters if any, social
security and medical services at hand; information concerning social, geographical and linguistic background (here, the statistics
available have to be consulted, as do accounts and papers from state
committees both in the source and the target country and papers
from other relevant scientific studies).

Persons receiving new immigrants at place of employment: policy of
employing immigrant workers (possible quotas, introductory phases,
e.g. the manner and elaboration of instructions given immigrant
workers by foremen, "old hands" and other persons); acceptance of
nationalities in a place of employment; acceptance of other languages (the language of notices and signs, explicitly stated policies
with regard to using immigrant workers' languages); interaction patterns in the place of employment during work, meal hours, rest
periods, before starting work, and after finishing a day's job,
observations made by foremen and "old hands"; how workers are allotted
tasks in respect of professional skills, age, sex, languages they
speak and know, and countries they come from; leisure activities
(adult education arranged by the place of employment, facilities
given by the employer for taking up sports etc.); duration of interactions between workers of different linguistic groups during
the working hours and leisure (the situations that allow for chatting
will be compared with the ones where this is restricted).

Representatives of immigrant organizations: number of immigrant organizations and size of their membership; nature of activities,
interest these arouse in the immigrant population; participation of
recently arrived immigrants in activities of organizations; formal
contacts between different immigrant societies; informal relations

(political, social, linguistic, and other relations members have
with other groups of immigrants, splits between various groups due
to the generation gap or to time of arrival in the host country);
other leisure activities (clubrooms, restaurants, immigrants' an-
nual festivities and possible campaigns to be acknowledged as a
minority); special groups and clubs dealing with immigrants' affairs
(e.g. professional social workers' gatherings).

(b) Participant observation. Participant observation in the early stages
of the project serves to gain an idea before data collection starts,
of the communicative interaction of TL and non TL-speakers (cf. 8.5).
It should then be possible to direct from the outset of data collection the relevant techniques towards recurring patterns of communication.

Participant observation, especially in the activities of immigrant organizations, may also help the researcher to become known,
and to gain trust in the SL community, and to establish contact with
informant networks.

(c) Personal contacts. The researchers' relationship with informants will
be discussed below in 9.3. It should simply be mentioned here that
the "snowball" effect of being introduced to friends of friends has
proved, overall, the most efficient way of finding informants. The
French team's pilot study, although smaller than the other two, also
used this method of contacting informants, to good effect.

(d) Personal research. In the period before data collection starts, researchers should become acquainted both with the general situation
of the SL community in the target country, and also with certain aspects of the source culture.

9.3 Motivation of informants

As was stated in chapter 8, it is essential to give (potential) informants a clear idea of the main characteristics of the project. At the
first contacts and in the first interview the learner should therefore be
informed about the following points:

(a) The interviewer is working at the university; doing these interviews is part of the job by which he earns his living.

(b)　The interviewer is interested, both professionally and personally, in the problems and difficulties of living and working in a foreign country, and especially in language problems.

(c)　The informant does not assume any obligation; nothing has to be signed, nothing will be sold, no propaganda will be made; we just want to talk to him about things he is particularly competent to talk about. No general guidelines can be given here about financial arrangements, as these may vary from country to country (see below).

(d)　In doing his job, the interviewer needs the help - the knowledge and the experience - of the informant; the informant is the expert, the interviewer is the learner in this field.

(e)　The results of this work may be of practical value for foreign workers, in helping to improve language courses, for example; they also help to gain a better understanding of foreign workers' language and social problems and thus may contribute to an improvement of their situation in general.

(f)　The interviewer is ready to help the informant with concrete problems.

(g)　The informant's co-operation will have no negative consequences for him; all information will be anonymous, and it will be exclusively used for the purposes mentioned above.

(h)　The recording on tape is necessary since otherwise important parts could be forgotten or incorrectly remembered; it also makes it possible to go back (possibly with the informant's help) over passages which the interviewer did not immediately understand or may have misunderstood in the conversation; finally, interviews with many informants could easily lead to confusion about who has said what; recording helps to avoid such confusion. This guarantees that the informant's opinion is correctly represented. Video recordings are sometimes necessary as we are interested in the way people can use movements to make themselves understood.

As the observation of informants goes on, they have to be informed in more detail about the objectives of the project; but these eight points should be given very early and to a large extent at the first interview.

The researcher should thus be seen as a committed observer, and fa-

miliarity with the SL-culture and with the situation of the SL-community
in the target country (cf. 9.2.3) should help him in being so perceived.
Progressively, he will become an enabler and a confidant. In this way, it
is hoped that informants will see encounters with researchers as meaningful and agreeable (cf. 8.1); in other words, that the different encounters
with researchers take place for a reason which they accept, and that these
encounters are enjoyable.

For the monthly encounters, the pretexts mentioned in 8.2.3 should
serve to avoid informants having either the impression that they are being
analyzed by a scientist or, at the other extreme, the impression that they
are dealing with a surrogate social worker interested exclusively in their
problems. It is hoped that in this way, the creation of a professional
stereotype will be avoided, as it could be de-motivating for an informant
to feel that once again it is time for the regular monthly interview.

Financial arrangements. The outline of researchers' relationship with
informants given above is not intended to disguise the fact that these latter are giving of their time, and providing an indispensible service.

The situations in the different countries are difficult to compare,
and do not allow us to state in detail what financial arrangements can be
made with the different informants. However, two broad principles must be
kept in mind:

(a)   Informants obviously must not suffer any material disadvantage from
       their co-operation with us. The implications of this (depending on
       the country and the type of informant) range from paying any trans-
       port costs incurred by informants, to buying lunch, for example, if
       an informant agrees to devote his lunch break to an encounter.

(b)   It may prove very worthwhile with informants of certain nationalities
       to pay them for specific services, or to offer a different type of
       compensation. In the pilot studies, the Swedish team found it was
       useful to give informants a small fee for a recording session and
       for work done outside encounters, such as self-recording or diary-
       keeping, whereas the German and French teams found that the organi-
       zation of dinners or parties for informants was better appreciated.

9.4 Ethical questions

The following statements are a representative selection of answers to a questionnaire given by a foreign worker, Saeed Anjum (1978), to foreign workers in Norway. "They" refers to researchers:

- They sell my feelings.
- They sell our ideas.
- They exploit us.
- They cheat us.
- I always cheat them, because they cheat us.
- They promise and do not fulfill.
- They do not want to listen to what I say.

On the (reasonable) assumption that Norwegian researchers do not differ from other researchers in that the former are exploiters and cheats and the latter are not, the above statements indicate the importance of the ethical aspects of our relationship with informants, and their complexity. It is only possible to summarize here what has been stated throughout this field manual, and indicate what concrete measures we are taking for protecting informants' anonymity.

Researchers go into this project in order to achieve a better understanding of the way in which informants acquire a second language and use it, and of the problems this can cause them, and will endeavour to make the results of the investigation benefit the communities from which the informants come.

We will try to build up a relationship of trust with the informants themselves. This means that they will be correctly informed of what we are attempting to do, that we will not make promises we cannot keep, that we will give help to the extent that we are able to. Very succinctly stated, we neither wish to be, nor give the impression that we are as Saeed Anjum's workers see researchers, and are aware of the great difficulties entailed in this.

Minimally, we must ensure that we take from informants only those data that they agree may be taken, and that these data are protected. It follows that:

No observation of them will take place without their prior knowledge.

In particular, no recordings will be made without their prior agreement, even in those countries where the law tolerates this;
- their anonymity will be guaranteed. A pseudonym will be used for each informant, and when necessary, other proper names will be deleted from transcriptions;
- audio- and video-recordings, and the complete transcriptions will only be available to researchers who have signed the Datenschutz (and corresponding documents in other countries);
- informants will be told of these measures.

Annexe: Social, biographical, propensity data

1. <u>Informant</u>

    Group: (longitudinal, long residence, etc.
                                              and source language)

    Informant's pseudonym:

    Sex:

    Age (estimated age):

    Religion:

2. <u>Source country</u>

    Place of birth:

    Region/province:

    Abode during childhood:

    Other abodes in source country: From: To:

    Reasons for change of abode:

    Parents' occupation:

    Noteworthy characteristics of upbringing:

268

Schooling: Where:
                                              How long:

Reasons for not attending/leaving school:

Reading/writing skills in source language:

Foreign language teaching in school:

Diplomas:

Professional qualifications in source country:

Professional occupation(s) in source country:
Occupation: Where: How long:

3. Languages

    Source language/dialect:

    Target language/dialect:

    Beginning of acquisition:

    Type of acquisition:

    Researcher's intuitive evaluation of target language skills:
    Speaking:

    Listening:

    Writing:

    Reading:

    Any other languages:

4. <u>Target country</u>

   Date of arrival:

   Reasons for coming:

   Circumstances of first weeks of arrival:

   Plan(s) for residence:
   Where: From: To:

   Previous periods of residence in target country:

5. <u>Work in target country</u>

   Employed/unemployed:

   Previous jobs:
   Where: Firm: From: To: Type of job:

   Present (last) job:
   Firm: Starting date:

   Type of job:

   Type of work place:

   Nationality of work mates:

   Language(s) spoken in work place:

   Language(s) written in work place:

   Meal breaks with:

   Other observations:

6. <u>Other outside activities in target country</u>

Contacts with authorities (including unemployment office):

Authority: Reason(s):   Frequency:

Free time activities:

Visits to/from:

Spends time with:

Reading habits:

Radio:

Television:
(sound on/off)

7. <u>Family circumstances</u>

Single/married: (since_____)

Period(s) spent separated from spouse:

Period(s) spent living with other family members in target country:

Other information:

<u>Spouse</u>

Nationality:

Abode:

Stay in target country:

Profession:

Target language knowledge:

Other information:

Children

	Age:	Abode:	Stay in target country:	TL knowledge:
Name:				
	Education:		Work:	Extra-family contacts:

Other information

Description of accommodation:

Neighbourhood:

Information on informant's search for accommodation:

Other information:

8.   Propensity data

8.1 Informant's experiences

Experiences of "being foreign", not knowing what is going on/
being made to feel at home, having things explained:

Key word: Cassette/protocol   Date:
                           reference:

Experiences of difficult/easy communicative situations:

Key word: Cassette/protocol   Date:
                           reference:

Experiences of discrimination:

Key word: Cassette/protocol   Date:
                                 reference:

8.2 <u>Attitudes to immigrant situation</u>

"Coping with" the immigrant situation (e.g., attitudes of resigna-
tion, expectation, resistance, assimilation; culture shock, etc.):

Key word: Cassette/protocol   Date:
                                 reference:

Feelings towards personal situation (e.g., feelings of contentment,
ambition, suffering, etc.):

Key word: Cassette/protocol   Date:
                                 reference:

Judgements on target country:

Key word: Cassette/protocol   Date:
                                 reference:

Judgements on/feelings towards TL-speakers:

Key word: Cassette/protocol   Date:
                                 reference:

Fears / wishes / hopes:

Key word: Cassette/protocol   Date:
                                 reference:

Future plans:

Key word: Cassette/protocol   Date:
                                   reference:

8.3 <u>TL-learning</u>

Situation with respect to TL-learning:

Key word: Cassette/protocol   Date:
                                   reference:

Attitude to TL-learning:

Key word: Cassette/protocol   Date:
                                   reference:

Attitude to TL:

Key word: Cassette/protocol   Date:
                                   reference:

10. Postscript

10.1 Eighteen months into the project

The Field Manual was completed in the summer of 1982, as the five teams were preparing to go out and look for informants, select them and start collecting data.

In the early fall of 1983, the project's steering committee (see chapter 2) met for the fourth time and decided that the project should go on with the informants and data-collection organization that it had at that time: no more informants were to be started, the data-collection schedule was definitive.

Thus it seemed appropriate to compare what we set out to achieve with what had concretely been achieved at the end of 1983, as the first eighteen months have, barring accidents, determined the type and quantity of data we will be analysing from the latter half of 1985 onwards.

As was stated in 9.2, the profiles of our "ideal" informants had to be confronted with the practicalities of the situation in each of the five countries. Some of the problems encountered by the research teams in matching the "ideal" profile proved to be intractible, others could be overcome. A brief description of all the SL informants engaged in the project is given in 10.2. The native speaker informants have not yet been interviewed, except in Aix-Marseille.

Chapter 8 gives the detail of the data-collection techniques which we use, and a sample schedule which indicates the quantity of work involved as well as the type of activities to be accomplished with longitudinal informants every cycle of three (audio-recorded, audio- and video-recorded) encounters.

With seven out of the ten SL-TL pairs, the schedule has proved impossible to keep exactly as had been planned. For these seven cases, informants' own commitments have meant that it is possible to meet with them on an average of once every six weeks rather than once every month (cf. 8.2.2). This fact, and the concomitant fact that accompanying observation (cf. 8.2.2

275

and 8.5.5) is totally dependent on the availability of informants, and on
their willingness to let us accompany them, led to the sort of co-ordinated
reappraisal of the data-collection schedule envisaged in 8.1.

However, this reappraisal went further than simply recognizing difficulties, and resulted in a much more ambitious and comparable data-collection
plan for the whole project than seemed at all possible in the summer of 1982.
This schedule is described in 10.3: all teams had accomplished half of it
(or slightly less, depending on the date when regular data-collection started
in each country) at the end of 1983.

10.2 Informants

Recall that for the main, longitudinal study, the "ideal" informant
(the "norm" of chapter 9) is aged between 18 and 30, has legal status, no
native TL-speaking spouse and no children of school age. His/her education is
limited. S/he is therefore probably working-class, with work (or some other
activity) providing day-to-day contacts in the TL. His/her proficiency is
very limited at the start of the investigation, thus s/he will normally
have been resident in the target country for a short while - preferably less
than one year - and will not be receiving regular TL tuition. The TL will
be his/her second language.

These characteristics also hold for the initial learner control groups:
both groups will therefore be dealt with in 10.2.1. The main characteristics
of the long resident informants will be discussed in 10.2.2. The native speaker informants have in most cases yet to be contacted.

10.2.1 Longitudinal and initial learner control informants. Immigration trends
from the source countries interacting with conditions of reception in the
target countries made it impossible to meet all the criteria defining the
"ideal" informant in all cases, more especially as in France, Sweden and
the Netherlands we were looking for homogeneous groups of sixteen informants
from each source language (see below). However, we had expected this (cf. 9.1).

The summer of 1982 therefore saw meetings take place between the teams
with a shared source language where they discussed the socio-biographical characteristics of the type of informant that preliminary field work had shown to
be available. These meetings were held to find a second best solution: namely,
that where one or more selection criteria could not be met, teams with a

shared source language "deviate" from the "norm" of chapter 9 in a co-
ordinated way, so that informants from one source country be kept comparable
in both target countries. This aim was achieved.

The main problems that proved to be intractable are listed below.
There then follows a brief description of the informants actually engaged
in the project.

Length of residence

The newly-elected French government passed a series of measures in the fall
of 1981 which restricted the influx of non-political immigrants, while
granting an amnesty to immigrants already illegally resident in France. Other
governments merely tightened already restrictive immigration rules at this
time. In the face of sometimes virtual impossibility to find newly-arrived
informants, it was decided to search for informants who had been resident
for less than a year and a half and whose TL proficiency was nevertheless
low.

Turkish informants

The situation in the Federal Republic of Germany (and in the Netherlands) at
the end of the project's pilot year is summarized in 9.2.2. It was decided in
Germany to look for informants where they could be found - i.e. in
the trade schools - and to follow their careers through the trade schools,
and afterwards at work.

Arabic-speaking informants

The one source country from which informants could be found in both France
and the Netherlands was Morocco. It was therefore decided to seek non-Berber-
speaking Moroccans in both countries: the disadvantage of the relatively
strong French colonial tradition in Morocco was thus counterbalanced by the
relative homogeneity of the spoken source language.

Spanish-speaking informants

There were virtually no newly-arriving immigrants from Spain in either country
(although Spaniards are traditionally an important immigrant group in France).
On the other hand, there was still a relatively large influx of Latin
American political refugees - and their families - in both countries. As was
stated in 1.1, immigrants to Sweden usually receive regular language teaching

on arrival: there are special language courses for refugees in that country, and this is also the case for France. Thus it was decided to sacrifice the criteria having to do with family status (children at school in particular), and language teaching (this latter being almost impossible to get round in any case in Sweden), for the linguistic interest of these pairings of source and target languages.

Numbers of informants

The table of 2.4 shows that we plan to end up with complete sets of data on 40 longitudinal informants (4 per SL-TL pair) and on 36 initial learner controls (6 per SL-TL pair). It was decided to play very safe at the beginning of regular data-collection, and to interview EIGHT informants for each individual group, if they could be found. They were.

Some informants have left us during these first eighteen months - for reasons ranging from lack of interest to illness, the birth of a child and, in one case, arrest and imprisonment.[1] The longitudinal informants mentioned below have therefore completed one half of the data-collection schedule and with the possible exception of the Latin Americans in Sweden - and barring unforeseen circumstances - should complete this schedule. The initial learner controls are being interviewed for a second time out of three at the time of writing. In Sweden, one Argentinian informant has already returned to his country after the elections there in 1983, and two others are quite reasonably envisaging the same move.

In what follows, the informants are discussed following the left to right organization of source languages in the table of 2.4. Their pseudonyms are given.

Punjabi informants: Longitudinal group

Eight Punjabi informants are working with us: Five men - their names are Ram,

---

[1] It should be pointed out that life affects researchers on the project, too. Five children have been born to members of the project so far: four in Sweden and one in England. Two more - in England and the Netherlands - are expected in the spring of 1984. One is planned in Paris for the spring of 1985. One member of the project has been victim to hepatitis, one to a sports accident and one, sadly, to the foolishness of a drunken driver. There seem however to be no permanent after-effects in these latter cases. So far, no project researcher has been arrested.

Malkit, Jagwinder, Amarjit and Gurdev - and three women - their names are
Polly, Balbir and Surjit.

The group corresponds generally to the "norm" of chapter 9, except
that all informants have a rudimentary knowledge of the related language
of the Punjab - Hindi. Ram, Malkit, Polly and Gurdev had, moreover, a small
amount of English teaching at school. This was, however, over ten years ago
and seems to have had little effect on their present command of English.

Malkit and Amarjit had been in England over a year and a half at the
outset of data collection.

Malkit is employed in a factory: his TL speaking and listening skills
were adequate at the start of data collection. The other men had very limited TL skills. They are, however, employed on a casual basis, and usually
by Indians, which means that their everyday contacts with the TL are not
optimal. The women are occupied as housewives, and also have limited everyday contacts with English. Balbir, however, started receiving English lessons
in September 1983.

Italian Informants: Longitudinal group
Eight informants are working with us in England, and seven in Germany.

In England, there are six men - Enrico, Antonio, Rudolfo, Carmine,
Raffaele and Salvatore - and two women - Maria and Laura.

All were educated for eight years (with the exception of Carmine, who
had only two years' primary school education). Rudolfo and Antonio had a
further five years' education and they, together with Raffaele, received
some formal French teaching. Raffaele has also been receiving TL-lessons
in England since January 1983.

The men are employed, part- or full-time, in manual jobs, thus coming
into regular contact with English. The women are mothers with babies and
have limited contacts with the English-speaking environment.

In Germany, there are five men - Alese, Casco, Tino, Vito, Marcello -
and two women - Angelina and Gina.

Again, all were educated for eight years, with Casco, Gina, Marcello
and Alese receiving two further years' vocational training. All received some
formal French and/or English teaching.

The men have similar employment to the informants in England. As for
the women: Angelina is married with a baby, Gina works as a house cleaner.

The two groups of informants are on the whole comparable. The most important difference between, on the one hand, these groups, and on the other hand the profile of the "ideal" informant, is the amount of formal (including language) teaching they received in their source country. The overall effect of this teaching is, however, unclear: certainly for those informants who left school after eight years, its benefits appear to have been very temporary. As regards foreign languages, they have forgotten almost all that they learned at the time.

Turkish informants

Germany: longitudinal group

Eight Turkish informants are working with us: seven young men - Abdullah, Cevdet, Ertem, Ertogan, Ilhami, Mustafa and Yaşar - and one young woman - Ayşe.

These informants form a homogeneous group. They were aged between 17-19 at the beginning of the data-collection period. All are single and live with their families and/or fathers. Ayşe is following the MBSE vocational course (which comprises some TL teaching, cf. 9.2.2). The young men all finished this course in July 1983, and most have found work by now. Ayşe has always had contacts with TL-speakers: such contacts were rare for the young men when they were taking their course, but the situation is now improving.

In all other respects, they correspond to the "norm" of chapter 9.

The Netherlands: longitudinal and initial learner control groups

There are six male longitudinal (L) informants - Mahmut, Osman, Ergün, Abdullah, Ahmet, Şenol - and eight male initial learner (IL) controls - Mehmet, Hüseyin, Haydar, Erdal, Yilmaz, Ayhan, Hikmet, Ferhat - being interviewed in the Netherlands.

These informants correspond to the "norm" of chapter 9 in all respects, except that some of them attend, or have attended vocational/language courses on a part time basis, and that one informant was 17 years old at the start of data collection.

The respects in which these informants are less than "ideal" would tend, therefore, to create greater comparability with the Turkish informants in Germany, as was expected.

Moroccan informants

The Netherlands: Longitudinal and initial learner control groups

There are seven L informants working with us in the Netherlands: five men - Mohamed, Hassan K., Hassan M., Mustapha and Rafa - and two women - Fatima and Fatna. The IL group also has five men - Abdeslam, Khalid, El Yazid, El Mofadel and Abdelkhalek - and two women - Khadija and Zeyneb.

These informants all correspond to the "norm" of chapter 9, except that eight of them have had some secondary school education involving some teaching in French, and that five informants are receiving some form of TL teaching. Two further exceptions are Mustapha and Fatna: both are aged between 30 and 35, Mustapha having a TL-speaking spouse, and Fatna having 3 children of school age.

France: Longitudinal and initial learner control groups

The longitudinal group in France comprises three men - Abdessamad, Abderrahim, Abdelmalek - and four women - Malika B., Malika H., R'quia D. and Zahra K. The IL group comprises six men - Abdelilah, Abdelsellem, Hassan, Mahani, Mohammed R., Mohammed B. - and six women - Aicha A., Aicha E., Babui, R'quia H., Zahra L. and Zahra S.

All these informants correspond closely to the "norm" of chapter 9, except that 5 are between 30 and 35, with two of them having children at school. Three other informants acquired some rudimentary Spanish on their travels before arriving in France.

Comparability both between and across these four groups is very high, the only noteworthy difference being the generally higher level of source country education and, in some cases, language teaching in the target country of the Netherlands group and the fact that, due to the French government's amnesty on illegal immigrants in late 1981, the French team's informants have generally been resident in France for a longer period.

Latin American informants

France: Longitudinal and initial learner control groups

There are eight informants in the L group: three men - Alberto, Pilucho, Ramon - and five women - Alicia, Bernarda, Gloria, Gladys and Palmira. The IL group comprises four men - Ariel, Enrique, Juan and Milton - and five women - Ana Maria, Carmen, Eva, Graciela and Zully.

All these informants are political refugees, and as such spent some months in refugee centres on arrival in France, where they received language and, optionally, professional training courses. Refugees tend to arrive with their families: all informants except Ramon, Rafaël, Ariel, Enrique and Graciela are in their thirties, married and with children of school age. The group is less well educated than many political refugees; the majority nevertheless received at least some secondary education in their home countries (Chili, Colombia, Uruguay, Argentina), with some (but in most cases negligible) English teaching. Gladys and Gloria received further training after secondary school.

Sweden: Longitudinal and initial learner control groups

There are seven longitudinal informants in Sweden: five men - Augusto, Carlos, Fernando, Gerardo, Leandro - and two women - Luisa and Nora. The IL group comprises six women - Bibiana, Camila, Laura, Magela, Raquel, Rubena - and two men - Pasquinel and Pedro.

The situation in Sweden is similar to that in France. Thus all informants but Pedro received TL courses in refugee centres on arrival. All but Bibiana, Luisa and Pasquinel are married with children, and in their thirties, except for Magela (28), Gerardo (45) and Raquel (50).

The two groups of informants are highly comparable. The only notable differences are that:

- the Paris informants have generally received more education in their home country;
- the average age of the Göteborg informants is four years higher than that of the Paris group.

Finnish informants: Longitudinal and initial learner control groups

There are six informants in the Finnish longitudinal group: three men - Mortti, Timo, Leo - and three women - Taria, Rauni, and Mari. The IL group comprises four men - Kunu, Ismo, Mikko, Voitto - and three women - Neiti, Raisa and Irja.

With the exception of Irja (26) these informants fall into two sub-groups: older (27-34: Timo, Rauni, Ismo and Raisa) and younger (19-23: the others). This division corresponds to a change in the foreign language teaching policy of Finnish schools; thus while all informants are relatively uneducated (for Finns) - 6 years (primary) Volksschule, 2 to 3 years secondary education plus in 4 cases a year's domestic science or mechanical training - the older informants had no foreign language training, whilst the younger informants received

at least three years' English language, and in some cases, some Swedish as
well. All informants were tested eight months or less after their arrival
in Sweden, and whilst the older informants' command of Swedish was extremely limited, the younger ones "go along" in speaking, listening, reading and
writing. Eight informants have enrolled in Swedish courses for Finns. In other
respects, these informants correspond to the "norm" of chapter 9.

10.2.2 Long resident informants

England

Four Punjabis - Mohan, Gurnam, Lal, Tara - and six Italians - Di, Lina, Elvira,
Elf, Steve and Fil - have been selected. All but Lina are men. Elvira, Steve
and Fil are in their fifties and have lived in England respectively, 25, 25
and 31 years. The others are in their forties, their residence varying between
17 and 27 years. All are employed in manual work.

Germany

Nine Turkish and eight Italian long resident informants have been found. The
Italian group comprises five women - Dina, Mani, Cusa, Gianna, Rubi - and three
men - Aia, Nello and Giulio. All are within the originally envisaged age range
except Nello (43), Mani (46) and Dina (55); their time in Germany varies from
6 to 21 years. Aia, Nello, Dina and Mani are employed in manual jobs; Giulio
was laid off last year; Cusa, Gianny and Rubi worked on arrival, but are
now married with children.

The Turkish group comprises six men - Yildaz, Akar, Kir, Bayrak H., Bakar
and Uyar - and three women - Bayrak M., Gezmiş and Özer. They are on average
older than the Italians; four are in their thirties, four in their forties
and one is about fifty. Their residence in Germany varies between 10 and 17
years. All are employed in manual jobs except Özer, who has five children to
look after.

Sweden

Six Latin American and eight Finnish informants have been found. The Latin
American group comprises two men - Julio, Domingo - and four women - Soledad,
Ana, Catalina, Mariana. All are in their mid to late thirties. All have taken
the compulsory refugee TL course. All except Julio (who is a driver) are presently employed as cleaners. They have been resident for a period of five to eight
years; Ana has, however, only been resident for three years.

The Finnish group comprises three men - Tipi, Kossi and Tiera - and five

women - Jatta, Jaska, Naimi, Ulpu and Asta. All are within the originally
envisaged age-range. All are employed in manual work. However, except for
Jaska (14 years) and Ulpu (6 years), their residence in Sweden varies from
4 to 2 years only.

10.3 Data Collection

10.3.1 A co-ordinated re-appraisal. As was mentioned in 10.1, it became quickly apparent that informants were not always available when we were available.
Conversely, conducting a longitudinal study with sixteen informants per team
initially entailed one recording about every two days if the monthly interval
between meetings was to be adhered to: The cross-sectional studies had to be
organized over and above this schedule, as did the varying forms of observation
(cf. 8.6.2). Thus in some countries, researchers were not able themselves to
adhere to the obligation of the monthly interval. These difficulties had to
be compensated for if a sufficient amount of comparable data was to be available
at the end of the longitudinal study.

Angelika Becker (Heidelberg) and Guus Extra (Tilburg) proposed an extension
of the "cycle" from its original three (audio, audio, video) encounters to a
more comprehensive structure lasting ten months, and repeated therefore three
times during the longitudinal study. This suggestion gave concrete form to the
generally felt need to safeguard comparability in the face of the differing
situations in each country. In elaborating on it, what was aimed for - and to
a large extent achieved - was a fairly ambitious overall plan of "core" techniques where both the type of recurring techniques and their order relative one
to another was specified, with the resulting schedule being divided into 6 to
9 encounters during the ten month period, depending on the resources of the
teams and the situation of the informants. This schedule allows longitudinal and
cross-sectional statements of the type: "In the first third of the first cycle
of data collection, technique x was used with this informant/all informants:
x was subsequently repeated twice, at ten-month intervals". This organization
had the further advantage that the relatively standardized initial interview
elaborated by each team to obtain relevant socio-biographical information on
informants as well as to gain a notional idea of their capabilities in the TL,
will itself be repeated twice. As a more comprehensive version of this interview is also used in most cases with the initial learner control groups, data
obtained from both types of informant is correspondingly more comparable than
initially envisaged.

Amongst the techniques being used by the different teams, the choice of those which should be included in the common "core" of the extended cycle was governed by the original choice of the authors of chapters 4 - 7 of this manual, who had suggested techniques which capture particularly relevant data for the major areas of research. The most frequently mentioned techniques, and their relevance, are listed in 10.3.2. Conversation is an integral part of every encounter, of course. For the others, all have been included at least twice in the extended cycle. This means in practice that, over and above conversation, particularly relevant data will be obtained at least twice per cycle for all topics of investigation except for (chapter 6) formulaic expressions, emotional attitude, modality, and (chapter 7) reference to future time. Data relevant for these topics will be found primarily (as originally envisaged) in spontaneous conversation.

All the techniques used were piloted (and are cross-referenced in 10.3.2 to the relevant paragraph of chapter 8) except one, elaborated by the Heidelberg team and used by all teams, which is worth describing here as the data obtained is proving to be particularly rich for two major research areas: the thematic structure of utterances and reference to people and time.

The Heidelberg team produced an edited version of Charlie Chaplin's silent film Modern Times. The plot is as follows:

Section 1 - Subtitle: America 1930 - poverty, hunger, unemployment
Charlie gets into a demonstration against unemployment, is taken for the leader and put into prison. At dinner one of his fellow-prisoners hides cocaine in the salt-cellar, and Charlie helps himself by mistake. With the drug he gains a heroical force: he foils an attempt to escape and frees the Director, who, in gratitude, releases him with a letter of reference for a job, which Charlie doesn't feel too enthusiastic about because in prison he is better off, he feels, than at liberty. However, he finds work in a shipyard, where he causes the launching of a ship that was not finished, is immediately fired and is all the more determined to go back to prison.

Parallel with this we see a second story: A young girl (whose father is unemployed and has no money to feed his three children, their mother being dead) steals food for her family. Her father is shot in a demonstration, and the children have to go to an orphanage. The girl manages to escape at the last moment.

Section 2 - Subtitle: Determined to return to prison

The girl roams through the streets hungrily, and steals a loaf of bread. When she tries to escape she runs into Charlie and both fall to the ground. A woman, who watched the theft, calls the baker. The policeman comes to arrest the girl. Charlie tries to claim responsibility for the theft but it doesn't work. The girl is marched off to prison.

Charlie tries again to get back to prison. He goes to a restaurant, eats as much as he can, calls a policeman from the street and tells him that he has no money to pay the bill. He is arrested.

In the police-car he again meets the girl who stole the bread. In an accident they are both thrown out. The girl suggests that he escape with her, and he does. In the garden of a middle-class house they rest for a while, and watch the couple who live there say a tender good-bye to each other in front of the door. Middle-class conjugal bliss. Charlie and the girl dream of an existence like that. A few days later the girl has a surprise for Charlie, having found such a house for both of them. It turns out to be a ruined cabin in a miserable condition, so that a series of accidents happen when they first come to see it. But they won't let this disturb their happiness. In the last picture we see them walking on a long road that disappears into the horizon.

This edited version is therefore in two sections. In the first (about 14 minutes), the two main characters are established, and their stories run in parallel. Researcher and informant watch this section together.

The researcher leaves the room, the informant watching the second part (about 10 minutes), where the main characters' stories converge. At the end, the researcher comes back into the room and the informant re-tells the second part.

The informant's production thus starts at a point where the knowledge of the researcher and himself is mutual ("given"). He relates events "new" to the researcher (and the established or "new" participants in these events), where the relative order that he assigns them and the relative importance that he attributes to them, can be checked back against the original film.

10.3.2 <u>The data-collection cycle</u>. Table 1 sets out the data-collection cycle with the principal data-collection techniques used, that is, techniques shared by three or more teams. Comparability of data-collection is in fact higher than the table indicates, as some teams with a shared SL also share additional techniques which are not mentioned.

The activities taking place in each encounter are listed in the left-hand column, together with a reference to the relevant paragraph of chapter 8. Each TL team has an identical schedule for both sets of SL informants except France, where the part of the team working with Moroccan informants in Aix-Marseille has adopted a nine-encounter cycle in line with the Dutch team, and where researchers working with Latin American informants in Paris have adopted a six-encounter cycle, more in line with the Swedish team. The columns to the right, under the various S- and TLs indicate the encounter during which a given activity takes place in a particular team's cycle. Discrepancies can be noticed when a number in a right-hand column does not correspond to the number of an encounter: these discrepancies are due mainly to the fact that the number of encounters per cycle vary, and to the fact that the extended cycle was being negotiated during the first months of data collection. The data-collection cycle of the Aix-Marseille team serves as a model for the ordering of the different techniques in the left-hand column.

See table 1 here

The schedule is based on the "particularly relevant activities" mentioned above. These activities are listed below, with the encounters in which they occur and with remarks on their relevance for the domains of investigation summarized from chapters 4 - 7.

(i) <u>Conversation</u> is relevant for all domains of investigation and occurs in all encounters. In some, the main theme of the conversation is chosen in advance.

(ii) <u>Play scenes</u> occur in encounters 1, 3 and 6. The dialogue elicited in play scenes is relevant for chapter 5 (question-answer sequences, ellipsis) and for chapter 7 (deictic shift). Completed by self-confrontation (encounter 4 and 7) they are relevant for chapter 4: explicating misunderstandings and processing the input.

A contrast of play scenes involving researchers with those involving non-researchers is relevant for chapter 4: conflict, cooperation and analyzing the speech stream. Furthermore, they are usually relevant for one of the lexical domains selected: for example, Tilburg and France have similar play scenes involving the domains "work" and "home/social relations".

(iii)<u>Film watching</u> occurs in encounters 2 and 5. It is relevant, in its original

Table 1:   Data Collection Cycle

	English / Punjabi	German / Italian	Dutch / Turkish	Moroccan / French	French / Spanish	Swedish / Finnish
	7 encounters	6 encounters	9 encounters	9 encounters	6 encounters	7 encounters
1) Conversation: socio-biographical information (systematic update),(cf. 8.3.1.-8.3.5)	1	1	1	1	1	1
vocabulary elicitation (home,work,social relations) (cf.8.3.4.2)	3	4	1	1	3	4
short play scenes (cf.8.4.2)	Ø	1	Ø	1	1	1
2) Conversation:	2	2	2	2	2	2
description of a picture of a street scene (cf.8.3.4.2)	1	2	Ø	2	2	4
3) (Video-recorded) Conversation:	3	3	3	3	3	3
stage directions experiment (cf.8.4.3)	2	3	3	3	3	5
play scenes (cf. 8.4.2)	3	6	3	3	2	2
film-watching: recounting the story	2	3	3	Ø	Ø	Ø
film-watching: elicitation of cultural background assumptions (cf. 8.2.3.1)	2	Ø	3	3	3	2
4) Conversation:	4	4	4	4	4	4
self-confrontation with recording of previous encounter's play scenes (cf.8.4.4)	4	Ø	Ø	4	3	2
5) Conversation:	5	5	5	5	5	5
broken-off film experiment (Modern Times) (cf. 10.2)	4	6	6	5	4	7
6) Video-recorded Conversation:	6	6	6	6	6	6
extended role-play with project-external professional (cf. 2.5.2. & 10.2)	6	5	6	6	4	5
7) Conversation (argumentative sequences) (cf.8.3.3):	7	1	7	7	Ø	7
self confrontation with recording of previous encounter's role-play (cf.8.4.4)	7	1	7	7	5	6
8) Conversation (briefing on accompanying conversation):	Ø	Ø	8	8	Ø	Ø
accompanying observation (everyday interactions in town)(cf.8.5.5)	5	Ø	8	8	6	3
9) Conversation	Ø	Ø	9	9	Ø	Ø
reactions to (confrontation of) accompanying observation	6	Ø	9	9	1	3
route directions (cf. 8.3.4.2)	7	6	9	9	6	7

xi
viii
xii

The ordering will be corrected in
the second printing of the book.

NEWBURY HOUSE PUBLISHERS, INC.
ROWLEY, MASSACHUSETTS 01969

version (cf. 8.3.2.1), to chapter 4: cultural background assumptions, and in its Heidelberg version (encounter 5, used by all teams, cf. above 10.3.1) generally to chapters 5 and 7, and specifically to controlling, in a story-re-telling task, the variable of given/new information in the structure of the learner's utterances, to foregrounding and backgrounding, and to the expression of temporal relations.

(iv) <u>Self-confrontation</u> occurs in encounters 4, 7 and, in less systematic form, in encounter 9. Its relevance, apart from what is already mentioned in (ii), is to investigate informants' use of metalinguistic vocabulary and their linguistic awareness (chapter 6).

(v) <u>Prepared experiments</u>: various vocabulary elicitation techniques relevant to the main domains of chapter 6 - home, work, social relations - occur in encounter 1.
A picture describing experiment occurs in encounter 2. This is relevant for chapter 7 - reference to people and space - and poses problems of linearization relevant to chapter 5.
A route directions experiment occurs in encounter 9. This, and also the (video-recorded) stage directions experiment of encounter 3, are relevant for chapter 7 - reference to space - and pose different problems of linearization relevant to chapter 5.

(vi) Finally, in order to guarantee some prepared and co-ordinated interactions with TL-speakers not involved in the project, an extended role play with such a person occurs in encounter 6, and a type of accompanying observation involving a trip into town with informants, and recording a series of short interactions in shops, information offices, travel agencies, etc. occurs in encounter 8. <u>Non-project-specific interaction</u> is relevant for all domains of investigation.

10.4 Conclusion

The previous paragraphs should give the reader a fairly clear idea of the extent to which the field-work of the first eighteen months of the project is producing the type and quantity of recorded data we set out to obtain.

To conclude simply for the main study: For informants, the situation is of course not perfect. Our Turkish informants are younger than we would have wished and our Latin American informants, older: we thus have an age-range of about seventeen years instead of the twelve years we had set ourselves. These two groups of informants have to follow some language, or vocational courses,

or a mixture of both, on arrival in the target country: we would have preferred this not to be the case. Other informants (particularly the Moroccans
in France, but also a few other individuals) had already been resident in the
target country for longer than we would have wished; similarly, the Punjabi
group, the mothers of young children, and some others, have less regular contact with their TL environment than would be ideal. The education system in
Italy and Finland in particular is such that these informants are relatively
well-educated, and some of them have some knowledge of another foreign language.
Finally, we have with our Moroccan and Punjabi informants, people who come from
an environment influenced respectively by the French and British colonial tradition.

These factors were of course for the most part beyond our control. What
can be said on the positive side is that local comparability has been achieved,
and that there is no major disturbing factor overall. We see no reason, in particular, for the moment at least, to regret having chosen to count language
teaching merely as one of a set of variables we would have to deal with
(cf. 1.2). And above all (with the caveats of the previous paragraph) sufficient
numbers of informants have been found of the type that we wanted to work with.

For data collection, the situation is again not perfect. The two black
clouds are that:
- While informants are being interviewed regularly, they will not (with the exception of Tilburg and Aix/Marseille) have been interviewed as often as we
  would have wished within the thirty month data-collection phase. We will have
  in the majority of cases, therefore, about twenty, rather than about thirty,
  interviews per informant.
- We are having difficulties in obtaining as much data from "authentic interactions" in relation to the amount obtained from "project-specific interactions"
  (cf. 2.5.2) as we would have wished. On the other hand, a certain amount of
  comparable data from "authentic interactions" is indeed being obtained.

What can be said here on the positive side is that large sets of highly
comparable data which are relevant for the main research areas are being collected,
transcribed and stored. The data-collection schedule is already proving to be
a very useful tool in choosing the data to store as a priority on the computer
in order to do pilot coding, and it will also be a very valuable tool in 1985
in selecting data for systematic cross-linguistic analysis. But that is a fence
to be jumped when we get to it.

Clive Perdue, Nijmegen, January 1984

Appendix: An overall scheme for analyzing interactions[1]

1 <u>Step one: forming a preliminary hypothesis</u>. We have said that the successful negotiation of meaning in any interaction depends on the extent to which cultural assumptions, and the linguistic tools used for signalling these assumptions, are shared by the participants.

The type of assumptions we have in mind are listed in 4.2.7: Variables of the Interaction. They can be grouped in the following way:

(a) the situation in which the interaction takes place, and especially such aspects of the situation as the participants' relative status and power, and how this determines appropriate behaviour;

(b) the purpose of the interaction: the attitudinal and instrumental goals of the speakers, and whether these goals are mutually compatible;

(c) speaker perspective, interpersonal relationships and co-operation: the signalling and interpreting of emotions and attitudes during the interaction, the effects of this on the positive and negative face-holding (cf. 4.2.3) of the interactants, and the overall co-operation of the participants in negotiating meaning.

The preliminary "top down" hypotheses will be formulated from what the analyst thinks the participants' perception is of the above factors: whether they have the same perception of the (in)equality of their relationship, whether they are aware of the (in)compatibility of their attitudinal and instrumental goals, and whether they feel they are interpreting each other's meaning correctly. These hypotheses are then checked against linguistic features of the text.

---

[1] This appendix is a detailed account of the "top down, bottom up" analysis elaborated by the English team, which was outlined in 4.2.6.

For example, one's overall hypothesis about role, status and power in the interaction can be checked by looking at features such as prosodic patterns, turn-taking, directness/indirectness, the structuring of the argument, etc. Alternatively, (the "bottoming up" approach) one might observe a feature like recurrent hesitation in the text, hypothesize that this indicates that the speaker perceives himself to have low status, and then check against other evidence in the data.

In either case, one would be examining whether the participants: shared the assumptions about status (or whatever); shared modes of signalling/interpreting feedback on these assumptions; shared ways of establishing and interpreting sympathy and goodwill.

We can expect that the more that is shared in the way of cultural assumptions and their linguistic signalling in the areas outlined in (a) - (c) above, the less language will be required to reach understanding, and conversely, the smaller the congruity of shared assumptions, the greater the amount of language required to negotiate meaning.

2 Step two: preliminary prosodic analysis. In order for the data to be processed, they have to be broken down into units that are both manageable and meaningful. The unit that fits the purpose is the information (or sense) unit.

In English, the information unit may be regarded as primarily syntactic, but it is coterminus with and only takes on its full meaning through its prosodic expression, the tone group.

However, when examining the prosodic and syntactic structure of immigrants' English, we found that prosodic features are frequently substituted for syntax, not supplementary to it as in English-English (EE). It emerged that in attempting to map the EE tone group system onto different SL speech, we were distorting our perceptual experience to fit our preconceptions and indeed overlooking patterns that might emerge if we had tried to derive them from the L2 speaker's discourse itself.

We felt the need therefore to find a system of notation that reflected a separate perception of stress-patterns (rhythm) and pitch-change, instead of perceiving the two inextricably linked together in the traditional notation of pre-head, head and nucleus.

As a result we decided to describe the prosody by:

(a) division into rhythmic feet;

(b) marking in the pitch contours.

As a guideline we assume that there will be patterns and rules of use of pitch and rhythm emerging that have definite identifiable discourse functions in L2 use and the analyst can begin to suggest what those patterns and functions might be. For example, are particular pitch or rhythmic changes or patterns used to signal important or new information; is pitch used within the clause to indicate focus; does pitch have a referential function, binding different parts of the discourse together?

This process of noting and interpreting patterns is a "bottom up" process in which one is attempting to derive "rules" from the data.

We can also begin to suggest whether these signals are being read by the other party to the interaction, and whether the L2 speaker is picking up on the prosodic signals of the TL speaker.

3 <u>Step three: modifying and elaborating the working hypothesis: i.e. re-write</u>. Relating the prosodic analysis back to the initial working hypothesis about the whole interaction will give a first check on whether the data appear to confirm, deny or modify the initial perceptions. It will certainly provide a more detailed view of what is going on than the initial "top down" process, and will also show points of interest or difficulty in the interaction.

In order to explore these points further, and to begin to look at prosody in conjunction with syntax and other features, it is useful to paraphrase those parts of the informant's discourse which appear to the TL observer to lack cohesion and coherence according to the preliminary interpretation of what the speaker meant.

Re-writing will take place in order to provide such information as is understood or elided, but not verbalized, and may involve:

(a) changes and additions in syntax;

(b) additional discourse markers; to make the discourse more cohesive and coherent it may be necessary to experiment with devices such as sequencing, feedback markers and connectives.

One cannot do everything at once, however, and so interactional features will be dealt with in 5 below;

(c) changes in prosodic features.

The purpose of re-writing is not to set a model for what "should" have been said, but is to alert the researcher to: recurrent features of interest or difficulty, and the kinds of relationship that exist between the formal features of the language used, and the whole communicative interaction.

It is worth re-writing more than one alternative of more than one part of the discourse, and checking these for internal consistency. By re-writing, one is conjecturing what the speaker perspective and goals may have been. One may re-write in different ways to give rise to different hypotheses. This may result in the generation of more hypotheses from which a final selection can be made, rather than narrowing down the range of choice.

In this way one can finally select which of the alternatives has the greater probability of carrying the speaker's meaning.

At the end of this process one should have a hypothesis of the interaction which is much more detailed than the initial one and which should reflect something of the way in which meaning is being negotiated throughout the interaction.

4 <u>Step four: prosody, syntax and lexis</u>. The process of relating prosody to syntactic and lexical features of the discourse involves an examination of the cohesive role they play at the clausal level, the inter-clausal level and at the discourse level (i.e. the whole interaction).

As relationships between prosody, syntax and lexis emerge they will either support or refute the initial hypothesis formulated by the researcher in step one and thus act as a bottoming up reality check on this hypothesis.

The researcher attempts to derive "rules" from the prosodic and syntactic features that may have definite signalling functions. These "rules" may then support/refute/modify the hypothesis about what is going on in the conversation. One is not therefore simply looking for and describing features that are different from native speaker practice. Rather, one is looking for factors of two types:

(a) features different from that of the TL which are used systematical-
    ly and meaningfully by the L2 speaker. For example, one may find a
    systematic use of the following features to indicate contrastive-
    ness:

    if it's my <wall>↑ or somebody else wall↓ | <emphatic stress>

    i.e. the speaker uses high pitch and loudness on the first noun,
    and "redundantly" repeats this noun. A result of this might be that
    while the L2 speaker feels a contrast is being made (the second
    noun is predicted by the pitch and stress of the first) the TL hear-
    er may not notice this contrast (since he would be expecting con-
    trastive stress on the determiners) and may consistently fail to
    retrieve the point being made;

(b) syntactic features similar to those used in the TL which may not
    actually have the same intended meaning but may be an expression
    of different "rules" imposed from the SL. An example of this would
    be the use of <u>even so</u> to replace emphatic particles used in Hindi.

The function of these differences or similarities to TL speech may
be to augment meaning (by, for example, using SL prosody as a substitute
for TL syntax), or to supplement TL syntax in order to express meaning
carried by devices common in the SL. Uses of prosodic and syntactic features may be the following:

	PROSODY	SYNTAX
Within the clause:	to signal focus;	to signal focus.
Interclausally:	to relativise/topicalise old/new, important/less important information;	to relativise and cohere: e.g. conjoining, embed-ding, repetition, structu-ral parallellism.
At the discourse level, i.e. the whole interaction:	pitch and rhythm changes used to signal cohesion between one part of the interaction and another;	deictic reference used to refer to something other than what a native speak-er would expect; structu-ral parallelism used to make connections between parts of the discourse which may be quite distant from each other.

Lexis will be examined in relation to syntax and prosody across
clauses in order to see how lexis is used to establish semantic links

through devices such as parallelism.

Throughout this process of correlating the formal features of the language with illocutionary intent, one should be constantly cross-checking with the initial hypothesis and refining one's views of the detailed operation of the variables of the interaction (cf. 4.2.7).

5 Step five: synthesis. We are now in a position to draw a much more detailed picture of what is going on in the interaction since we have gained insights into the way that the informant makes use of his L2 (cf. steps two, three and four). This means that we can now look more meaningfully at features of discourse management from two points of view: (a) the progression of speaker intent, and (b) co-operation between speakers.

(a) Progression of speaker intent. This will involve an examination of how the informant achieves coherence in the TL through:

   - topicalisation; modes of focussing to distinguish important/less important, old/new information;
   - relativisation; demonstration of relationships between informa-
     tion units; deixis; reference to person, place and time; con-
     trastiveness;
   - speaker perspective; signalling, display or indication of emo-
     tions and attitude; involvement in what speaker is saying;
   - illocutionary meaning; signalling through prosody, choice of
     lexis;
   - structuring the argument; e.g. repetition or elaboration; se-
     quencing of content; reference and correctives.

(b) Co-operation between speakers. Here, the interactants' strategies for production and interpretation of the following features will be examined;

   - opening, closing, turntaking; introduction of self, politeness
     formulae, phatics. Such interactive features may be crucial to
     the development of attitudes on either side, particularly if the
     informant uses conventions different from those of the native
     speaker;
   - feedback elicitation and giving: verbal/non-verbal backchannel-

ling; self / other correction; maintenance/alteration of perspective. Are the participants aware of the intention behind the
techniques the other employs?;
- recognition and repair of misunderstandings: acknowledgement,
  perlocutionary effect in relation to illocutionary intent, miti-
  gation;
- appropriacy: of content (sequencing); of register (status, role);
  of non-verbal gesture and body language; directness/indirectness
  in relation to respect for the other; agreeing/disagreeing;
- meta-talk: confirmation, summary of own or other's meaning.

As a result of this examination we can make a choice between the
hypotheses made at re-writing stage.

We can also make an assessment of the success of the interaction in
relation to the goals. Success is likely to be influenced by the mutual
compatibility of goals. For example, the speaker's intention may be conveyed to the hearer, but the instrumental goals of one speaker may still
not be achieved if they are incompatible with the goals of the other.
Conversely, an attitudinal goal (such as wishing to show respect) may
not be attained (e.g. because the perlocutionary effect fails to match
the illocutionary intent) but, given goodwill and sympathy on the part
of the TL speaker, the informant may still be successful in achieving
his/her instrumental goal (cf. 4.2.3).

References

Allwood, J.: The complex NP constraint as a non-universal rule and some
semantic factors influencing the acceptability of Swedish sentences
which violate the complex NP constraint. University of Gothenburg
1974.

Allwood, J.: Linguistic Communication as Action and Co-operation. University of Gothenburg 1976.

Allwood, J.: On the analysis of communicative action. Gothenburg Papers in
Theoretical Linguistics 38 (1978).

Anjum, S.: What foreign workers think about... In: Papers from the First
Scandinavian-German Symposium on the Language of Immigrant Workers
and their Children, Eds. N. Dittmar et al. Roskilde (Denmark) 1978,
283-284.

Arditty,J. and M. Mittner (Eds.): Acquisition d'une Langue Etrangère I
(Encrages numéro spécial). University of Paris VIII 1980.

Arditty,J. and C. Perdue: Variabilité et connaissances en langue étrangère.
Encrages numéro spécial, 32-43 (1979).

Åslund, J.: Araber skriver svenska - arabisk syntax och arabers syntaxfel
i svenskan. University of Stockholm 1976.

Bannert, R.: Ordprosodi i invandrarundervisningen. University of Lund 1979.

Bannert, R.: Svårigheter med svensk uttal: inventering och prioritering.
University of Lund 1980.

Barkowski, H. et al.: Handbuch für den Deutschunterricht mit ausländischen
Arbeitern. Scriptor, Königstein (Ts) 1980.

Bates, E.: Processing strategies in second language acquisition. University
of Colorado, Boulder 1981.

Becker, A. et al.: Sprachliche und soziale Determinanten im kommunikativen
Verhalten ausländischer Arbeiter. In: Sprachstruktur-Sozialstruktur,
Ed. U. Quasthoff. Scriptor, Königstein (Ts) 1978, 158-192.

Becker, A. and W. Klein: Eine Gesprächsanalyse. In: HPD Arbeitsbericht V.
University of Heidelberg 1979, 126-173.

Becker, A. and C. Perdue: Ein einziges Mißverständnis: wie die Kommunikation schieflaufen kann und weshalb. To appear in: Osnabrücker Beiträge zur Sprachtheorie, Osnabrück 1982.

Belder, S., H. Hulshof, B. Visser and J. de Vries: Een probabilistische grammatica voor Nederlandse nominale groepen van enkele Turken. GLOT 3, 99-116 (1980).

Benveniste, E.: Problêmes de Linguistique Génêrale. Gallimard, Paris 1966.

Berthoud, A.-Cl.: Rôle de la mêtalangue dans l'acquisition de la dêixis spatiale. Encrages numêro spêcial, 109-117 (1980).

Besse, H.: Le discours mêtalinguistique de la classe. Encrages numêro spêcial, 102-108 (1980).

Bhutti, S. and H. Kanitkar: Ethnic Minorities and the Adult Education Service. Commission for Racial Equality, London (in prep.).

Bodemann, Y. and R. Ostow: Lingua Franca und Pseudo-Pidgin in der Bundesrepublik: Fremdarbeiter und Einheimische im Sprachzusammenhang. In: Sprache ausländischer Arbeiter, Ed. W. Klein. Vandenhoek and Ruprecht, Göttingen 1975, 122-146.

Bourdieu, P.: L'êconomie des êchanges linguistiques. Langue Française 34 (1977).

Bourdieu, P. and J.-Cl. Passeron: La Reproduction. Editions de Minuit, Paris 1970.

Boutet, J., F. Gauthier and M. Saint-Pierre: La notion de phrase chez les enfants de 6 à 12 ans: une êtude expêrimentale. Encrages 8/9, 131-138 (1982).

Brown, P. and S. Levinson: Universals in language usage. In: Question and Politeness, Ed. E. Goody. O.U.P., Oxford 1978.

Brown, R. and A. Gilman: The pronouns of power and solidarity. In: Style in Language, Ed. Th. A. Sebeok. M.I.T. Press, Cambridge, Mass. 1960, 253-276.

Bühler, K.: Sprachtheorie: die Darstellungsfunktion der Sprache. Fischer, Jena 1934. Reprinted in 1965 by Gustav Fischer Verlag, Stuttgart.

Cadiot, P.: Ordre des mots et interlocution. In: Pratiques et Thêories de la Sociolinguistique, Eds. J. Marcellesi and B. Gardin. Rouen 1980.

Cazden, L., H. Cancino, E. Rosansky and J. Schumann: Second language acquisition in children, adolescents and adults. Research Report, Cambridge, Mass. 1975.

Clahsen, H.: Psycholinguistic aspects of L2-acquisition: word order phenomena in foreign workers' interlanguage. In: Second Language Development. Trends and Issues, Ed. S. Felix. Narr, Tübingen 1980, 57-79.

Clahsen, H. and J.M. Meisel: Eine psycholinguistische Rechtfertigung von Wortstellungsregeln. Papiere zur Linguistik 21, 3-25 (1980).

Clahsen, H. et al.: Deutsch als Zweitsprache. Der Spracherwerb ausländischer Arbeiter. Narr, Tübingen (in prep.).

Clark, E.: Awareness of language: some evidence from what children say and do. In: The Child's Conception of Language, Eds. A. Sinclair, R. Jarvella and W. Levelt. Springer, Berlin 1978, 17-44 (= Clark 1978a).

Clark, E.: From gesture to word: on the natural history of deixis in language acquisition. In: Human Growth and Development, Eds. J. Bruner and A. Garton. Clarendon Press, Oxford 1978, 85-120 (= Clark 1978b).

Clark, H. and C. Marshall: Definite reference and mutual knowledge. In: Elements of Discourse Understanding, Eds. J. Aravind, B. Webber and I. Sag. C.U.P., Cambridge 1981, 10-63.

Clyne, M.: Zum Pidgin-Deutsch der Gastarbeiter. Zeitschrift für Mundartforschung 35, 130-139 (1968).

Deulofeu, H.-J.: Y a-t-il un dialecte propre aux enfants de migrants? Champs Educatifs 1, 25-31 (1980).

Deutsch, W.: Sprachliche Redundanz und Objektidentifikation. University of Marburg 1976.

Dietrich, R.: "Bestimmtheit und Unbestimmtheit im Deutschen eines türkischen Arbeiters - Eine Hypothese", University of Kassel, April 1982.

Dittmar, N.: Ordering adult learners according to language abilities. In: Papers from the First Scandinavian-German Symposium on the Language of Immigrant Workers and Their Children, Eds. N. Dittmar et al. Roskilde (Denmark) 1978, 119-147.

Dittmar, N.: Fremdsprachenerwerb im sozialen Kontext. Das Erlernen von Modalverben - eine lexikalisch-semantische Analyse. Zeitschrift für Literaturwissenschaft und Linguistik 33, 84-103 (1979).

Dittmar, N.: On the verbal organization of L2 tense marking in an elicited translation task by Spanish immigrants in Germany. Studies in Second Language Acquisition 3, 136-164 (1981).

Dittmar, N.: Ich fertig arbeite, nicht mehr spreche Deutsch: semantische
Eigenschaften pidginisierter Lernervarietäten des Deutschen. Zeitschrift für Literaturwissenschaft und Linguistik 45 (1982).

Dittmar, N., W. Klein et al.: Untersuchungen zum Pidgin-Deutsch spanischer
und italienischer Arbeiter in der Bundesrepublik. Ein Arbeitsbericht.
University of Heidelberg 1974.

Dittmar, N. and E. Thielicke: Der Niederschlag von Erfahrungen ausländischer Arbeiter mit dem institutionellen Kontext des Arbeitsplatzes
in Erzählungen. In: Interpretative Verfahren in den Sozial- und
Textwissenschaften, Ed. H.G. Soeffner. Stuttgart 1979, 65-103.

Dubois, C., C. Noyau, C. Perdue and R. Porquier: A propos d'une prê-
enquête sur l'utilisation du français en milieu naturel par des
adultes hispanophones. GRECO 13 numéro spécial, 57-78 (1981).

Emonds, J.: A Transformational Approach to English Syntax. Academic Press,
New York 1976.

Erickson, F.: Gate-keeping encounters: a social selection process. In:
Anthropology and the Public Interest, Ed. P. Sanday. Academic Press,
New York 1976.

Ervin-Tripp, S.: Sociolinguistics. In: Advances in Experimental Social
Psychology 4. Academic Press, New York 1969, 91-165.

Faerch, C. and G. Kasper: Processes and strategies in foreign language
learning and communication. Interlanguage Studies Bulletin 5(1)
(1980).

Felix, S.: Psycholinguistische Aspekte des Zweitspracherwerbs. Narr,
Tübingen 1982.

Felix, S. and Simmet, A.: L'acquisition des pronoms personnels en milieu
scolaire. Encrages 8/9, 33-41 (1982).

Fillmore, Ch.L.: Towards a descriptive framework for spatial deixis.
In: Speech, Place, and Action, Eds. R.J. Jarvella and W. Klein. Wiley,
Chichester 1982, 31-59.

Frauenfelder, U., C. Noyau, C. Perdue and R. Porquier: Connaissance en
langue étrangère. Langages 57, 43-60 (1980).

Friedrich, P.: Structural implications of Russian pronominal usage. In:
Sociolinguistics, Ed. W. Bright. Mouton, The Hague 1966, 214-253.

Gardin, B. (Ed.): L'Apprentissage du Français par les Travailleurs Immigrês
(Langue Française 29). Larousse, Paris 1976.

302—References

Gårding, E. and R. Bannert: Projektrapporter: optimering av svensk uttal. University of Lund 1979.

Garrod, S. and A.J. Sanford: Understanding written language. Wiley, Chichester 1981.

Gilbert, G. and M. Orlović:"Pidgin-German spoken by foreign workers in West Germany: the definite article", Honolulu, Hawai 1975.

Givón, T.: From discourse to syntax: grammar as a processing strategy. In: Syntax and semantics 12. Discourse and syntax, Ed. T. Givón. Academic Press, New York 1979, 81-111.

Gleitman, L. and H. Gleitman: Phrase and Paraphrase. Norton, New York 1970.

Gumperz, J., T. Jupp and C. Roberts: Crosstalk. The National Centre for Industrial Language Training, Southall 1979.

Gumperz, J. and C. Roberts: Developing awareness skills for inter-ethnic communication. National Centre for Industrial Language Training, Southall 1978.

Gumperz, J. and D. Tannen: Individual and social differences in language use. In: Individual Differences in Language Ability and Language Behavior. Academic Press, New York 1979, 305-325.

Gutfleisch, I. et al.: Bibliographie zur Zweitspracherwerbsforschung 1967-1978 (Parts I and II). Linguistische Berichte 64 and 65 (1979 and 1980).

Hakuta, K.: Prefabricated patterns and the emergence of structure in second language acquisition. Language Learning 24, 287-297 (1974).

Hammarberg, B. and Å. Viberg: Felanalys och språktypologi: orientiering om två delstudier i SSM-projektet. University of Stockholm 1977.

Hammarberg, B. and Å. Viberg: Platshållartvånget, ett syntaktist problem i svenskan för invandrare. University of Stockholm 1979.

Hawkins, J.: The semantic diversity of basic grammatical relations in English and German. Linguistische Berichte 75, 1-25 (1981).

Heeschen, V.: The metalinguistic vocabulary of a speech community in the highlands of Irian Jaya (West New Guinea). In: The Child's Conception of Language, Eds. A. Sinclair, R. Jarvella and W. Levelt. Springer, Berlin 1978, 155-187.

Heidelberger Forschungsprojekt "Pidgin-Deutsch" (HPD): Sprache und Kommunikation ausländischer Arbeiter. Scriptor, Kronberg (Ts) 1975.

HPD: Untersuchungen zur Erlernung des Deutschen durch ausländische Arbeiter (Arbeitsbericht III). University of Heidelberg 1976.

HPD: Die ungesteuerte Erlernung des Deutschen durch spanische und italienische Arbeiter. Osnabrücker Beiträge zur Sprachtheorie, Beiheft 2. Osnabrück 1977.

HPD: Zur Erlernung des Deutschen durch ausländische Arbeiter: Wortstellung und ausgewählte lexikalisch-semantische Aspekte (Arbeitsbericht IV). University of Heidelberg 1978.

HPD: Studien zum Spracherwerb ausländischer Arbeiter (Arbeitsbericht V). University of Heidelberg 1979.

Huang, J.: A Chinese child's acquisition of English syntax. Manuscript, Los Angeles 1971.

Hulstijn, J.: Monitor Use by Adult Second Language Learners. Krips, Meppel 1982.

Hyltenstam, K.: Implicational patterns in interlanguage syntax variation. Language Learning 27 (2) (1977).

Hyltenstam, K.: Progress in Immigrant Swedish Syntax: A Variability Analysis. University of Lund 1978.

Jakobson, R.: Closing statements: linguistics and poetics. In: Style in Language, Ed. T. Sebeok. M.I.T. Press, Cambridge 1960, 350-377.

Jansen, B. and J. Lalleman: Interferentie en woordvolgorde, het Nederlands van buitenlandse arbeiders. Publ. Instituut Algemene Taalwetenschap Amsterdam 27, 1-48 (1980) (= Jansen and Lalleman 1980a).

Jansen, B. and J. Lalleman: De invloed van de moedertaal op de zinsbouw van het Nederlands van Turkse en Marokkaanse arbeiders. In: Taalproblemen van Buitenlandse Arbeiders en hun Kinderen, Eds. R. Appel et al. Coutinho, Muiderberg 1980, 137-150 (= Jansen and Lalleman 1980b).

Jansen, B., J. Lalleman and P. Muysken: The alternation hypothesis: acquisition of Dutch word order by Turkish and Moroccan foreign workers. Language Learning 31(2), 315-336 (1981).

Jespersen, O.: The Philosophy of Grammar. London 1924.

Karmiloff-Smith, A.: Psychological processes underlying pronominalization and non-pronominalization in children's connected discourse. In: Papers from the Parasession on Pronouns and Anaphora, Eds. J. Kreiman and A. Ojeda. Chicago Linguistics Society, Chicago 1980, 231-250.

Kay, P. and G. Sankoff: A language-universal approach to pidgins and creoles. In: Pidgins and Creoles: Current Trends and Prospects, Eds. D. Decamp and I. Hancock. Georgetown University Press, Washington DC 1974.

Keenan, E.: Remarkable subjects in Malagasy. In: Subject and Topic, Ed. C. Li. Academic Press, New York 1976.

Keim, I. et al.: Gastarbeiter-Deutsch: Untersuchungen zum sprachlichen Verhalten türkischer Gastarbeiter. Narr, Tübingen 1978.

Kempen, G.: Conceptualizing and formulating in sentence production. In: Sentence Production: Developments in Research and Theory, Ed. S. Rosenberg. Erlbaum, Hillsdale 1977.

Klein, W.: Variation in der Sprache. Scriptor, Kronberg (Ts) 1974.

Klein, W.: Knowing a language and knowing to communicate. In: Language Problems of Minority Groups, Ed. A.R. Vermeer. Tilburg Studies in Language and Literature 1, 75-95 (1981) (= Klein 1981a).

Klein, W.: L'acquisition des pronoms personnels par des travailleurs espagnols et italiens. GRECO 13 numéro spécial, 19-31 (1981) (= Klein 1981b).

Klein, W.: Spatial orientation in route directions. To appear in: Spatial Orientation, Eds. H. Pick and L. Acredolo. Plenum Press, New York 1981 (= Klein 1981c).

Klein, W.: Der Ausdruck der Temporalität im ungesteuerten Spracherwerb. In: Essays on Deixis, Ed. G. Rauh. Narr, Tübingen 1982.

Klein, W. and N. Dittmar: Developing Grammars. The Acquisition of German Syntax by Foreign Workers. Springer, Berlin 1979.

Klein, W. and B.O. Rieck: Der Erwerb der Personalpronomina im ungesteuerten Spracherwerb. In: Zweitspracherwerb, Eds. W. Klein and J. Weissenborn. Zeitschrift für Linguistik und Literaturwissenschaft 45 (1982).

Kotsinas, U.-B.: Kommer och predikatet GO: funderingar kring tempus och aspekt i invandrarsvenska. In: Tvåspråkighet, Föredrag från Tredje Nordiska Tvåspråkighetsymposiet, 4-5 juni 1980, Eds. E. Ejerhed and I. Henrysson. Umeå Studies in the Humanities 36 (1980).

Krashen, S.: The critical period hypothesis and its possible bases. In: Developmental Psycholinguistics and Communication Disorders, Eds. D. Aaronson and R. Reiber. The New York Academy of Sciences, New York 1975.

Kuno, S.: Newness of information and order of deletion. Cahiers Charles V
1, 211-221 (1979).

Labov, W.: Sociolinguistic Patterns. University of Pennsylvania Press,
Philadelphia 1972 (= Labov 1972a).

Labov, W.: Language in the Inner City. University of Pennsylvania Press,
Philadelphia 1972 (= Labov 1972b).

Lemos de, C. and J. Bybee: The acquisition of past reference in Brazilian
Portugese. Working paper for MPI Workshop on language acquisition.
Nijmegen 1981.

Levelt, W.J.M.: The speaker's linearization problem. Philological Trans-
actions of the Royal Society of London, Series B, 295, 305-315 (1981).

Levelt, W.J.M.: Linearization in describing spatial networks. In: Processes,
Beliefs and Questions, Eds. S. Peters and E. Saarinen. Reidel,
Dordrecht 1982, 199-220. (= Levelt 1982a).

Levelt, W.J.M.: "The speaker's linearization of discourse", XIII International
Congress of Linguists, Tokyo, September 1982 (= Levelt 1982b).

Linde, C. and W. Labov: Spatial networks as a site for the study of
language and thought. Language 51(4), 924-939 (1975).

di Luzio, A.: Untersuchungen zur Muttersprache von Gastarbeiterkindern
im Kontakt mit Deutsch. In: SFB 99 - Linguistik, University of
Konstanz, Ergebnisbericht 1980-1982. Konstanz 1982, 151-206.

Lyons, J.: Introduction to Theoretical Linguistics. Cambridge University
Press, Cambridge 1968.

Lyons, J.: Semantics. Cambridge University Press, Cambridge 1977.

Marshall, J. and J. Morton: On the mechanics of Emma. In: The Child's
Conception of Language, Eds. A. Sinclair, R. Jarvella and W. Levelt.
Springer, Berlin 1978, 225-239.

Marslen-Wilson, W., L.K. Tyler and E. Levy: Producing interpretable
discourse: the establishment and maintenance of referents. In:
Speech, Place, and Action, Eds. R. Jarvella and W. Klein. Wiley,
Chichester 1982, 339-378.

Meisel, J.: Ausländerdeutsch und Deutsch ausländischer Arbeiter. In:
Sprache Ausländischer Arbeiter, Ed. W. Klein. Vandenhoek and Ruprecht,
Göttingen 1975, 9-53.

Meisel, J.: The language of foreign workers in Germany. In: German in
Contact with Other Languages, Eds. C.H. Molony et al. Scriptor,
Kronberg 1977, 184-212.

Meisel, J.:"The role of transfer as a strategy of natural second language acquisition/processing", University of California at Los Angeles (Lake Arrowhead), September 1981.

Meisel, J.: Strategies of second language acquisition. In: Pidginization and Creolization as Language Acquisition, Ed. R. Andersen. Newbury House, Rowley, Mass. 1983.

Meisel, J., H. Clahsen and M. Pienemann: On determining developmental stages in natural second language acquisition. Studies in Second Language Acquisition 3(2), 109-135 (1981).

Meyer-Ingwersen, J. et al.: Zur Sprachentwicklung türkischer Schüler in der Bundesrepublik. Scriptor, Königstein (Ts) 1977.

Miller, G.A. and Ph.N. Johnson-Laird: Language and Perception. Harvard University Press, Cambridge, Mass. 1976.

Miller, M.: Psycholinguistische Probleme der Referenz. In: Sprache und Kontext, Ed. W. Klein. Vandenhoek and Ruprecht, Göttingen 1977, 83-97.

Mittner, M. with G. Kahn: Réflexions sur l'activité métalinguistique des apprenants adultes en milieu naturel. Encrages 8/9, 67-75 (1982).

Morsly, D.: Interférences de l'arabe sur le français des travailleurs immigrés à Paris. University of Paris V 1976.

Morsly, D. and M.-T. Vasseur: L'emploi des verbes français par les travailleurs immigrés arabophones et portugais. Langue Française 29, 80-92 (1976).

Neufeld, G.: Vers une théorie de la capacité d'apprentisage linguistique. Encrages numéro spécial, 9-15 (1979).

Noyau, C.: Les "français approchés" des travailleurs migrants: un nouveau champ de recherche. Langue Française 29, 45-60 (1976).

Noyau, C.: Deux types de connaissance de la langue étrangère dans l'acquisition en milieu naturel? Champs Educatifs 1, 6-16 (1980).

Noyau, C. (Ed.): Les Travailleurs Étrangers et la Langue. Centre National de la Recherche Scientifique, Paris 1981.

Oksaar, E.: Linguistic and pragmatic awareness of monolingual and multilingual children. In: Child Language - An International Perspective, Eds. P. Dale and D. Ingram. University Park Press, Baltimore 1981.

de Oliveira, E.: Influences du contact entre les deux systèmes linguistiques d'un ouvrier portugais immigré en France (I) & (II). University of Paris V 1974 & 1975.

Orlovič-Schwarzwald, M.: Zum Gastarbeiterdeutsch jugoslawischer Arbeiter im Rhein-Main-Gebiet. Franz Steiner, Wiesbaden 1978.

Perdue, C. and R. Porquier (Eds.): Encrages: Numéro Spécial de Linguistique Appliquée. University of Paris VIII 1979.

Perdue, C. and R. Porquier (Eds.): Apprentissage et Connaissance d'une Langue Etrangère (Langages 57). Larousse, Paris 1980.

Pfaff, C.W.: Sociolinguistic problems of immigrants: foreign workers and their children in Germany (a review article). Language in Society 10, 155-188 (1981).

Pichel, L.: Les interférences linguistiques (phonétiques, syntaxiques et culturelles) des Espagnols immigrés en France. University of Paris III 1980.

Porcher, L. (Ed.): Des Migrants Confrontés au Français (Etudes de Linguistique Appliquée 30). Didier-Larousse, Paris 1978.

Quirk, R., S. Greenbaum, G. Leech and J. Svartvik: A grammar of contemporary English. Longman, London 1972.

Rieck, B.O.: Die Interlingua spanischer Arbeitsimmigranten. M.A. Thesis, University of Heidelberg 1975.

Rosansky, E.: Language acquisition from the Piagetian and the Chomsky-Lenneberg points of view and the implications for second language learning. Harvard University 1973.

Rosansky, E.: The critical period for the acquisition of language: some cognitive developmental considerations. Working papers in Bilingualism 6, 93-100 (1975).

Saifullah Khan, V.: The "mother-tongue" of linguistic minorities in multicultural England. Journal of Multilingual and Multicultural Development 1, 71-88 (1980).

Santos-Pereira, C.: Problèmes de bilingualisme et interférences chez les travailleurs portugais immigrés en France. University of Paris V 1981.

Schumann, J.: The Pidginization Process: a Model for Second Language Acquisition. Newbury House, Rowley 1978.

Silberman, R., Y. Monlier, S. Harchaomi and H. Chekir: Les femmes
    immigrées et l'emploi: nouvelles tendances. Centre de Recherche
    Economique, Ecole Normale Supérieure, Paris 1980.
Sinclair, A., R. Jarvella and W. Levelt (Eds.): The Child's Conception of
    Language. Springer, Berlin 1978.
Slobin, D.: Cognitive prerequisites for the development of grammar. In:
    Studies of Child Language Development, Eds. Ch. Ferguson and
    D. Slobin. Holt, Rinehart and Winston, New York 1973, 175-208.
Slobin, D.: Language change in childhood and in history. In: Language
    Learning and Thought, Ed. J. Macnamara. Academic Press, New York
    1977, 185-214.
Slobin, D.: A case study of early language awareness. In: The Child's
    Conception of Language, Eds. A. Sinclair, R. Jarvella and W. Levelt.
    Springer, Berlin 1978, 45-54.
Snow, C., R. van Eeden and P. Muysken: The interactional origins of
    foreigner talk: municipal employees and foreign workers. Interna-
    tional Journal of the Society of Languages 28, 81-91 (1981).
von Stechow, A.: Three local deictics. In: Speech, Place, and Action,
    Eds. R. Jarvella and W. Klein. Wiley, Chichester 1982, 73-99.
Stölting, W.: Wie die Ausländer sprechen: eine jugoslawische Familie. In:
    Sprache Ausländischer Arbeiter, Ed. W. Klein. Vandenhoek and
    Ruprecht, Göttingen 1975, 54-67.
Stölting, W. et al.: Die Zweitsprachigkeit jugoslawischer Schüler in der
    Bundesrepublik. Harrassowitz, Wiesbaden 1980.
von Stutterheim, C.: When language barriers become mind blocks. Max-Planck-
    Institut für Psycholinguistik, Nijmegen 1982.
Svennung, J.: Anredeformen. Vergleichende Forschungen zur indirekten An-
    rede in der 3. Person und zum Nominativ f.d. Vokativ. Skrifter
    utgivna av K. Humanistika Vetenskapssamfundet, Uppsala 1958.
Talmy, L.: The representation of space by language. Cognitive Science
    Program, University of California at San Diego, 1980.
Tanz, C.: Studies in the Acquisition of Deictic Terms. Cambridge Univer-
    sity Press, London 1980.
Thompson, S.: Modern English from a typological point of view: some
    implications of the function of word order. Linguistische Berichte
    54, 19-35 (1978).

Thorpe, D.: Cross-cultural communication in an industrial job interview. National Council for Industrial Language Training, Southall 1981.

Trévise, A.: Spécificité de l'énonciation didactique dans l'apprentissage de l'anglais par des étudiants francophones. Encrages numéro spécial, 44-52 (1979).

Trévise, A.:"Adult Spanish speakers and acquisition of French negation forms: individual variation and linguistic awareness",University of California at Los Angeles (Lake Arrowhead),September 1981.

Trévise, A. (Ed.): Acquisition d'une Langue Etrangère II (Encrages 8/9). University of Paris VIII 1982.

Tropf, H.: Phonologische Variation im ungesteuerten Spracherwerb. University of Heidelberg 1982.

Ullmer-Ehrich, V.: Da and the system of spatial deixis in German. In: Here and There. Cross-linguistic studies in Deixis and Demonstration, Eds. J. Weissenborn and W. Klein. Benjamins, Amsterdam 1982.

Ullmer-Ehrich, V. and C. Koster: Discourse organization and sentence form. The structure of static arrangement descriptions. Max-Planck-Institut für Psycholinguistik, Nijmegen 1981.

Van Heuven, V. and J. de Vries: Begrijpelijkheid van buitenlanders: de rol van fonische versus niet-fonische faktoren. Forum der Letteren 22(4), 309-320 (1981).

Van Heuven, V., J. Kruyt and J. de Vries: Buitenlandsheid en begrijpelijkheid in het Nederlands van buitenlandse arbeiders, een verkennende studie. Forum der Letteren 22(2),171-178 (1981).

Vermeer, A. (Ed.): Language Problems of Minority Groups (Tilburg Studies in Language and Literature 1). University of Tilburg 1931.

Véronique, D.: La variabilité dans le français des travailleurs migrants maghrébins. Champs Educatifs 1, 17-24 (1980).

Véronique, D. and D. Faïta: Sollicitation de données syntaxiques auprès d'un groupe de travailleurs maghrébins. Encrages 8/9, 47-56 (1982).

Véronique, D. and H. Stoffel: Linguistique et variation: à propos du français des travailleurs migrants maghrébins. Cahiers de Linguistique, d'Orientalisme et de Slavistique 13, 147-163 (1979).

Vries de, J.: Een taalontlokkingsgesprek met buitenlandse arbeiders. Toegepaste Taalwetenschap in Artikelen 10(2), 104-131 (1981).

Weinrich, H.: Tempus. Besprochene und erzählte Welt. Kohlhammer, Stuttgart 1964.

Weissenborn, J. and W. Klein (Eds.): Here and There. Cross-linguistic
    Studies on Deixis and Demonstration. Benjamins, Amsterdam 1982.

Werkgroep Taal Buitenlandse Werknemers (WTBW): Nederlands tegen buiten-
    landers. Instituut Algemene Taalwetenschap Amsterdam 18 (1978).

WTBW: Taalattitude, taalvaardigheid, en sociale omstandigheden van
    Marokkaanse arbeiders in Nederland: een verkennend onderzoek. Toege-
    paste Taalwetenschap in Artikelen 6, 38-62 (1979).

WTBW: Krom praten tegen buitenlanders. In: Taalproblemen van Buitenlandse
    Arbeiders en hun Kinderen, Eds. R. Appel et al. Coutinho, Muiderberg
    1980, 63-175 (= WTBW 1980a).

WTBW: Taalattitude, taalvaardigheid, en sociale omstandigheden van
    Marokkaanse arbeiders in Nederland: een verkennend onderzoek. In:
    De Verwerving van het Nederlands door Buitenlandse Arbeiders, Ed.
    P. Muysken. Instituut Algemene Taalwetenschap Amsterdam 27, 49-106
    (19   WTBW 1980b)

WTBW: De   Nederlands. In:
    Taa   *Wode 82*   ren, Eds.
    R.   = WTBWc).

Wildgen,   chbeherrschung
    bei   d. W. Haubrichs.
    Gö

Wode, H.   f language
    acquisition. Narr, Tübingen 1981.

Wong-Fillmore, L.: The Second Time Around. University of Stanford 1976.

Yakut, A.: Sprache der Familie. Narr, Tübingen 1981.

Zweitspracherwerb Italienischer und Spanischer Arbeiter (ZISA): Hand-
    reichungen zur Ermittlung von Erwerbsstufen und Arten des Verlaufs
    beim natürlichen Erwerb des Deutschen durch italienische Arbeiter.
    Gesamthochschule Wuppertal 1979.

AUTHOR INDEX

SUBJECT INDEX